WHEN MEN KILL
Scenarios of Masculine Violence

KENNETH POLK

Department of Criminology
University of Melbourne

CAMBRIDGE
UNIVERSITY PRESS

Published by the Press Syndicate of the University of Cambridge
The Pitt Building, Trumpington Street, Cambridge CB2 IRP, UK
40 West 20th Street, New York, NY 10011-4211, USA
10 Stamford Road, Oakleigh, Melbourne 3166, Australia

First published 1994

National Library of Australia cataloguing in publication data

Polk, Kenneth.
When men kill: scenarios of masculine violence.
Bibliography.
Includes index.
1. Homicide – Victoria. 2. Homicide – Case studies. 3. Men –
Psychology. 4. Violence. I. Title.
364.152

Library of Congress cataloguing in publication data

Polk, Kenneth.
When men kill: scenarios of masculine violence/Kenneth Polk.
p.   cm.
Includes bibliographical references and index.
1. Homicide – Australia – Victoria – Sex differences. 2. Violence –
Australia – Victoria – Sex differences. 3. Masculinity (Psychology) –
Australia – Victoria. I. Title.
HV6535.A82V536 1994
364.1' 523' 081 – dc20   94-8969
                                                                CIP

A catalogue record for this book is available from the British Library.

ISBN 0 521 46267 3 Hardback
ISBN 0 521 46808 6 Paperback

Transferred to digital printing 1999

Contents

Acknowledgements

This research was supported by grants from the Australian Criminology Research Council. Throughout, the work has depended upon the close collaboration of Dr David Ranson, a forensic pathologist with the Victorian Institute of Forensic Pathology, who was responsible for the effective access that was gained to the Office of the Coroner of Victoria for the homicide data studied here. Dr Ranson participated in all stages of the research and was the co-author of the early research reports. He prepared major sections of Chapter 2 of this book, specifically those dealing with the homicide investigation and the role of the forensic pathologist in this process. This work could not have been done without the support of both Dr Ranson and the Victorian Institute of Forensic Pathology.

Several colleagues have helped in reviewing early drafts. Professor Don Gibbons of Portland State University has read sections of the manuscript, and has provided valuable advice through the years this work has taken. Margo Wilson and Martin Daly have given careful reading to drafts of the manuscript, and have been patient in their attempts to convey their important view of homicide. The exchange of ideas with the staff of the Institute for the Study of Social Change at the University of California, Berkeley, has been most helpful, and appreciation needs to be expressed to its Director, Professor Troy Duster, and others in that Institute such as David Minkus, David Wellman and Deborah Woo.

There were many research assistants who helped in collecting data from the files of the Office of the Coroner; these include Nick Hartland, David Ballek, Maj-Britt Englehardt, Santina Perrone and Hillary Little.

I am grateful for the constant support of Dr Christine Alder throughout the course of this research.

Excerpts from Wallace (1986), Katz (1988) and Daly and Wilson (1988) are reprinted with permission.

CHAPTER 1

Introduction

This book is about masculinity and homicide. It is an exploration of various patterns whereby men take the lives of others. Its empirical data are drawn from records of homicide which occurred in Victoria, Australia, between 1985 and 1989. Victoria is a state of Australia with a population of 4.5 million; 3.2 million live in the radius of the capital city, Melbourne. Throughout, the focal point of the analysis will be on the relationship between the offender and victim, and following on from that an investigation of the social dynamics which resulted in the homicide. The basic method consists of an examination of the themes which emerge from a review of a large number of case studies of homicide. As such this research is fundamentally qualitative in that it is seeking to identify the elements of the masculine scenarios of violence which are being played out in the dramas found within the narratives of homicides surveyed.

Setting the stage

The information available suggests that the rate of homicide in Australia in recent years has been running at just under 2 per 100,000 (Wallace, 1986, reported a figure of 1.9; Grabosky *et al.*, 1981, report a figure of 1.8, per 100 000; the National Committee on Violence, 1990, and Strang, 1992, show that the average figures for the past two decades would fall between 1.8 and 2.1 per 100 000). While a number of problems are encountered when comparisons are made between countries, these levels are well below the exceptionally high rates reported in nations such as Guatemala (with a rate of 63.0 per 100 000), or the high rates observed in the United States (9.1 per 100 000) (Wallace, 1986:

1

22). On the other hand, the observed rates tend to be higher in Australia than in such European countries as the Federal Republic of Germany (1.1 per 100 000), the Netherlands (0.8 per 100 000) or England and Wales (also 0.8 per 1000) (Wallace, 1986: 22). This 'middling' position of the homicide rates of Australia has also been confirmed by the recent report of the National Academy of Sciences in the United States (Reiss and Roth, 1993).

In general, Australia's homicide rate has tended to remain relatively stable over recent years, with the rate in most years falling between 1.7 and 2.1 per 100 000. As Wallace (1986: 24) points out, this stands in sharp contrast to the situation in the United States which between 1960 and 1980 experienced an increase of almost 100 per cent in the level of homicide. Of further interest is that fact that in one State in Australia, New South Wales, there were sharp drops in the level of homicide observed after the opening decade of the century, that is, the highest rates of homicide were observed prior to 1920 (Wallace, 1986: 24). There was probably much more, not less, murder on a per person basis in the 'good old days'. Certainly, the frequent assertion found in media accounts in Australia that 'violent crime is rising' does not appear to apply to homicide, especially if one takes a longer view of the time dimension.

The picture of persons who commit this offence in Australia tends to conform to observations in overseas research. The studies uniformly show that unlike property offences which involve predominantly younger offenders, slightly more than half of the offenders will be over 25 (Law Reform Commission of Victoria [LRCV], 1991; Wallace, 1986; Grabosky et al., 1981). In Australia, as elsewhere, homicide offenders are not likely to come from backgrounds of economic privilege. In both Victoria and New South Wales, where occupational data are available, less than 5 per cent of those who take the life of another come from occupations at the professional, managerial, or semi-professional levels (LRCV, 1991: 24; Wallace, 1986: 47). Quite often, these offenders are in fact unemployed, as was found among just over half (54 per cent) of the Victorian homicide offenders (LRCV, 1991: 22) and roughly one-third of the New South Wales offenders (Wallace, 1986: 47).

Turning to the circumstances of the offence, about half the time the offence occurs in the home (of either the victim or the offender), it is somewhat more likely to occur on weekend nights, and is highly likely to occur in evening hours (Strang, 1992; LRCV, 1991; Wallace, 1986). In sharp contrast to the United States where a majority of homicides will involve the use of guns, in Australian jurisdictions guns are involved in one-third of homicides or less (23 per cent in the recent national study, Strang, 1992), with knives and fists/feet accounting for significant proportions of the remainder (Wallace, 1986; LRCV, 1991; Strang, 1992).

One major difference between Victorian homicide and that seen overseas, especially in the United States, concerns the variable of race. There are few residents in Australia whose origins are from Africa, so that this important component of homicide in the United States (for example, see Reiss and Roth, 1993: 51) will not be found in the present investigation. While in Australia overall the Aboriginal population contributes a disproportionate amount to the total number of homicides (21 per cent of all homicides, with the national homicide rate for Aboriginal males being 52 per 100 000, in contrast to the overall rate of 3.6), in Victoria the Koori population is much lower, and they made up only 5 per cent of homicides reported in 1990–91 (Strang, 1992).

The victim-offender relationship

In much of the research on homicide, in Australia and elsewhere, a major focal point has been the relationship between the victim and the offender. This flows out of the recognition that homicide is fundamentally a social act, and therefore it is important to explore the relationships that exist among the key actors in the event. Wolfgang's (1958) early research has played a major role in establishing the basic understandings and categories within which research on victim-offender relationships is carried out.

Wolfgang (1958) argued that a weakness of much of the criminological work that existed at the time was it examined either offenders, or victims, separately, rather than as interdependent participants in an inherently social event. Drawing upon the observations of von Hentig (1948), Wolfgang urged that the homicide scene be examined within a 'duet frame of crime', where the victim can be seen as 'shaping and moulding' the offender as the homicide unfolds.

This central idea that homicide research should examine the victim-offender relationship continues to echo in the current literature, as in the recent observation of Silverman and Mukherjee (1987: 37) that murder is a social event involving at least two actors in a 'social relationship that plays a dynamic role in the way that the homicide unfolds'. Luckenbill widens this somewhat when he observes that: 'By definition, criminal homicide is a collective transaction. An offender, victim, and possibly an audience engage in an interchange which leaves the victim dead.' (Luckenbill, 1977: 176)

One of the major observations which has emerged, first, from Wolfgang's investigation, and then others which have followed, is that homicide is not commonly an event involving people who are unknown to each other. In the 1958 Philadelphia study, for example, only 12 per cent of the homicides involved persons who were strangers to each other (Wolfgang, 1958: 207). Later studies in the United States have suggested somewhat higher levels of 'stranger' homicide, such homicides accounting for 28 per cent of all homicides in the report of Zahn and Sagi (1987), and 32 per cent in the work of Hewitt (1988), although data prepared for the more recent National Academy of Sciences report on violence suggest a level of 'stranger' homicide in the range of 19 per cent (Reiss and Roth, 1993: 80). In Canada, 26 per cent of all homicide victims in 1979–83 were strangers to the offender (Langevin and Handy, 1987).

As is the case in the United States, homicide in Australia is not likely to occur among strangers. In South Australia, stranger homicides made up only 9 per cent of all reported homicides (Grabosky et al., 1981: 40), a figure close to the national 6 per cent observed by Strang (1992), although in New South Wales it was somewhat higher at 18 per cent (Wallace, 1986: 83). The figures were even higher in a recent study in Victoria, where 29 per cent of all homicides were reported to be 'stranger' homicides (LRCV, 1991: 16). Possibly these last figures are higher because the other two Australian states used police reports as their source of data, while the Law Reform Commission of Victoria investigation picked up the cases at the point of prosecution.

To put the matter properly, in Australia as elsewhere; homicide is an event most likely to involve some form of close relationship between the victim and the offender. As Wallace comments:

> Homicide in New South Wales is a crime which typically occurs between intimates; four out of five victims knew their attacker, and in a majority of cases, their relationship was a close one. The family was the most common venue for these homicides.   *(Wallace, 1986: 93)*

This information hardly provides an explanation for homicide, however. Knowing that homicides take place among people who share some amount of intimacy helps to locate the problem, but it only carries us part of the way to understanding the dynamics of violent behaviour. To go farther, it is necessary to go beyond the valuable foundation found in the work of writers such as Wolfgang, Luckenbill or Wallace. The present investigation will proceed from the assumption that a primary focus of exploration should be the relationship between victim and offender. It will be argued, however, that there are important limits to what can be explained from the use of such terms as 'stranger', 'friend/acquaintance' or 'family' to describe the bond between offender and victim. Such terms in fact provide few clues as to why the homicide has occurred. Knowing, for example, that the offender and victim were bound by a family or friendship tie, or even that they were previously unknown to each other, by itself does not suggest what has provoked the killing. A major thrust of this research is methodological, and argues that it is time to re-enter raw data on homicides to establish more effective ways of describing victim-offender interactions that are richer in theoretical content.

But at the same time, there is a clear theoretical orientation of this research. Previous investigations suggest two major social vectors that run through homicide data. The first of these is social class. Writers from Wolfgang (1958) onward have pointed out the distinctive lower- and working-class distribution of violence in general, and homicide in particular. In the New South Wales data, for example, 5 per cent or less of all offenders, and all victims, were drawn from professional and managerial backgrounds (Wallace, 1986: 38). Explanations of why that should be the case have been less than compelling. Wolfgang and Ferracuti (1967) advanced a potentially helpful set of ideas in their discussion of the role of a 'subculture of violence' in supporting behaviour which could result in homicide.

Messerschmidt (1986) has opened up some interesting lines of inquiry in his discussion of the linkage between class, gender and violence. What such a discussion contributes is an explicit recognition of the second vector, gender, which is an important feature of homicide data. While there are some differences between Australia and countries such as the United States in terms of variables related to homicide (such as weapon use), one uniform finding across jurisdictions is that homicide is a masculine offence. Homicide offenders in Australia are predominantly male, the proportion of males being 86 per cent in a recent Victorian study (Naylor, 1993), 83 per cent in New South Wales (Wallace, 1986), and 90 per cent in South Australia (Grabosky et al., 1981) and in recent national data (Strang, 1992). These figures are comparable to the 90 per cent of males reported being arrested for homicide in the United States as a whole in 1991 (Bureau of Justice Statistics, 1992: 442), or such figures reported in individual studies as the 88 per cent reported for two up-state New York counties (Falk, 1990) or 82 per cent in Wolfgang's (1958) early study in Philadelphia.

It then follows that an important theoretical task is to account for why homicide should be such a distinctively masculine matter. The present investigation will draw heavily upon the work of Daly and Wilson (1988) in terms of their conceptual framework describing the role played by masculinity in homicide. It is their observation that across time, and across cultures, it has been established firmly that homicide is fundamentally masculine.

Daly and Wilson go well beyond this simple point, however, and describe a number of different ways that masculinity becomes played out in homicide data. One obvious dimension is that where the violence arises out of sexual intimacy. Certainly, other writers have pointed out the contribution of sexual intimacy to homicide (Silverman and Mukherjee, 1987; Easteal, 1993), and Wallace (1986: 83) was led to conclude that 'the marital relationship provides the context for some of the most violent encounters in our society'.

As important as such observations are, it also needs to be emphasised that a large proportion of lethal violence involves situations where both the offender and the victim are male. Wallace (1986), for example, reported that 54 per cent of all homicides were male-on-male.

One of the contributions of Daly and Wilson (1988) is that their account includes a description of major forms of such male-on-male violence, such as confrontations over 'honour' and the risk-taking involved in robbery homicides. Their work is important because it: (1) provides specific directions regarding particular forms of victim-offender relationships that might be explored; (2) identifies the critical gender basis of such relationships; and (3) argues for a diversity of forms of masculine violence.

There are, of course, a wide range of other sources which can be drawn into the present analysis. Katz's (1988) imaginative analysis of homicide within his framework of the 'seductions of crime' raises theoretical and methodological issues that are difficult to ignore. Especially relevant for the present analysis is his urging that we examine the 'foreground' of crime which gives emphasis to the 'lived experience of criminality' (Katz, 1988: 4). Gottfredson and Hirschi (1990) also advance hypotheses about homicide which, if not entirely accurate, nonetheless help point to directions which analysis might follow. Specifically, they identify elements of 'typical homicide' which are helpful in focusing data collection and analysis.

There are several large sets of homicide data that help set the context for the present work, including the reports of Wolfgang (1958), Wallace (1986) and Strang (1992). Wolfgang's study was carried out in one city, Philadelphia, and constitutes the starting point for contemporary analyses of homicide. In addition to opening up the discussion of victim-offender relationships, the Philadelphia data contribute a number of helpful concepts which continue to add to our understanding of homicide. Wolfgang's notion, for one example, the importance to some males of what to others are 'trivial altercations', is one that will feature in the present analysis of male-on-male homicide.

Wallace's (1986) investigation of homicide between 1968–81 in New South Wales provides one of the soundest compilations of statistical data on homicide available in the research literature. Time and again it will prove useful as a source of comparative statistical information. As well, it contains a number of important theoretical insights, especially into the nature of masculine violence toward female sexual intimates. As a helpful backdrop of national Australian data, the work of Strang (1992) will be drawn upon at several points to help set the statistical context of homicide.

Other analyses of large data sets will contribute to the present analysis as well. Maxfield (1989) has carried out an extensive analysis of the victim-offender relationships information available in the vast Supplementary Homicide Reports collected as part of the Uniform Crime Reporting system maintained by the Federal Bureau of Investigation in the United States. Similarly helpful, especially for insights and comparisons regarding the form of the analysis of victim-offender relationships, is the study of homicide in up-state New York conducted by Falk (1990), and the analysis of the Canadian national data by investigators such as Langevin and Handy (1987).

In summary, the present research will continue the well established tradition which calls for a focus of homicide research on the nature of the social relationship between offender and victim which leads up to the killing. Consistent with such writers as Wolfgang (1958), Luckenbill (1977), and Silverman and Mukherjee (1987), the assumption is that this relationship is a dynamic one, with the victim and the offender often moving through complex social manoeuvres such that a description of the role of both parties is essential to understand the nature of the homicide. In many respects, the present analysis will follow the model of Lundsgaarde (1977) who has provided in his investigation of homicide in 'Space City' a rich source of case study material valuable for contrasts with the case study material of the present research.

More substantively, given that homicide overwhelmingly involves lower- or working-class males as offenders, this investigation will specifically probe into the scenarios of masculine behaviour involved in homicide. Empirically, it will attempt to establish the major patterns which indicate how men become caught up in lethal violence. It will then move to the much more difficult theoretical question of why it is that such violence is so distinctively lower class and masculine in character.

CHAPTER 2

Procedure, data and method

Since this is an empirical study of homicide, a number of matters have to be dealt with to enable the reader to make sense of the data as they unfold. In particular, it is essential that we: (1) clarify what we mean by the term 'homicide', (2) provide specific information on the body of data to be used in the study, and (3) review the particular approach to be used in the investigation.

Homicide defined

It is possible to define homicide, as a dictionary might, simply as 'the killing by whatever means of one human being by another'. Such a definition captures the spirit of what is inherent in the general understanding of the term. There are, of course, complications that arise as we proceed from this common sense interpretation of the concept to a more precise meaning which provides the focus for research analysis.

One of these is the issue of criminality. While there is some tragedy that lurks in all homicides, it has long been recognised that there will be a few killings that are either lawful or justifiable (most killings in war, for example, or those where it is possible to claim legitimate self-defence). Some investigations exclude these and focus exclusively upon those homicides which are unlawful. For an important example, Wolfgang (1958) in the very title of his landmark study, established the scope of his work as 'criminal homicide'.

While it is a matter of some interest to examine in the data which follow the conditions under which some homicides are deemed justifiable (as in cases where it is decided that the killing was in self-defence), as an empirical matter it is often difficult to discern how or why such

8

decisions are made by police, prosecutors or courts. As Daly and Wilson (1988) argue, if our aim is to study the behaviour of victims and their killers rather than decisions made by officials at one point or another in the criminal justice system, it is necessary to enter the problem at the earliest juncture, notably where the police have identified a case where a victim, or victims, have been killed by another person or persons.

The definition offered by Daly and Wilson, and which appears appropriate for purposes of the present research, is that the term homicide refers to: 'those interpersonal assaults and other acts directed against another person (for example poisonings) that occur outside the context of warfare, and that prove fatal' (Daly and Wilson, 1988: 14).

A number of implications follow from the statement of this approach. For one, in the pages which follow little attention will be paid to examining differences between murders and manslaughters. Central to the distinction of murders from manslaughters, from the viewpoint of legal process, in most instances will be the issue of intent, as found in the phrase 'malice aforethought' laid down early in English law. In actual practice, of course, other matters arise to cloud this distinction, including the process of plea or charge bargaining. As such, the ultimate designation between murder and manslaughter provides important information about how the justice system has responded to a killing. The focus here will be on the killing itself, and as such throughout this text the appropriate term will be homicide, rather than such terms as murder or manslaughter which are the eventual results of complex legal processes. This is in no way intending to minimise the importance of the issues raised in legal discussion of homicide (for example, see the lengthy account of Fisse, 1990: 25–130, or of Ashworth, 1991: 227–74). It is rather that, for present purposes, the mental and physical elements that are important for determining the meaning of murder and manslaughter are not central to the empirical task of examining how it is that people come to the point where one takes the life of another.

A further implication of the definition to be employed here, as Daly and Wilson (1988) are careful to point out, is that it implies an entry into the events at an early point, specifically at the police investigation stage. As such, quite different data result than if the focus were limited only to individuals who had been convicted of murder in a criminal court. In a strict legal sense, only those so convicted can be treated as 'murderers'. Yet, data after conviction are notably biased because of the various social factors that are involved both in the killing and the response of the justice system to that killing and its circumstances. As Daly and Wilson (1988: 15) establish in their discussion, data restricted to convictions in Detroit would result in the conclusion that wives are much less likely to murder husbands than are husbands to murder wives, when in fact in that city (at least in 1972, the year being examined) more wives killed husbands than husbands killed wives.

The focus of the present research, as was that of Daly and Wilson, is on the dynamics of the killing itself, rather than the complicated, and certainly important, response of the justice system to that killing. As such, the entry point will be at an early point in the investigation, rather than drawing upon data much deeper in the justice process, such as files based on either murder convictions or murderers sent to prison.

A further implication of this approach is that some cases will be treated as homicide even where an offender ultimately may be found not guilty of a killing in the courts. For a number of reasons, a large proportion of cases where killers have been identified will not proceed through the criminal courts, such as instances where persons have committed suicide, or where the homicide is deemed lawful. Even in some cases where the preponderance of evidence lead the police or coroner to conclude that a person is responsible for the death, the exacting requirements of proving a case 'beyond reasonable doubt' may not be met.

Again, since our interest is in the killing itself, and not the complications that arise in the legal processes, here we will accept the conclusions drawn jointly by the coroner and the police as to the events relating to the homicide. As such there may be a few errors, but in no instance will accounts be considered if there is not a plausible case to be made from the case study that we are dealing with a homicide. The few inaccuracies that may result are much to be preferred to the gross distortions that would result if convicted killers were the only focal point of the investigations.

Finally, it should be obvious that homicides which go undetected or unreported cannot be considered. There are a number of ways this might happen. Some killings are carefully planned, and part of the plot may consist of disposing of the body in such a manner that its discovery is unlikely. The few illustrations within these files of bodies accidentally found in disused mine shafts, or which bob to the surface of water months or years after being killed, hint that there are more which remain successfully hidden from view.

There are, as well, homicides that take place within family circles that do not become part of the official record. At one end of the age continuum, death may result from 'elder abuse' and be recorded as an accident. At the other end of the continuum, examples can be found where babies died of horrific injuries not consistent with an ordinary household accident, and where the subsequent autopsy revealed indications of previous similar injuries which had healed (a pattern consistent with battered children which in other cases are prosecuted as homicide), all of which suggest homicide, yet from the information available the death is classified as an accident.

Deaths at work which result from extreme negligence of employers by law in Victoria and most English-speaking jurisdictions might be treated as either murder or manslaughter, and have been in some cases in the United States (Reiner and Chatten-Brown, 1988) or the Netherlands (Field and Jorg, 1991). In Victoria, however, these events are not investigated by either the homicide squad or by other trained police investigators, and to date even if there has been an investigation (usually conducted by a government department such as the Department of Labour), the matter has not been carried forward to successful prosecution as homicide by the Director of Public Prosecutions. This is not for want of cases (see Polk, Haines and Perrone, 1993), but rather a consequence of a legal process which elects to deal with these in a different manner (where prosecutions are sought, they are likely to fall under sections of the *Occupational Health and Safety Act*, so that it is the violations of safety regulations, rather than the death, that becomes the focal point of the charge). Despite the examples of death at work resulting in convictions of employers either for manslaughter or murder, in none of the current systems of classifying homicide (including the Supplementary Homicide Reports which are part of the Uniform Crime Reports of the US Federal Bureau of Investigation) are such killings considered as a form of homicide.

In homicide, as in other forms of crime, then, there is no easy way to resolve this problem of the 'dark figure of crime', and answering the question of how much homicide 'really' exists. What can be pointed out, however, is that of all offences, homicide is the one taken most seriously both by the community and the justice system. There are examples, including instances among our case studies, where individual victims were identified even in circumstances where the body has not been discovered. In other circumstances, the homicide is uncovered after relatives of the victim have complained to the police, and it was this complaint that resulted in the discovery of both the crime and the body. While some unknown and unknowable number of killings, presumably small in contemporary Australian society, go unreported, of all forms of crime homicide is probably the one best approached through study of official data.

Homicides in Victoria 1985–89

This investigation will draw its data from files of the Office of the Coroner for the State of Victoria and utilises information on all cases of homicide reported in the years 1985–89. In Victoria, the law provides that a death is reportable to the Coroner if it is appears to have been unexpected, unnatural or violent or to have resulted directly or indirectly from accident or injury. Among these will be deaths due to car and work accidents. Those deaths that occur during an anaesthetic, or occur as a result of an anaesthetic, and are not due to natural causes, will also be reported, as will be the death of a person who immediately before death was a person held in care or custody. Reportable deaths, further, include deaths of persons whose identity is unknown, and deaths where a death certificate has not been signed by a legally qualified medical practitioner. Finally, all cases of suspected homicide must also be reported to the Coroner.

More specifically, the *Coroners Act* (Vic.) of 1985 makes an inquest mandatory in cases of suspected homicide. There are a number of steps which are undertaken which lead up to this inquest. The likely sequence of a homicide investigation will begin with a report of the death to the police, followed by the police investigation, the analysis by forensic specialists, including the forensic pathologists, an autopsy, with the results of all of these brought together in the inquest conducted by the Coroner.

The police investigation

Although a dead body may be found in a variety of ways, the reporting of the suspicious circumstances of the death is usually made directly to the police either to a police station or to a Central Police Control Room. In either event it is the Central Police Communications Room that takes the first steps initiating the investigative process. While some discretion is left to the senior officer controlling the communications room, the usual scenario would be for the Senior Communications Officer to instruct a local uniformed police unit to attend at the scene and to report its findings. The local police who respond are responsible for completion of a 'Report of Death' form ('Form 83') which provides a brief summary of the events as these appear at the time, and information on the deceased including name, address, age, and when last seen alive.

The Communications Officer will, under most circumstances, also notify the Coroner of the death and an investigation crew from the local Criminal Investigation Branch. If the case appeared suspicious, the detectives would make arrangements for the Homicide Squad to be contacted and to take over the investigation.

The Homicide Squad officers are divided into a series of crews comprising approximately half a dozen police officers who work an on-call rota system. They would attend the scene and be briefed by both the uniformed officers and the local Criminal Investigation Branch officers and make arrangements with the local police for preservation of the scene and control of access to the scene. At the same time, the various specialist investigatory teams will be contacted and will arrive at the scene to be briefed by the Homicide Squad officers. Such specialist teams include the scene photographers, the crime scene examiners, the specialist scientific staff of the State Forensic Science Laboratory in the appropriate area (ballistics, for example). At the same time, the Coroner's Office would make arrangements for a pathologist from the Victorian Institute of Forensic Pathology to attend at the scene and to assist in the investigation of the death.

Whilst the role of the police in this investigation is to investigate the death in relation to any criminal activity that may have taken place, the Coroner's duty is to investigate all aspects of the death explicitly excluding issues of direct criminal liability. As part of the Coroner's investigation it would be normal practice for the Coroner to attend at the scene of death, personally accompanied by a pathologist from the Victorian Institute of Forensic Pathology and perhaps other members of staff from the Coroner's Office. The role of the pathologist at the scene is to gain first-hand knowledge of the circumstances surrounding the death and the environment in which the body was found. The pathologist also assists in the general process of investigation by providing medical expertise regarding the issues of mode and time of death to the Coroner and the investigating police officers. The remainder of the specialist work at the scene includes the analysis and examination of the body in situ together with its environment with a report being compiled by the crime scene officer regarding the body at the place of death.

The autopsy

When all evidence has been examined at the scene, the body is removed to the mortuary at the Coronial Services Centre in Melbourne and a full autopsy performed, with photographic evidence of all injuries regardless of their immediate relevance to the death. The autopsy examination will include all portions of the body and will normally involve x-ray examination of the body as well as detailed section of not only internal organs but the skin and subcutaneous tissue. During this process, officers from the Homicide Squad will attend the autopsy to obtain information regarding the circumstances and cause of death from the pathologist in order to assist them in the investigation of the death.

The significance of the information arising out of the autopsy is often not fully appreciated. The identification of the cause of death is the one area of expertise that is generally recognised and yet it usually represents one of the simplest of tasks for the pathologist. It requires but little skill to recognise that a man with his head disrupted by a shotgun wound has a fatal wound and will have usually died following a 'gunshot wound to the head'. If the forensic pathologist is to assist in the investigation and subsequent prosecution of the offence it is at this point that the real detail of the work begins.

It has been long recognised by forensic pathologists that wound patterns are not random but that both the type and site of wounds play an important part in reconstructing the events surrounding the killing. In this way a body of expertise has developed that has been accepted and applied by the courts which often have little else but such medical evidence to use in order to arrive at a conclusion regarding the scenario surrounding the killing. In the past such medical opinion has gone towards elucidating individual elements of the physical interaction surrounding a killing that has resulted in macroscopic or microscopic injury. At a general level, pathologists have observed that different patterns of injury are not only associated with different specific physical interactions but also with the type of social relationship or interaction between the parties to the killing. Little qualitative or quantitative research has been carried out in this area, and this study with its unique source of data provides an opportunity to compare injury patterns with the social interaction patterns surrounding a homicide (for an overview, see Ranson, 1992).

In cases in Victoria, upon completion of the autopsy a full report is prepared by the forensic pathologist, and this is added to the file of the case to be considered by the Coroner at the inquest. In addition, various samples are obtained, and sent to the State Forensic Laboratory, and the resultant toxicology reports also become part of the file prepared on the death.

The police prosecution brief

It is the responsibility of the police to prepare a thorough report, a 'prosecution brief', of the various investigative steps regarding the homicide. Included in this report will be numerous witness statements, including lengthy transcripts of interview with individuals close to the victim, those who know the offender, and perhaps even the offender where such are available. The focus of these, of course, is on the circumstances which surround the death in question. As well, this report usually includes statements from forensic scientists and crime scene examiners regarding specialist investigation of evidential items removed from the scene and at the time of autopsy. These components of the investigation are collated together by the police responsible, most often members of the Homicide Squad, with the statements from any suspect or individual subsequently charged with a criminal offence in relation to the death. The completed brief of evidence is then summarised by one of the investigating officers from the Homicide Squad and the total brief of evidence is then placed into the judicial process of prosecution and following this process, before the Coroner's Court for a coronial finding.

The inquest

As indicated previously, the law specifies that an inquest by the Coroner is required in all cases of suspected homicide. A Coroner's inquest occupies a unique niche in the structure of Anglo-Australian law since its proceedings are intended to establish the facts relating to the death, and its procedures are defined as inquisitorial, rather than adversarial (for an overview, see Selby, 1992). The inquest considers statements from relevant witnesses, police reports (including the Police Prosecution Brief), testimony regarding the autopsy, and if relevant, specialist testimony which throws light on the circumstances of the death. The report of the findings of the Coroner is relatively brief, in most cases roughly half a page in length. It states the identity of the deceased, the location of the death, and the causes and circumstances of the death. Regarding the circumstances, a typical entry might read:

> At approximately 8.55 pm on the 27th February 1988 the deceased, a Tattslotto Agent in Bourke Street Melbourne was shot by an unidentified person at his residence ... A quantity of money of approximately $8500, being the days takings from the Agency was removed from the deceased's premises by the person who shot the deceased. *(Case No. 839–88)*

In another case, the Coroner found that:

> the death occurred on or about 11.11.1988 ... [cause of death] ... gunshot wounds to the head and chest in the following circumstances. The deceased and R.H. had an argument and a confrontation in the loungeroom ... R.H. picked up a gun which the deceased had brought to the house and shot the deceased once and then several more times. And I further find that R.H. contributed to the cause of death. *(Case No. 4950–88)*

This report then becomes a part of the records on the homicide maintained in the Office of the Coroner.

The files

These various investigations and inquiries carried out in Victoria for cases of homicide result in a set of documents which constitute the files available in the Office of the Coroner. In most instances, the individual files will consist of the following source documents: (1) a form prepared by the initial attending police officers which reports the death (Form 83), this document providing a source of information about selected social characteristics of the victim, as well as a brief initial statement of the circumstances surrounding the killing; (2) a report of the autopsy performed by the forensic pathologists, this document providing a detailed description of the physical state of the deceased, including for present purposes a medical assessment of the cause of death; (3) a Police Prosecutor's Brief, which in most cases is an extensive document containing transcripts of interviews conducted with various witnesses relevant to the event, including in many cases transcripts of interviews with the offender; (4) the report of the Coroner's inquest, which provides a summary finding from the Coroner regarding the cause of death and who was responsible for the death; and (5) reports of toxicology and other relevant tests conducted upon the victim.

By their very nature, these files provide data about victims of homicide. Other points of entry, such as court records, are likely to be made up of data on offenders. Victim files can be expected to be somewhat more extensive than offender files, because there will be some instances where there is a known victim, but the identity of the offender cannot be determined. Further, there will be instances where a homicide occurs, but the authorities decide for one reason or another not to prosecute an offender.

A further characteristic of these files on homicide in Victoria is that all cases officially known to the police (by virtue of the processing of Form 83) will also be known to the Coroner. The situation in Victoria is unlike that in Philadelphia, where Wolfgang (1958: 12) observed that Coroner's records 'lack details of the offence which police files possess'. In contrast, in Victoria the Coroner's files will have most of the information contained in official police files, especially since it is the responsibility of the police to prepare the Prosecutor's brief which provides much of the data considered by the Coroner at the inquest. Unlike the Philadelphia records, however, these Coroner's files do not contain a record of the trial outcome, and these had to be obtained separately through the Director of Public Prosecutions (DPP).

One of the early tasks in reviewing these files was that of removing those cases which had been referred to the Coroner as homicides, but where the death did not result from the act of another person, at least in the judgment of either police or the Coroner. Some bodies are found in what might be suspicious circumstances, but where further investigation shows the death to be the result of self-administration of drugs.

In other cases, persons have died from wounds which might have been inflicted by others, but where the circumstances suggest that a reasonable case could be made that the death was a result of an accident. For an example, a body of a well-known chronic alcoholic is found in the park with wounds to the head. These might have resulted from a fight, but the wounding is also consistent with an accidental fall, and the latter is the conclusion of the authorities in the absence of any other information. Similarly, there are cases where infants die from wounds where the circumstances are remarkably similar to the battered child syndrome, yet the authorities ultimately conclude that the death was accidental. Further information might have led some of these to be treated as homicide, but the preponderance of the available information suggests that for now the deaths are best treated as accidental, and thus they are excluded from further consideration in the present research.

Preparation of case studies

Each case of homicide for the period 1985–89 was examined, and a working file was prepared which pulled together the information from these various sources of information. From these working files, a case study was written for each case. The central focus of these case studies was the dynamics of the interaction between the victim and offender. In some cases, little would be known, particularly in some of the unsolved killings. Thus, the entry might consist of a brief observation that a body was found late at night at a service station, with a bullet wound to the head, with the homicide apparently occurring in the course of an armed robbery. In other cases (as can be seen in the sections which follow) much more information is available, and an extensive narrative can be developed which can run to several paragraphs. In all cases, names have been altered to protect the privacy of those involved.

At times, it appears that a reasonably accurate accounting of the events is possible, including many of the utterances which passed between victim and offender in the events leading up to the killing. This occurs because in the great bulk of the cases homicide is emphatically a public and social act, and the tragedy is played before a social audience who afterwards are able to provide an account where the various participants agree as to what was said. The multiple grievances that lead to lethal violence are frequently spread through time, and relatives and close friends have a clear view of the precipitating events.

While in virtually all cases some narrative account can be prepared, some problems in the procedure need to be recognised. A major difficulty is that in homicides the viewpoint of the victim is not available afterward to provide an interpretation of what transpired, except in the few cases where the victim lingers for a period of time after the fatal wounding. In most instances it is possible by means of witness statements to obtain a reasonable account of what the victim apparently did and said in the precipitating events. Often strong advocates of the victim's point of view are present, such as their close friends or relatives, who may have seen the playing out of the whole tragedy.

Nonetheless, victims obviously cannot have the opportunity of the police interview, the Coroner's inquest, and the trial itself to tell the tale from their point of view. Furthermore, there are at times inherent conflicts in the homicide scene which carry over into the interpretations which follow. In some cases, the homicide results from conflict between two groups, each of which has a vital stake in selling a view as to who initiated the violence. In other cases, perhaps because of high levels of alcohol intake during the lead up to the homicide, the offender or other witnesses may not provide a clear account of what happened.

In the preparation of the case studies which provide the basic data for the present study, it is recognised that there are likely to be distortions in the accounts that are available. As much as possible, an attempt has been made to bring in viewpoints from those close to the victim. In the great majority of the cases, in fact, most observers available after the fatal wounding appear to agree on the basic outline of what happened. Where that is not the case, within the case study itself it is indicated that the interpretation of the events is open to some amount of confusion.

The study actually proceeded in two stages. The first stage was an investigation of general patterns of homicide, and was designed as part of a national initiative concerned with violence (Polk and Ranson, 1991a), and examined data for 1985 and 1986. The second stage evolved as a result of the emergence in the initial phase of the masculine scenarios of violence, and called for a further exploration of these by adding the data for the 1987–89 period.

An approach to the study of homicide

There are two important features of the approach to be followed in this book. First, the procedures are fundamentally qualitative in nature. Specifically, the investigation focuses on a detailed thematic analysis of case histories which are prepared for all homicides in the files. Second, these case studies are prepared to throw light on the particular dynamics which characterise the interactional dynamics which link victims and offenders. In criminology the investigation of homicide is unique in its persistent emphasis on the critical role of the social interaction between victim and offender. Few have put the matter as well as Wolfgang (1958), who set criminologists off on the chase for an understanding of such social relationships when he argued that:

> homicide is a dynamic relationship between two or more persons caught up in a life drama where they operate in a direct, interactional relationship. More so than in any other violation of conduct norms, the relationship the victim bears to the offender plays a role in explaining the reasons for such flagrant violation.
> *(Wolfgang, 1958: 203)*

In virtually all sociological studies since that time, close attention is paid to what transpires between victim and offender. As a consequence, each researcher has developed an approach to the analysis of particular forms of relationship which are found between the victim and offender prior to the homicide.

If there is agreement that such a focus should guide research, there is little consistency in dealing with the question of how such analyses should proceed. It is interesting that over thirty years ago, at the beginning of this long line of investigation, Wolfgang could comment that: 'The usual difficulties of incomparable classifications are met when the distribution of victim-offender relationships is compared with other research.' (Wolfgang, 1958: 217)

It is a matter of empirical fact that in the ensuing period this problem of 'incomparable classifications' has not only continued, but arguably has worsened. None of the major investigations following the Philadelphia research has maintained the system of classification suggested by Wolfgang. Some writers follow a path of parsimony, as did Hewitt (1988) in reducing the scheme to but three categories, while others have gone for a more exhaustive listing, as found in the Supplementary Homicide Reports (Maxfield, 1989) where over thirty categories are employed. More important, of course, is the unfortunate diversity in the content of the categories. Most, in fact, suggest one or another form of relationship which is unique. Of Wolfgang's (1958) original list of eleven categories, subsequent researchers have tended to ignore such forms of relationship he proposed as 'paramour, mistress, prostitute', 'enemy', or 'innocent bystander'. Wallace (1986) employed a grouping referring to a 'residential' relationship not mentioned by others, Maxfield's (1989) lengthy list proposed 'employee' and 'employer' relationships which are not found in other classifications, while Falk's (1990) category of 'neighbors' similarly appears to be unique.

In fact, among the many investigations on homicide carried out over the years, it would be fair to say that each tends to employ its own description of victim/offender relationships so that it is highly likely that no two lists will be the same. There may be agreement regarding what should be done (that is, analyse the dynamics occurring between victim and offender), but there is no clear agreement regarding how such analyses should proceed.

One should be careful not to overstate this case, however, since a review of the various classification schemes shows some minimum amount of consistency. Using the term 'relational distance' suggested by Silverman and Kennedy (1987), it is reasonable to argue that all of the classification schemes pose an underlying continuum which ranges from the most intimate relationships at one extreme, to the most distant (strangers) at the other. This idea of relational distance is brought into sharp perspective in the briefer of the classification schemes, such as Hewitt (1988) where provision is made for three groupings: 'relative', 'known' and 'stranger'; or Zahn and Sagi (1987) with their suggested 'family', 'acquaintance', 'stranger felony' and 'stranger non-felony' groupings.

For all that, the various classification schemes are more diverse than they are consistent. It can be argued that the reason for the diversity rests in the nature of the task itself, and the inadequacy of the common terms to carry us very far in understanding what is happening between offender and victim.

It is for this reason, of course, that many researchers have turned to another grouping, one which deals more directly with the particular conditions which produce lethal violence. Here, again, a starting point is Wolfgang (1958), who proposed a classification of 'motives' of homicide consisting of thirteen categories (which begins with his particularly well known 'altercation of trivial origin', which accounted for 35 per cent of all homicides in Philadelphia).

The consistency of this grouping fares even worse as we look at subsequent investigations. As a matter of fact, in the research which has followed there has not even been agreement regarding what it is that is being classified. For example, the Supplementary Homicide Reports used by Maxfield (1989) provided thirty separate groupings of what are termed 'homicide circumstance' (rather than motive), with only minimal overlap with the list suggested by Wolfgang.

A different approach is employed in the Chicago Homicide Project (Block and Block, 1992) which identifies various 'homicide syndromes', including homicides which are 'expressive' (where the immediate goal is to hurt, maim or kill, this grouping including 'competitive confrontations', neighbour or work-related killings, bar-room brawls, child abuse, elder abuse, revenge killings, etc.), those which are 'instrumental' (robbery homicide, burglary homicide, arson for profit, etc.), those which involve rape, or are street-gang related, one residual category designated as 'other', and a second residual grouping in which are placed cases involving some 'mystery' (including homicides which are unsolved or in which there is no evidence of motive).

The fundamental problem with existing codes of either relationships or motives/circumstances is that as these stand they do not provide enough information to inform theoretical analysis of why people kill. Knowing that persons are related by marriage provides a possible hint as to why the homicide occurs, since it would appear reasonable that the source of the violence resides somewhere in the marital bond. It does not speak to why either the husband or the wife has killed, however. Even more critical is a category such as 'stranger', since it becomes an enormous puzzle to determine what would generate the exceptional emotions most often found in a homicide when the people involved are previously unknown to each other.

While these various approaches to classifying either forms of relationship or motive may have some descriptive value, it can be argued that they are not of much use in helping to direct theoretical analysis of homicide. As Daly and Wilson put it:

> the prevailing criminological conception of motives in homicide is a woolly amalgam of several potentially independent dimensions: spontaneity versus premeditation, the victim-offender relationship, and only a relatively small dose of those substantive issues that murder mystery and ordinary speakers of English mean when they speak of 'motive' ... Violence arises from conflicts *about something*, difficult though it may be to pinpoint exactly what, and notwithstanding that the bones of contention may be multiple.
>
> (*Daly and Wilson, 1988: 173–4*)

It is the present contention that while there is some minimal amount of value in existing classification procedures, it is time to re-examine the actual data of homicide to observe if it is possible to obtain more concise and theoretically meaningful groupings of homicides. Such categories, it will be argued, should make reference not simply to the relationship between the individuals, but what it is that has transpired to bring the victim and the offender to the point where lethal violence is employed. In the terms used by Daly and Wilson immediately above,

it is assumed that the conflict was 'about something', and the task of the
present research is to see if it is possible to obtain a better understanding of what constitutes such events.

Such a view starts from a similar point to that of Luckenbill (1977),
who argued for viewing homicide as a 'situated transaction'. The aim of
the analysis will be to identify the various themes which govern such
social transactions, in order to see if an ordered and small set of
groupings emerge.

The present investigation is not completely blind in carrying out
such an analysis. Daly and Wilson in their work have emphasised the
masculine character of homicide, pointing out that across time and
across cultures homicide is a masculine matter. These writers have
identified at least three dimensions of masculine violence which can
help point the way for the present study. It is their view that males are
more likely than females to employ violence: (1) in sexual relationships
as a form of reproductive control, especially around the issue of
jealousy; (2) in killings arising out of sexual rivalry; (3) in altercations
involving 'honour'; and (4) in the situation of 'robbery homicides'
(Daly and Wilson, 1988).

The present case studies were analysed in order to identify the major
themes of victim-offender interaction in scenes of lethal violence. Each
of the case studies was reviewed in terms of the key elements in the
scenario of violence which unfolded. These were then grouped into
those which seemed to share common themes. Thus, the process was
fundamentally qualitative (in that it focused on the emergent themes of
interaction based on case history accounts) and inductive in that the
defining themes, or key elements of the scenarios, emerged from the
close reading and then grouping of the individual case studies.

As the patterns began to emerge, guidelines, or a set of check lists,
were developed to guide the coding. For each particular form of homicide, in other words, a series of questions could be used to provide for
the accurate placement of cases into the various categories. It must be
emphasised that the process was a highly emergent one, and the process gradually unfolded, with some types being altered as new data were
added. The resulting set of groupings are discussed briefly below, and
in the chapters which follow. In a chapter dealing with methodological
issues, some of the specific issues which arise in the process of
classification of homicide are addressed.

In general, the themes which emerge are consistent with the forms
suggested by Daly and Wilson, although somewhat more clusters
emerged from the present case studies. The various groupings will be
discussed briefly here in order to establish the overall pattern, with a
more detailed description of the major patterns to be elaborated in the

Table 1: *Forms of victim-offender relationships in homicide, Victoria, 1985–89*

Homicides in the context of sexual intimacy	(N=101)			
Female victim/male offender (Chapter 3)		73		
Jealousy/control			58	
Depression/suicide			15	
Male victim/male offender (Chapter 3)		13		
Sexual rivals			13	
Homosexual killings			0	
Male victim/female offender (Chapter 7)		12		
Provoked by violence			8	
Control/other			4	
Female victim/female offender (Chapter 7)		3		
Sexual rival			2	
Homosexual killing			1	
Homicides originating in family intimacy (Chapter 7)	(N=40)			
Children victims		31		
Victims of trauma			13	
Battered children				7
Victims of shooting, other				6
Victims of parental suicide			9	
Neonaticides			8	
Victims of neglect			1	
Other family victims		9		
Sister victim/brother offender			2	
Parent victims/son, step-son offender			5	
Other (in-law, grandparent victims)			2	
Confrontational homicides (Chapter 4)	(N=84)			
Homicide originating in other crime (Chapter 5)	(N=61)			
Double victims		31		
Reverse victims		18		
Killed by police			11	
Killed by citizen			7	
Professional killings		5		
Police killed		5		
Prison killings		2		
Conflict resolution homicides (Chapter 6)	(N=38)			
Victims of mass killers (Chapter 7)	(N=15)			
Unsolved (and unclassifiable) (Chapter 8)	(N=22)			
'Special' cases (Chapter 8)	(N=18)			
Mercy killing (Chapter 8)	(N=1)			
Total	(N=380)			

chapters which follow. Clearly, from the present data a large proportion of homicides have their origins in matters concerning sexual relationships. Just over one-fourth of all homicides (101 of 380, or 27 per cent) evolved in one way or another in the context of sexual relationships (Table 1).

In examining this major cluster, however, it became apparent that it was necessary to differentiate the cases by gender of both victim and offender. There were a total of 86 cases where males were the offenders. In the largest proportion of these (73 of the 86), the victim was the female partner of the male. Most of these female killings resulted from the attempt of the male to assert control over the behaviour of his partner through the use of violence (58 of the 73 female victims of male offenders), often in the context of jealousy. A significant proportion (15 of the 73), however, were in a situation where the male was extremely depressed, and the homicide was part of the planned suicide of the male. Masculine violence in cases of sexual jealousy is not limited to females, so that in addition, there were 13 cases where males killed their male sexual rival. Among these case studies there were no cases of homicide arising out of sexual jealousy among male homosexuals, although a longer time span would be likely to produce examples of such homicides.

Women were much less likely to kill in the context of sexual relationships. There were in all 15 such cases, of which 12 were made up of males being killed by their female sexual partners. Most of these (8 of the 12) were females killing in response to the violent behaviour of the male partner. Only 3 killings arose out of an attempt of the woman to exert possessive control over the partner's behaviour (there were no cases where the woman killed her male partner because of jealousy), and there was one case where a woman and her lover contracted for another male to kill her husband so that the two could live together. There were 3 cases where women killed women because of sexual relationships, 2 of these representing the removal of a sexual rival, while the remaining case was an instance of a killing with its origins in homosexual jealousy.

A second major pattern consisted of distinctively masculine 'confrontations' arising out of defence of honour. There were 84 of these homicides (accounting for 22 per cent of all killings). A major characteristic of these is that in most cases they emerged quickly out of some exchange, often involving insults, sometimes nonverbal gestures. The events would move rapidly and spontaneously from these initial events, often starting with a fight, then leading to the fatal injuries. Virtually all of the individuals engaging in this scenario were male, but there were four examples (5 per cent of all confrontational killings) where this pattern involved women as both offender and victim.

A third pattern involved homicides which arose out of other criminality, which accounted for 61 (or 16 per cent of the total). Most common here were double victims (31 of the 61) who were the victim first of some crime such as robbery or burglary, and then became the victim of homicide. In another 18 of the 61 cases, the ultimate homicide victim was an offender in an original crime (11 of these 'reverse victims' were killed by police, the remainder, 7, by the victim of the original crime). Included here as well are 5 professional killings, 5 police killed while on duty, and 2 cases where the death occurred in prison.

A fourth pattern involved what is termed here 'conflict resolution' homicides, where the killing resulted from the planned and rational intention to employ violence to resolve some form of personal dispute, over such issues as debts, shared resources or the like, between victim and offender. Most often this pattern, which accounted for 38 homicides (or 10 per cent of all homicides) involved persons well at the boundaries of conventional society, such that their close ties to a criminal way of life closed off any possibility of the use of conventional conflict resolution procedures.

While the present analysis will focus on four scenarios of masculine violence that can be derived from the major patterns reviewed up to this point, there are, of course, other forms of homicide. A further pattern, for example, involves multiple homicides. Within the present data, we found 2 examples of mass killings which contributed a total of 15 victims. There were no examples of the serial killings in this time period that feature so prominently in the analysis of homicide in the United States.

Killings within the boundaries of family relationship contributed another 40 cases (making up 10 per cent of all homicides), with most of these being 31 cases of children killed by parents. The largest group of these child killings were made up of deaths resulting from trauma (13 cases), with smaller numbers where the death was part of the suicide plan of a parent (9 cases), where the death was a neonaticide (8 cases) and there was one child who was a victim of parental neglect.

There was one case of a 'mercy killing' which could not be placed within any other category.

There were, in addition, 18 cases which were so odd, bizarre or different that it was impossible to trace an easy interpretation from the relationship to the killing, and these have been grouped together and placed within a category of 'special' killings and are discussed in Chapter 7. This same chapter will provide an analysis of the 22 killings which were both unsolved and unclassifiable within the other categories.

As analysts such as Wallace (1986) or Daly and Wilson (1988) have argued, gender is a fundamental issue which projects through these figures. From the hypotheses sketched out by Daly and Wilson, the first three of the masculine scenarios of violence might have been expected, these consisting of the masculine use of violence around issues of sexuality and sexual control, the use of violence in the confrontational scene as a defence of masculine honour, and the masculine willingness to take risks involved in engaging in crime which threatens life. The fourth pattern, homicide as a form of conflict resolution, emerged inductively out of the present analysis. It is the task of the following pages to round out each of these four scenarios of masculine violence, and to provide the case study material which illustrates the empirical content of such patterns. After this, a brief discussion of the other forms of homicide will help to set the context for these four scenarios.

CHAPTER 3

Scenarios of masculine violence in the context of sexual intimacy

Homicide is most likely to occur between people who not only know each other, but in fact share some form of close relationship. In the words of Wallace (1986: 93), homicide 'is a crime which typically occurs among intimates'. Similarly, in their study of 'intimate homicide', Silverman and Mukherjee commented that lethal violence often occurs in relationships that initially were forged 'on the basis of some positive attachment'. (Silverman and Mukherjee, 1987: 37)

Among the many forms of intimacy, the one which accounts for the largest share of these homicides is that arising out of sexual relationships. In the analysis of national patterns, Strang (1992) observed that 21 per cent of homicides in Australia took place between 'spouses', a figure close to the 23 per cent observed in Wallace's (1986) study of New South Wales. As is true of homicide generally, the dominant picture, at least in Australia, is one of masculine violence. Wallace observed that:

> Marital murder in New South Wales is, as it was 100 years ago ... , a practice largely confined to men: 73.3% ... of the marital murders were committed by husbands; 26.7% ... were committed by wives. Thus, women were three times more likely than men to be killed by their spouse. Both numerically and proportionately, more women than men were killed by their marital partner.
> *(Wallace, 1986: 84)*

How is it that what begins as a relationship of closeness and intimacy can turn in such a direction that exceptional violence is provoked? The case study data enable us to draw out the threads that run through this particular scenario of masculine violence. For present purposes, it will be presumed that intimacy refers to couples who have established a

27

sexual relationship, so that this will include persons who are married, persons involved in a de facto relationship, as well as persons who have been going together to the point where a sexual relationship has been established. There were 73 homicides where males took the lives of their sexual intimates (accounting for 19 per cent of all homicides). There were, in addition, 13 homicides where a male killed what he presumed was his sexual rival, a form of homicide which also derives from some initial sexual intimacy. In total, then, there were as a consequence 86 homicides where males killed and where a sexual relationship provided the bond with the victim (23 per cent of all homicides).

There appear to be two distinct major sub-patterns to the homicides where men kill women, one concerned with sexual possession where violence is employed as a control strategy, the other with a pattern of suicidal masculine depression which also encompasses the female partner in a control process, but to quite a different end. The elements of these patterns can be seen in the various case studies which follow.

The theme of masculine possession

Wallace (1986) in her study of homicide in New South Wales observed that either separation (or its threat) or jealousy were the major precipitating events of homicides where men took the lives of their spouses. This, she argued, was a reflection of the ultimate attempt of males to exert 'their power and control over their wives' (Wallace, 1986: 123). In all, among the present case studies 58 of the homicides (15 per cent of all homicides) could be considered as a reflection of male use of violence to control their sexual partners.

It is commonly the threat of separation, and the feelings of jealousy aroused by such a separation, that prompts the violence. Daly and Wilson (1988) have argued that sexual jealousy and rivalry are the dominant motives in homicide involving women as victims and men as offenders. This arises, they postulate, out of the inherent desire of men to control women and their reproductive capacities: 'we find it highly significant that *men the world around think and talk about women and marriage in proprietary terms*' (Daly and Wilson, 1988: 189, emphasis in the original). They observe that jealousy and sexual ownership constitute the major 'dangerous' issue in marriage (Daly and Wilson, 1988: 200). Rasche (1989), in support of this observation, reports that the single most important motive for murder among intimates was the inability of the offender to accept the termination of the relationship.

Certainly, the theme of jealousy and control run consistently through the many case studies of intimate homicide. Consider the following account:

Some six years previously, Rita B. (age 39, home duties) after a divorce had formed a de facto relationship with G.K. (who was born in Cyprus). In the last few months of her life, this relationship turned stormy and violent. Her son later observed that: 'I was aware that there were many arguments between them ... I was aware of injuries received by my mother which I know were inflicted by G.K. I have seen G.K. physically strike my mother. I have seen bruises and she has complained of sore legs and back.' The son also stated that he: 'heard G.K. threaten to kill my mother. G.K. had been away for a while and my mother was going out with another man, a butcher from Kew.' The son testified that when G.K. found out about her other relationship, he again threatened his mother, saying: 'if I can't have you, no one will ...'.

Because of these assaults and threats, the police were called, and G.K. was subsequently charged with assault. Rita attempted to solve her problems by moving out. She made every attempt to keep her new address a secret, even pleading with the removalist not to divulge her address to anyone. The removalist later stated that Rita had told him that 'if anyone comes looking for me, don't tell them where I live because if he finds out he will kill me.'

Rita was correct in her assessment of G.K.'s intentions, but underestimated his inventiveness. When G.K.'s attempts to find Rita were unsuccessful (he did contact that removalist, who refused to provide the new address), he then hired a private detective who was successful in identifying the new address.

Shortly afterwards, Rita's mother received a call from her terrified daughter. G.K. had just called and said he was coming over to kill her. The mother told Rita to call the police immediately, which she did. By the time the police arrived she was already dead, having been killed by multiple gunshot wounds to the head. G.K. immediately left Australia, and has not yet been found and brought to trial.   *(Case No. 1731–85)*

This male was obsessional in his desire to maintain control over his sexual partner. He would destroy his intimate 'possession' rather than let her fall into the hands of a competitor male. In addition, in this account a deep level of premeditation can be observed. The killing is not the spontaneous outgrowth of an argument which gets out of control. This male planned carefully, including going to the extraordinary lengths of employing a private investigator to locate the residence of his victim. Such elaborate steps are common in these intimate homicides:

It was just at the end of the working day, 5 pm, when A.L. walked into the Laverton Police Station and announced 'I have just shot my wife'. Police went to A.L.'s house, and found Clara L. (age 43, home duties) dead of multiple gunshot wounds. In the interview which followed, A.L. explained how he had purchased a percussion revolver (a 19th century weapon) from a gun shop by claiming he was a collector of antique firearms some two months prior to this, then taking the weapon home and testing it to make sure he knew how to make it work.

A.L. then related how he had carefully studied his wife's movements, and knew which train he could expect her to travel on after she finished her shopping (she had moved out some three months before). As she stepped down from a train carrying her to her new home, A.L. approached Clara, and talked her into coming with him to his residence. As she was putting the kettle on to fix him a cup of tea, he fetched his revolver from an adjoining room, and shot her in the head. He said that he 'just had enough of her', and when questioned about his motives, he said that 'she's been sticking it to me for many years . . . she's had a number of different men'.

Subsequent questioning of Clara's friends revealed a different story. They related that they knew her well, but, as one put it: 'I have been in close contact with Clara and she never had an interest in other men, nor was she having an affair with anyone.' This same friend related how Clara had been mistreated by A.L., including occasions where her face was so severely cut and bruised that several stitches were required to close the wounds. Finally, 'She couldn't stand A.L. because he was beating her up and tormenting her', so she moved out of the marital household. After she left, Clara received several telephone calls from her husband, calls which were abusive and threatening. A.L. then obtained the weapon, and successfully plotted her death. After the crime, A.L. showed no remorse over the killing, expressing instead a sense of relief.   *(Case No. 3858–85)*

Here, too, can be seen the careful planning which led to the homicide. The wife's movements were plotted, and the difficult steps were taken to obtain the murder weapon (hand guns are controlled weapons in Victoria). In both this and the first case, there is the presence of considerable violence prior to the homicide, that violence being a major factor in the decision of the woman to try to separate from the male.

The careful tracking of the movements of the victim as part of the plan illustrates the intentional character of many of these homicides. When the rage has reached the point where the male is ready to kill, he often scouts out the movements of his victim, determining where and when she will be vulnerable to attack:

In April 1987, Vicki (age 25, kindergarten teacher) ended a four-year de facto relationship with P.L. The breakup was impossible for P.L. to accept. He began to harass her in various ways, including constant telephone calls (it finally reached the point where co-workers would refuse to put telephone calls through to her at the school). One Monday, P.L. was successful in reaching Vicki by telephone, and insisted that she stop by the next day to return some crockery which he thought was his, and for her to pay him money for the car she was driving (which P.L.'s delusions drove him to believe he was owed). She ignored the request. Vicki's failure to show up Tuesday night tipped P.L. over the edge. The following morning, he armed himself with a knife and at 7.30 arrived at the school parking lot, awaiting Vicki. He had left plenty of time to make sure that he would be there before her. When Vicki arrived shortly after 8 am, P.L. confronted her, an argument developed, and he then stabbed her several times with the knife. Afterwards he stated that when Vicki told him to 'fuck off', he 'snapped', and that he remembered little of what happened after that.   *(Case No. 3732–87)*

These killings, however, are not sudden outbursts of violence provoked by an argument or other moment of passion (in the above account, for example, P.L. may claim that he 'snapped', but as well he plotted Vicki's movements, arranged to be where he knew she would be, even arriving early, and he brought the weapon with him). While the degree of intentionality varies, it is possible in close to two-thirds of these cases (37 of the 58, or 64 per cent) to find some clear element of prior planning in the events leading to the death. To be sure, they may not all 'stalk' their victims as found in these previous cases, but in most these are planned homicides rather than a swift upswelling of passionate rage.

Another element common to this scenario of masculine violence is the delusional character of the masculine response (as in P.L.'s conviction that Vicki owed him money, or A.L.'s belief that his wife had been having affairs with other men). A more convoluted form of such delusions is found in the following case:

After some twelve years of marriage, mounting financial pressures meant that Natalie H. (age 33, process worker) had to take a job to help support the household and two children. At the factory where she worked she met a man with whom she struck up a friendship that widened into a sexual relationship. Eventually she decided to leave her husband, A.H., leaving to move in with her new lover.

The husband, who had migrated from Yugoslavia some twenty years previously, still clung to some of his old world values, and found himself unable to cope with the breakup of the marriage. As they were arranging the formal details of the separation through their solicitors, Natalie mentioned to her new partner that A.H. had threatened to kill her. A.H. had experienced a transitory sexual encounter with a prostitute immediately after the initial separation. Curiosity led him to look through the handbag of the woman, where he said he found a picture of himself. He then constructed an elaborate fantasy whereby his wife and her boyfriend had arranged for the prostitute, whom he convinced himself had AIDS, to infect him with AIDS in turn so that he would die and they could inherit his property.

As this fantasy became more fixed in his mind, and as he began to detect (in his imagination) the symptoms of AIDS, A.H. decided to murder his wife. He illegally purchased a hand gun through connections in St Kilda (a Melbourne suburb). He began to plot his wife's movements. One day when he knew she would be shopping, he decided to act. He took the gun and searched the shopping centre until he found her, an argument started, and he shot her in the head with the pistol, killing her instantly.

When asked by the police what had happened that afternoon he replied:
A.H.: 'Something cross my mind, I am not a man any more because of my health' [referring to the AIDS].
Q: 'Had you made up your mind that you wanted to shoot her?'
A.H.: 'Yes, I have in the mind, that is why I buy the gun.'
Q: 'When did you make up your mind to shoot your wife?'

A.H.: 'When the pain getting worse and I can't sleep, probably three weeks ago.'
Q: 'Why did you shoot her?'
A.H.: 'Because I have to die and I never do anything wrong with her, never look at another girl, and I look to keep the family going and because she go the other way. She meet another person and go to New South Wales and gamble. I believe she must die, too ...'
Q: 'Do you feel any regret that your wife has now died?'
A.H.: 'I don't know. I just worry for the kids. She no worry for me when she leave. I worry for the kids only.'

One of the witnesses who helped apprehend A.H. as he attempted to flee from the scene of the killing testified that A.H. had said: 'She's my ex-wife ... she deserved it.'   *(Case No. 231–86)*

Fuelled by the jealous rage, delusions can build in the minds of these men tormented by the thought of their lovers moving out of their control and into the arms of another man (for a more detailed account of the role of 'morbid' jealousy in homicide, see Mowat, 1966). This goes to the lengths in this case where the male became convinced that an elaborate plot had been concocted to infect him with a fatal illness, even to the point where he imagined the symptoms of the disease. Consumed by jealousy which strikes deep at his manhood, driven by his delusional pain, he decided that since he was dying, she 'must die, too'. This exceptional jealousy is a common thread through many accounts of masculine, intimate homicide:

Terri (age 32, machine operator) had been married to Mack (age 43) for fourteen years. Over the past couple of years, Mack had become increasingly jealous of his wife, making many unfounded allegations that his wife was having affairs with other men. His controlling behaviour edged into the extreme when it reached the point where he forbade Terri to leave the house without him. At one point (a year before the homicide) he threatened Terri with a gun.

In June 1988 Mack and Terri had an argument because Terri wanted to visit her grandmother in a nearby town, and Mack stormed out of the house. Terri packed the children in the car and began the journey toward her grandmother's. Mack was waiting for them, parked by the side of the road. As his family passed, Mack pulled a shotgun from the boot of his car, and began to pursue them. Terrified, Terri pulled into a rest area and asked people there to call the police because she feared that Mack would shoot her. Seeing him approach, she took off in her car. Mack followed, and was able to force her off the road. He came up to the car and yelled: 'You've got to come home. You have to stay inside the house, and you are not to see your parents any more. You're going to be all right, because I'm going to control your life.' Terri pleaded with Mack, saying 'I'm not doing anything, I'll come home.' Mack pushed the gun through the window, and shot and killed Terri. He then reloaded the weapon, and killed himself.

It was established afterwards that Mack had been seeing a psychiatrist, who had observed that 'his main concern was his perceived loss of control of his wife ... if she continued in the same way, he would get his gun and shoot his wife and then himself.'   *(Case No. 2474–88)*

This male wanted virtually to lock his wife away, and his inability to exert this extraordinary level of control was a feature of his jealous rage. While for some men it is the threat of separation that generates masculine rage, in this case the woman's desire was simply to see her family, which the husband found literally intolerable.

It is hard to estimate the full level of delusional behaviour among these males, but a reading of the case accounts indicates that in one-third (19 of the 58, or 33 per cent) there is evidence that the male alleges sexual misconduct which others in the scene (family and friends of the victim) deny. While the male in some cases might have been correct, the point here is that many close to the victim allege that the male had deluded himself into believing that his partner was unfaithful, and the weight of the evidence suggests that males are too ready to not only believe in their partner's infidelities, but to react to these with violence. In some instances, as these previous case histories demonstrate, these delusions can go to rather extraordinary lengths.

It is not uncommon that males, trapped by the heat of the anger, express feelings of relief as with A.H. in the account above, rather than remorse, in the time immediately following the killing. The lack of remorse is captured in other accounts as well:

After going out with Michael (age 25, bouncer) for several months, Eileen (age 26, secretary) began to attempt to withdraw from the relationship. Michael found this difficult to accept, and began to utter threats concerning Eileen's growing independence (Michael had a history of violence with previous girlfriends). His jealousy grew, and resulted in such actions as his attempt to break into Eileen's flat early one morning (Michael had managed to convince himself, without foundation, that she was sleeping with someone else).

The crisis came on Christmas day. At the holiday gathering of Eileen's family the relatives noted an air of tension between the two. A minor incident flared when Eileen was, in Michael's view, overly friendly with other male guests at the party. When it came time for Michael to leave, Eileen went with him, indicating that she would return shortly. The couple parked their car in Errol Street, North Melbourne, and were overheard to argue. Police were summoned to the scene shortly afterward, and found Eileen dead (she had been strangled). When asked what happened by the police, Michael stated: 'I strangled the bitch, that's all.' When told that she was dead, Michael stated further: 'Fucking good, the bitch deserved it ... I wasn't going to let her hurt anyone again. I knew I had to do it ... I just lost it, she wasn't going to hurt me or anyone else again.'   *(Case No. 5524–88)*

The words 'the bitch deserved it' convey how far the mind's journey of these men has carried them. Their 'loved one' is now dead, but rather than remorse at the awesome act of killing, the men had convinced themselves that their partner deserved to die, that the fate was a justifiable one. The power of this rage to push out any feelings of remorse is also found in the following case:

> After living for a few months with T.K. (originally from Yugoslavia) in a de facto relationship in Melbourne, Hanna M. (age 46) decided to move to the country with T.K. to establish a dairy farm. The move, the economic stresses, and other factors brought unexpected pressures into their relationship. T.K. began to drink heavily and the couple began to fight. A young Yugoslav who worked as a hand on the farm, and who lived there, commented that they began to fight all the time, and that T.K. would: 'push Hanna, he push her into walls, doors, all the time. He kicked her in the bum. When he did this he called her names. She would never hit him back, he was too big. She was scared of him.' Hanna's daughter testified that she had seen bruises on her mother several times, while another friend commented that Hanna had told her that T.K. had even tried 'to kill her on numerous occasions'.
>
> Late one afternoon events seem to boil over. First, T.K. started after Hanna with a hammer. When the young farm hand intervened, T.K. backed off, only to return a few minutes later carrying an axe, leaving little doubt that he intended to use it on both Hanna and the farm hand.
>
> Hanna, the hand, and the girlfriend of the hand made a quick exit from the farm. They approached the police, but were told there was little that the police could do. When the young farm hand explained that they had no place to spend the night, he said that the police told him: 'You go to motel or friends.'
>
> Lacking money, and having no friends in the country area, the three made the mistake of returning to the farm after dark. They attempted to sneak into the bungalow at the back of the property which was the residence of the farm hand, but were discovered by T.K.
>
> The young hand and his girlfriend indicated that they did not want to stay. Hanna decided that she would be able to remain there safely, at least for the night. The farm hand stayed long enough to be assured that she would be safe. T.K., when he came into the bungalow, said: 'Don't scream, I don't want to touch you.' The farm hand surreptitiously looked on for a few minutes, then left, since, as he said he: 'didn't hear any screaming ... I thought it was the same as before. One minute scream, one minute quiet.'
>
> While somehow Hanna and T.K. managed to get through the night, the police were called to the scene the following morning. They found T.K. covered in blood, and Hanna dead from knife wounds. When asked what happened, T.K. answered: 'I grabbed her and told her that I will not let her leave ... She begged me not to kill her because she said she still loved me, but I said it was a lie, she did not love me any more ... I only wanted to destroy her ... I wanted to get rid of her then I can go to the jail and stay in peace.' *(Case No. 3028–86)*

In this account the anger is manifest, and in these immediate utterances can be found an expression of a sense of relief after the killing has been accomplished (and, certainly, no sense of remorse). The death freed the male so that he then could live 'in peace'. We see in this narrative a further issue, the ineffectiveness of the justice system when called upon by potential victims. The absence of police action is found in the following narrative as well:

Diane B. (age 32, on mother's pension) had met T.Y. (age 21, originally from Lebanon) at a disco a few months after she had broken up with her husband. The relationship went in fits and starts for about a year and a half. Finally, Diane cooled altogether and decided to call the relationship off.

T.Y. became enraged. First, he called her and abused her, then threatened to kill her. He then came over to her flat, banging on doors and windows, brandishing a shotgun. Diane stayed hidden, and successfully deceived T.Y. into thinking that she was not at home. T.Y. then went to the house of her sister, threatening the sister and her husband with the gun, demanding that they tell him Diane's whereabouts. The couple was able to calm T.Y. down, and when he left he seemed to have himself under control.

A few days later, however, he was again after Diane. This time he had lain in wait until he spotted her car, and then forced her off the road. In the argument which followed, TY.. said that he desperately 'wanted her back', and that 'if he couldn't have her, no one else would'. This time, though, as they talked T.Y. gradually calmed down and finally left.

After this episode, Diane sought help from the police, informing them that she had been threatened with a gun. Their advice was that she should move, and cease further contact with T.Y. The police made no attempt to apprehend T.Y., and no formal record of Diane's complaint was made by the attending officers.

One day shortly after, T.Y. again went to Diane's flat, this time being successful in gaining entry. What happened is not clear, but T.Y. first fired two shots from the shotgun into the ceiling of the flat, then one shot to the head which killed Diane, then turned the gun on himself, the result also proving fatal.   *(Case No. 1026-85)*

A repetition can be seen here of the attempt to claim exclusive rights over the intimate partner. A fact which stands out in this account is that the intentions of the male were well established. The unwillingness of the police to take action is notable, especially given that both witnesses and the victim made clear that the male had made threats with a gun.

Even if the police take aggressive action, however, they may not be able to contain the violence of the male:

Iris H. (age 33) had lived for some years with G.R. (age 48), and the couple had one child together (an older boy from Iris's previous marriage lived with them as well). G.R. became progressively more violent toward his de facto wife, and she finally decided to move out. At the same time, she struck up a close relationship with an older workmate of her oldest son. This male friend later recounted that the boy (age 14) had told him that G.R. often threatened him and his mother, including threats 'to kill them and burn the house down'. The friend became very close to the mother, since 'she was

under severe stress and looked to me to talk to and seek advice about her
domestic situation'.

G.R. broke in on the two while the two friends were having one of their
chats, and proceeded to assault the male whom he saw as a rival, accusing
him of 'back-dooring his missus'. The man told the police that: 'I defended
myself but he was acting like a crazy person ... he threatened to kill me and
Iris.' The police were called, and it was clearly established that the two had
not been in bed together. The police were able to calm G.R., at least for that
day, and he left.

Iris continued to be apprehensive, and sought help and advice from both
police and the Salvation Army. Early in the evening a week after the previous
incident, the police received a call from a woman saying that she had
suffered a gunshot wound to the chest. Police arrived to find Iris on the floor,
with her 3-year-old child kneeling beside her. She claimed that G.R. had shot
her, but 'at least I saved my baby'. She died in hospital as a result of shock
and haemorrhage due to multiple gun shot wounds. G.R. committed suicide
after he shot his wife.   *(Case No. 1979–86)*

In this account, the police attended, and to all appearances had
brought calm into the situation. Further, there was no indication to the
police that the male had a deadly weapon in his possession. As in other
of these cases, this male could not tolerate the separation of his sexual
partner, and the images his mind created of her sexual activity with
other men. There is, also, the background of prior physical violence
that so often is responsible for the decision of the woman to leave her
spouse.

In another account, the police gave the woman the good advice to
remove her self well away from the scene, that advice was followed, but
then the woman made the unfortunate mistake of returning for some
goods she had left behind:

Polly K. (age 25, home duties) had been living in a de facto relationship with
Abe R. (age 48) for ten years, with the couple having two children in that
time. In recent months, the two had experienced what the police reports
referred to as 'serious domestic difficulties' (that is, reports of physical
assault of Abe on Polly).

Polly decided finally that it was time to make a break, accepting police
advice that she remove herself from the home. She left the house for a few
days, hiding with friends in a country area well removed from their
Melbourne home. Abe became frantic, searching out all of Polly's known
haunts, making various threats of what he would do when he found her.

After being away for a few days, Polly returned home for the purpose of
gathering up her things. Abe happened to be home, and Polly made the
mistake of attempting to negotiate a separation. An argument developed,
which was followed by an assault by Abe on Polly. After the argument had
cooled a bit, Polly collected some bedding and clothes, according to Abe's
testimony, and retired to the caravan which was parked at the back of the
house to get away from Abe.

Later that night, Polly was found dead in the caravan. A single shot had been fired into her body at close range. Abe claimed that she had committed suicide, but the police found the story unconvincing, and he was charged with the murder of his de facto wife.   *(Case No. 99K1–85)*

The police in this case had offered advice which might have avoided the final clash. Neither the police nor the woman were able to predict, however, the lengths to which this male would go when gripped by his possessive rage.

From these accounts one can draw the pessimistic observation that the justice system can offer little real protection from the jealous rage of a male determined and set on the course of homicide. Even when orders are issued explicitly restraining the male from further violence, the protection offered can prove sadly inadequate:

The de facto relationship between Sally (age 31, shop assistant) and Richard was complicated, difficult and littered with a history of violence. The two had begun their relationship in early 1986, but separated after four or five months. For a brief period, Sally reunited with her first husband, and Richard in turn initiated a new de facto relationship with another woman. Neither of these new relationships worked, and in the middle of 1987 Sally and Richard once again resumed living together.

The new pattern was a repeat of the old. The relationship became progressively more violent, and to friends Richard stated that he was considering killing Sally. The couple split again on 1 January 1988. On 4 January Sally went to the local police station, alleging assault and stating that Richard had indicated his plan to take her life. A restraining order on Richard was issued on 6 January.

That same day, Sally became fearful of Richard's mounting anger, and his capacity for violence, and approached a male friend and asked for protection. The friend agreed to stay with Sally at her house. That night, Richard broke into Sally's house, and bludgeoned both Sally and her friend to death. He then dragged her body out of the house, and disposed of it in a place which has still not been uncovered.   *(Case No. 2290–88)*

In this narrative there is again the theme of persistent physical assault prior to the final outburst. Unlike some of the previous accounts, the woman attempted to extricate herself from the danger posed by the relationship, seeking help both from the justice system in terms of the restraining order, and from a male friend. As is common, the separation itself served to escalate the violent anger of the male. Neither the restraining order, nor the help of a friend, served as a barrier to this determined and violent male. A similar pattern is found in the following case:

After enduring many years of humiliation and violence in the marriage, Dorothy (age 35, textile worker) finally separated from her husband Harold

(age 38) after police had been called to the marital home because of a
domestic dispute. At first she moved with her two children to a nearby
refuge, returning to the home after a few days in the hope that Harold had
cooled down. A court order was obtained restraining Harold from bothering
Dorothy, and because of the difficulties it was arranged that the turnover
point for Harold's access visits to the children would be the local police
station.

It was only a matter of days before Harold violated the court order, and as
a result he was arrested and spent eight days in gaol. The police then applied
for a more restrictive restraining order, and also cancelled his firearms
licence, and all of his firearms were seized after the order had been issued.

Dorothy continued to be fearful of her husband, and asked for and
received further assistance from the police. The police undertook initiatives
to gather evidence on Harold's threats, and spoke to him about the potential
consequences of his behaviour. Harold was persuaded to see a psychiatrist on
a voluntary basis, and began a course of treatment, including taking various
medications (mostly tranquillisers).

One evening, after consuming both a large dosage of drugs and a large
quantity of alcohol (his blood alcohol level was later measured at 0.23), he
broke into his wife's home. When the wife and the children arrived at the
house later, they were confronted by Harold, armed with a shotgun. They
attempted to evade him by running into a bedroom and slamming the door.
Harold shot through the door, wounding one of the children. He then broke
into the bedroom, and shot his wife, killing her instantly. Following this, he
went into the kitchen, reloaded the gun, and then killed himself.

(Case No. 4541–89)

In many ways, this might appear to be a textbook case of proper
management of a domestic dispute on the part of the justice system.
When called, the police did intervene. Arrangements were made to
remove the woman initially to a refuge. As a result of court orders, the
male was prohibited from having unauthorised contact with the family,
and his firearms were seized. He was persuaded, successfully, to begin a
course of psychiatric treatment. Still, the rage of the male was so
overwhelming that all of these protections were brushed aside in the
final burst of lethal violence. It is worth noting that early on in this case,
during one of the first of the police interventions, the male had told
police: 'If that bitch takes the kids, I shoot her and then myself, I don't
care if you lock me up, if it takes weeks or months or years, I get a gun
somehow and shoot her and then myself.'

It was clear afterwards how serious he was. Since the state employed
virtually all of its preventive powers in this account, what this makes
obvious is how vulnerable a woman can be to the calculated anger of a
determined male, and how ineffectual the protections offered by the
state can be. There were in these files at least six homicides in which at
some point the woman had obtained a restraining order of some kind
on the male, and this is probably an underestimate since this

information might not have been recorded in all cases. In all, 23 of the 58 show some contact with the legal system (police, court, solicitor) prior to the homicide.

At times, there arise human ambivalences that reduce the power of the courts to extend even what limited protection might be available:

> After many years of marriage Sally (age 41, process worker) arranged an amicable separation from her husband. Shortly after, she met Larry (age 45) and the two began a de facto relationship. This was not a successful relationship, and within six months Sally had taken out an interim intervention order to prevent Larry from 'contacting, harassing, molesting or assaulting' her, and he was further ordered to surrender all firearms. Within a week, Larry had persuaded Sally to let him return, and as a consequence the police had no choice but to allow the order to lapse.
>
> Larry began to feel personal pressures mounting as a result of financial pressures (he was unemployed) and the fact that he was facing court charges on other matters. In addition he was drinking heavily, and was suffering from alcoholic hepatitis. The arguments of the couple began to build in intensity. Finally, once again Sally told Larry to leave. Two days later, he broke into the house, shot and killed Sally with a .22 rifle, and then took his own life.
>
> *(Case No. 3468–89)*

These relationships are complicated. Women may find themselves caught in a crossfire of conflicting emotions, among them some residue of close attachment to the male, or perhaps economic and psychological dependence. Feeling the pull of such forces, they allow themselves to be swept back into the cycle of violence which in the above case proved lethal.

There are other instances where court events themselves provide a spark for masculine violence. In one case (4032–89), the husband broke into his wife's house (they had been separated for about a year and a half) and shot her in the early morning of the day on which family court proceedings had been scheduled. A similar response is found in the following narrative:

> Carol (age 28, antique-shop owner and prostitute) and Keith (age 41, unemployed) had lived for a number of years in a violent relationship (she had suffered black eyes, a broken nose, broken jaw, as well as multiple bruising). Carol had been running an antique business, but found it hard to support her two children and her unemployed husband. As the bills began to get out of control, Carol began working as a prostitute. With the passage of time, Keith became more withdrawn and obsessive. Carol found the strains of managing work as a prostitute with the other demands of her life difficult, and decided to give up the work as a prostitute (a decision which Keith resisted).
>
> Finally, Carol had enough of the difficulties in their married life and separated from Keith, filing for a divorce. A few days after, Keith came by

Carol's new residence to mind the children while she went to see her
solicitor. When she returned, Carol showed Keith the Family Court
documents relating to the divorce proceedings. Keith left the room to fetch a
.22 rifle which he had brought with him earlier in the day, returned to the
room and shot Carol three times, killing her instantly.   *(Case No. 5055–87)*

While emphatically not the cause of the death, in this narrative the
issue of the court proceedings provided the spark which triggered the
final violence. It was as if the documents themselves epitomised the act
of separation, an act which was simply not to be tolerated by this male.
There are other stories in which the court or justice system plays some
background role in the violence:

After a number of years of marriage, Joan (age 34, factory worker) and Carl
(age 39) separated and obtained a divorce. Carl retained custody of their
child, with Joan having weekly access visits. Carl became concerned with
Joan's behaviour during these access visits (his daughter had told him of
seeing naked men, and of men sleeping with her mother during her visits).
On five different occasions, Carl returned to the Family Court to attempt
various modifications of the visitation rights, but was unsuccessful in all such
attempts.

Despite the difficulties between them, Carl apparently still wanted Joan to
return to him and to resume their married life. On one occasion, he took
both the daughter and his ex-wife on a long holiday to Adelaide in an
attempt to re-establish their relationship. This failed, and Carl was left with
the impression that Joan had been using him financially and otherwise (she
was born overseas, and their marriage had been the factor that had allowed
her immigration into Australia).

Shortly after the Adelaide trip Joan visited Carl at his flat. According to his
account of events, he offered her all the money he possessed ($10 000) if she
would remove herself from his life. He stated that she laughed, saying 'Is that
all you're going to give me?' Carl's anger flared, and he said that at this point
he pushed her. Joan in turn used her long fingernails to scratch his throat
and chest. The two fell to the floor, with Carl grabbing her about the neck.
He continued to apply pressure to the neck, and Joan died of strangulation.
(Case No. 2856–89)

There were, from Carl's point of view, two possible options. He would
have preferred his ex-wife to return to the marital home, and for them
to resume married life. Failing that, he apparently would be content
only if she were to be completely out of his life. The courts, it seems,
would not grant him this second option, and Joan's behaviour closed
off the first. From Carl's point of view, the inability of the Family Court
to come to grips with what he defined as the unacceptable behaviour of
Joan would be a major factor leading to this killing. In terms of both the
law and the facts, of course, there would be little choice available to the
court other than the one that it chose. And, when all is said and done,

the underlying issue was Carl's inability to cope with his wife's separation and divorce. It was not the Family Court that wrapped its fingers around Joan's throat.

A point demonstrated by this case, however, is that not all of these intimate homicides show the pattern of careful premeditation. There are instances where the anger does flare suddenly (although in most cases there is a well-established base of masculine resentment, if not prior violence). As in the case involving Carl, the violence can erupt suddenly when the female partner openly challenges the male, especially around issues of sexuality:

Alice N. (age 38, home duties) had been married to G.N. for twenty years. Their relationship had begun to crumble after the death of their 10-year-old daughter in a traffic accident in the previous year. Alice had become extremely frightened of her husband because he regularly beat and threatened her. As one neighbour said: 'Alice ... was frightened of G.N. She would tell me that he carried a gun and that he had pointed it at her and at the children. G.N. had often given Alice a belting ... earlier this year, G.N. gave Alice a belting in the driveway out the front of their house. He was kicking into her and she was lying in the driveway.'

Family had also become worried, including Alice's sister who explained 'when Alice would come to my place after these fights, she would be a nervous wreck ... I told her to leave him, but she was too scared of what he would do to her. He was a very jealous man and he had a very bad temper ... At one time, I recall Alice saying to me that she was frightened G.N. would kill her.'

Alice had approached police seeking help, but seemed indecisive when it became necessary for her to act in order to have the police take action. Things took a rapid turn for the worse.

G.N. became convinced that Alice was having an affair with one of his best friends (other family and the friend deny this). One morning Alice and G.N. had another argument. G.N. alleged to his son that when he had confronted Alice with the fact the affair had been going on for weeks, she replied to him 'For weeks? ... it's been going on for seven months!' G.N. stormed into his room, picked up his hand gun, came back and shot Alice as she sat on the couch in the loungeroom. G.N. then dashed over to the house of the friend whom he suspected of having the affair, and shot him as well. G.N. then fled, and some six days later turned himself in to a local police station in the company of his solicitor. Alice's wounds proved fatal, but the friend, although severely wounded, lived.   *(Case No. 3247–85)*

It can be seen in this narrative that a challenge on sexual matters can provide a spark for the flaring of sudden violence. It must be added, however, that there was a solid base of hostile violence which had been constructed over time, and the presence of the hand gun, and the seeking out of the sexual rival, suggest that the argument had provided the pretext for actions which the offender had given prior contemplation (although, to be sure, on the basis of the available evidence this cannot be considered a planned homicide). As well, there is in this case study an illustration of the indecisiveness in the woman that can be caused by a high level of violence, when there is fear that there might be an escalation of risk if a separation is threatened. The victim did attempt to reach out for help, both to family and to the police, which proved ineffectual apparently because of the profound level of tension and fear of potential consequences that any steps might provoke in the male.

In a similar case, a woman had separated for a few days from her de facto husband, and when confronted on the night that she informed him she wanted to terminate the relationship completely and announced that she had begun a sexual relationship with another man. The man flew into a rage and bludgeoned his partner to death (later committing suicide in a police cell). (Case No. 2985–88)

In another case, it was the husband's demand for sex and the refusal of the partner to comply (coupled with the fact that he felt he was losing control over her), which provoked the violence:

> Mary T. (age 34, bank teller) had been married for some years to V. when the marriage began to cool for her. She began to move outward and establish a life outside the marital home, away from her husband and two children.
>
> For the husband, this became difficult to bear when it involved Mary initiating a sexual relationship with another man. Mary finally approached a solicitor, instructing him to draw up the arrangements for a separation and divorce from V. This was a difficult period, and Mary's new lover later testified that Mary had told him there had been several heated arguments with V., and there had been instances of sexual assault.
>
> Mary chose to stay in the marital home during this troubled time. On her birthday the lover sent flowers and a card to Mary, which provoked a major argument between husband and wife.
>
> Later that night, according to V.'s testimony to the police, he attempted to make love to his wife. She refused to have anything to do with V. Angered, the husband persisted but Mary continued to resist. As his rage grew, V. began to use physical violence to force his wife to comply with his sexual demands. Mary began to scream, and V. put some clothing over her face to stop her from crying out. This resulted in her death through suffocation.
>
> In an attempt to conceal what had happened, V. placed his wife's body in a car, poured petrol over her, and set the car alight. This clumsy attempt to disguise what had happened was penetrated by the police within a short time. When confronted, V. broke down, saying: 'I did it, I did it, I loved her so much, I loved her. I didn't mean it, I loved her.'   *(Case No. 3062–86)*

Some of these cases, then, fit a pattern of rage which boils over to the point where the homicide results. As in most such cases, however, a foundation of marital discord has been laid down, including previous threats to separate on the part of the female, and prior violence on the part of the male.

It is also the case that the violence may spring from the desire of the woman to separate, regardless of whether the woman has become involved with a sexual rival:

> Tommy had been living with Jill and her three children for three years, but what had started as a good relationship had gone very sour. Tommy was a heavy drinker, and friends described him as drunk and a 'no hoper'. When Tommy would drink heavily (which he did often), it would lead to violent arguments with Jill, with friends commenting that this would result in Jill evidencing visible bruises and black eyes. As time passed, Tommy's violent behaviour increased and became more and more bizarre. On one occasion when Jill and the children were visiting at a friend's house, Tommy poured petrol around the outside of the house and threatened to burn the house down. On another occasion, he discovered that his teenage daughter was going out with a boyfriend, and he started slapping her around. When Jill intervened, he went outside, and started hitting the outside of the house with an axe, and would not stop until the police came and took him away. Some time after this episode, one night when Tommy came home drunk, Jill informed him that she was going to separate. His first response was to point to a short piece of rope and say that he was going to hang Jill and her children with it. Some time later, he went out into the shed, found a fishing knife, returned and stabbed Jill fatally.   *(Case No. 2191–89)*

Rather than jealousy, the issue in this case is sheer possessiveness. The threat of the separation, especially given the history of violence, was enough to push this male to the point where lethal violence resulted. The following is similar in the inability of the male to accept the fact of separation:

> Holly L. and R. had been going together for four years, but Holly had come to the conclusion that their relationship should be finished. R. had difficulty accepting this, and for a while Holly vacillated back and forth, but finally decided that it had to be terminated. R. took it badly, began drinking heavily, and commented to a woman friend that he planned to kill himself. He began to follow Holly around, and would plead with her to return. One night Holly and her friends were at a pub where R. was also present. One of Holly's woman friends went over to R. and asked him why he had been following Holly, and tried to tell him that the relationship was over. R. then approached Holly, and she, too, again told him that he had to accept that what they had was finished. Friends say that she was gentle in her language. He left the pub early in the evening: R. then went home and picked up his rifle. He returned to the pub, and waited some hours for Holly and her party to leave. When she came out, R. approached, and a scuffle broke out between him and one of Holly's woman friends who tried to intervene. He shoved her aside, and shot Holly at close range. Holly was killed instantly.

> *(Case No. 2959–87)*

For some men, then, it is sheer possessiveness that drives them, and faced with the loss of the partner their response is violence. The power of the male to control is demonstrated by the very act of destruction of his 'possession'.

Masculine depression and homicide followed by suicide

In several of the preceding accounts, the powerful motives of jealousy and loss of control resulted in the male taking his own life as well as that of his sexual partner. There is another pattern involving sexual relationships which evolves out of a theme of control mixed with exceptional depression. In these events, the male is going through some form of depressive crisis which is severe enough to lead him to consider suicide. These events revolve, then, around the decision of the male to take his own life, with the killing of the woman being a secondary consequence of this decision. These males are not primarily focused on the destruction of their partner, but reach the point of insisting, after they have concluded that their own lives must end, that their partner should be a part of this decision as well. In these files there were 15 such homicides, these making up 20 per cent of the cases where males killed their female sexual partner. A major differentiating characteristic of these cases is that the major focus is on the suicide of the male:

One afternoon, the telephone operator of the Victorian Ambulance Service answered the telephone, and the following conversation ensued:
    A male voice, later identified as F.M. began: 'Ambulance, can you send an ambulance to (he gave his address in Carnegie, a Melbourne suburb)?'
    O: 'What's happened there?'
    F.M.: 'There's a couple of gunshot, gunshot, ... ah ... mmm, or people with gunshot wounds to be picked up.'
    O: 'And, who's got the shotgun?'
    F.M.: 'There's no shotgun.'
    O: 'But you just said there's been a couple of shotgun wounds.'
    F.M.: 'I said there's been gun shot wounds which is definitely small calibre.'
    O: 'But, who's ... who's ... who's got the gun?'
    F.M.: 'I've had the gun.'
    O: 'And, who have you shot?'
    F.M.: 'I've shot my wife, and I am about to shoot myself.'
    O: 'You are going to shoot yourself in Carnegie?'
    F.M.: 'That's correct, yes.'
    O: 'Right, can I talk you out of this?'
    F.M.: 'Well, I don't think it's possible ... It's a case of euthanasia and all ... as far as I'm concerned, it's double euthanasia, and, ah, I've made up my mind ... we've reached the end of the road.'
    By that time, a physician had come on to the line in an attempt to help the operator. They were not successful in their attempt to keep the telephone conversation going. By the time the ambulance arrived at the address, the

officers found both F.M. and his wife, Bonnie M. (age 47, pensioner) dead from gunshot wounds to the head.

The couple were both married for the second time, and had met in a psychiatric hospital in Shepparton where each had been undergoing psychiatric treatment. The husband had experienced exceptional depression in recent weeks. The wife had expressed the fear to neighbours that F.M. might take her life, since he threatened her previously with a rifle. One of the neighbours reported that she had said that F.M. 'was very depressed and she feared she would be killed and that F. would also kill himself.'

(Case No. 1499–86)

There is no jealous rage in this account, no threat of separation, in fact no anger or particular animosity toward the woman. While the woman expressed fear of the possible violence of her husband, that violence is of a fundamentally different quality to that in homicides provoked by jealousy or separation. In some of these cases, the depression appears to be brought on by various effects of the aging process which begin to accelerate upon retirement:

Helen H. (age 67, retired pensioner) had been married to F.H. for forty years when the husband retired from work. The period after the retirement had been difficult for the couple, with both being treated for serious medical and psychiatric problems. In the case of F.H., this included a history of deep psychological depression, such that for many days on end F.H. would spend virtually all day in bed, rising only for meals.

Helen was quite close to her son, whom she would generally call two or three times a day. She expressed to her son concerns for her safety, confiding to him that F.H. had attempted to strangle her on at least two occasions. She told him that F.H. 'did not want to live, and he wished that they could both go together'.

One afternoon the son received a call from his wife saying that she had just had a call from F.H. and that he 'was acting strangely'. The son immediately called his father, who tried to assure him that 'mum's all right, everything is all right'.

Still, the son found the tone and manner odd. He decided he had better go and have a look for himself. When he arrived at his parents' house, he found his mother dead from strangulation on the couch. Hearing water running in the bathroom, he went in where he found his father, also dead, had stabbed himself in the bath.   *(Case No. 859–85)*

In this narrative, the element of masculine control can be seen in the husband's view (not shared by the wife) that the couple should 'both go together'. There is some indication of the possibility of lethal violence, but the prior indications have a different quality to those originating in jealous rage. In some of the cases involving older couples, the impact of rapid breakdown in health contributes, and there are sometimes hints that the decision to end life is a joint one:

Molly H. and A.H. were both in their seventies, and retired pensioners. Two years previously, they had sold their family home (in which they had lived for thirty years) and bought into a property which they shared with their son and his wife.

Over time, Molly and A.H. became increasingly unhappy over the new arrangements. They were now several miles from their friends, and as their health started to fail it became increasingly difficult for them to maintain contact with friends. A.H. became convinced that his son had coerced him into buying the property, and that they were trying to force them out of the house, even though the couple owned a half interest in the property. In fact, the son was trying to set them up in their own self-contained unit on the property (which the couple refused), and had even offered to buy out their half interest so they could return to their former community (also refused).

The health of the two began to fail drastically. Molly had several operations on her abdomen, and had reached the point where she had to be assisted to get up from bed and to go to the toilet. A.H. had been diagnosed as having cancer of the prostate, and was beginning to suffer from severe bleeding of the bowels. Both were suffering from obvious signs of depression as well, but when advised by both friends and the son to consult a psychiatrist, A.H. replied that 'They can't do anything for us now ... '

On 11 May, the son and his wife went out for the evening, and then off for a couple of days to see other relatives. As they were leaving, the son reported that his mother clung to his wife, 'and thanked us for Mother's Day and for the present. Mum was upset and crying ... Dad just remained at the table and glanced at me ... '

Early the next morning a friend called the house, and A.H. answered. The friend reported that: 'He was terribly agitated, and kept saying "it's all my fault" over and over again. He stated that Molly couldn't come to the phone, and kept repeated that "he'll have to go", whereupon he then abruptly ended the call.' Their bodies were found when the son and his wife returned home the next day. The Coroner found that Molly had died from a gunshot wound inflicted by her husband, and that the husband had then died from the effects of a self-inflicted gunshot wound.   *(Case No. 1388–86)*

This pattern of physical deterioration and mutual agreement to end life was repeated in another account where the note left behind stated: 'My head hurts more and more. I am very sorry, but it's all too much' which was signed by the husband, with the words 'ditto' written in and signed by the wife. (Case No. 5141–87)

Couples confronting their final period together under conditions of physical deterioration may see few options open to them in terms of maintaining adequate care and dignity in their lives:

Nellie M. (age 74) and C.M. (age 75) had been married for fifty-three years. Nellie had suffered severe strokes and epilepsy, and was totally dependent on C.M. since she was incapable of leaving her bed (she was also virtually blind). If anything, C.M. was in worse medical condition, having previously had a cancerous larynx removed, and more recently two operations for lung cancer. C.M.'s increasing loss of weight and debilitation was making it more and more difficult for him to manage the household chores. When neighbours called in to check on the couple early one June day, they found Nellie dead from a rifle wound to the head, and C.M. dead from self-inflicted gunshot wounds.   *(Case No. 2337–87)*

For these two who faced almost complete physical breakdown, the choice of homicide and suicide might be viewed as their way of maintaining some control over their lives. When couples are younger, the theme of depression can run through the homicide-suicide, with the source of that depression being the press of economic circumstances:

D.L. (age 42) had been a highly successful owner of a car dealership, but had been out of the business for several months. In late 1987 he purchased a new car dealership expecting to continue his pattern of success, only to run head-on into the consequences of the economic downturn. Instead of making money, the losses began to mount rapidly, and gradually built up to debts totalling hundreds of thousands of dollars. Friends noticed that he was deteriorating both mentally and physically. Arguments broke out between D.L. and his wife Joan (age 42, homemaker).

On 11 February, D.L. attempted to enter several hospitals, finally finding one which assessed him as having a major depressive illness. The hospital agreed to admit D.L. the following day when a bed became available. Instead, on 12 February, D.L. first shot and killed his wife, shot his mother-in-law (who survived) and then turned the gun on himself.   *(Case No. 669–88)*

When the male is younger in these depressive suicide/homicide cases, the provocation appears from these case studies to be found in economic breakdown as well as, or instead of, an erosion of physical health. In the following case there was a mix of economic and health factors which contributed to the ultimate decision of the husband to take both his wife's and his own life:

For many years I.K. (age 49) had been an ideal parent and husband. He was known to be a hard worker, and made a good living as an independent builder. Then, in early 1985 he underwent a dramatic change. He became moody and depressed, and began to go from doctor to doctor seeking medication and help. He began to take heavy doses of tranquillisers. He stopped work.

As money began to dry up, and economic stresses mount, arguments began to develop between I.K. and his wife Kathy K. (age 47, home duties). No violence between them was observed. As one daughter said: 'My father never hit or struck my mother, and I didn't think he was capable of doing anything like that. With a sound, rational mind, I don't think my father was capable of doing anything violent.'

Then one day, an argument with Kathy over money seemed to trigger I.K. Perhaps it was that during the argument Kathy had asked for her half of the money which she was entitled to as a result of a recent sale of a residence, and she obviously intended to use the money to begin to function more independently of I.K.

The next morning, as one of the daughters was leaving the house for work, he called her back, gave her $50, and kissed her. This was so different from the normal pattern that the daughter recalled afterwards: 'It was on my mind that he might commit suicide.'

A friend called in later that day and found Kathy dead in the kitchen. She had been strangled with a bit of rope. A few minutes later I.K. was found, also dead, in a shed at the back of the house where he had hanged himself.

(Case No. 1144–86)

As is true in the other cases within this pattern, there is no indication of jealousy, nor any signs even of prior attempts at violence in connection with suicide. Trapped by the closing down of the economic dreams, this male saw no option but to commit suicide, but also to 'protect' his family from the fate that would befall them without his sources of support. There is one account in which physical injury, financial pressures, and cultural differences are woven together in the factors which produce the final tragedy:

T.P (age 34, factory worker) had arrived in Australia from Vietnam with her husband, V.P., some five years previously. Apparently their married years in Vietnam were stable and happy, as were the first four years in Australia, according to later testimony from the family. V.P. had sustained an injury at work which apparently brought about a significant change in his outlook and behaviour.

Lacking a job, under financial stress, V.P. began to worry about money and became noticeably depressed. To one of the family members, who thought it was a joke, he had said he might have to kill his wife.

It was the couple's two young children, the eldest being only 5, that can provide an account of the event leading up to the homicide. The child indicated that there had been some violence between the couple on earlier evenings: 'Daddy would hit mummy. Mummy would hit him back, then stop.' One night the daughter heard her father say: 'If I die, you'll die as well.' The mother replied that she did not wish to die. A struggle broke out on the couple's bed. T.P. attempted to fight V. off, but V. was too strong, and he was able to strangle his wife, using a chain.

The daughter, who observed these events, recalled that: 'Daddy told me to go back to bed, saying "your mother must die, your father must die. We cannot live." ' The father then went into the lounge room and managed to strangle himself using rubber bands.   *(Case No. 415–85)*

The common themes running through these accounts are masculine control coupled with depression. These cases require a careful reading to distinguish this particular pattern from other situations where males take their own lives after killing their sexual partner. There were, in fact, almost an equal number of males who killed their wives out of a sense of possessiveness or jealousy and then committed suicide, as there were males who fitted this pattern of depression-homicide-suicide (14 compared to 15). The key element of the sub-pattern identified here is that a reading of the case narrative indicates that it is profound depression which has pushed these males to the point where they contemplate the step of committing suicide. Their primary goal is self-destruction. In a way analogous to that of jealous males, these husbands view their wives as possessions which should be carried along in this final journey. Their female partners are not to be left behind and alone. In contrast, most of the masculine killings of women in the context of sexual intimacy are primarily about the destruction of the women, then when that goal is accomplished some of the males (14 in all) took their own life.

Some other cases

While a high proportion of cases where men take the lives of women with whom they are sexually involved are characterised by themes of jealousy and manifest possessiveness, or perhaps of depression/suicide, it needs to be recognised that there are some cases which do not fit easily into either of these two moulds. In the broadest sense, these cases fit into a pattern where violence is a distinctively male form of control, or attempt to extend control, of the sexual partner. It needs to be recognised, however, that empirically the patterns are diverse. Indeed, Easteal (1993) was led to conclude, regarding patterns of spousal homicide that:

> The findings have confirmed that there is no one simple cause and effect formula to be found. On the contrary, not only do most of these cases appear to represent the climax of numerous factors intermingling but they also show that those factors vary somewhat depending upon gender, ethnicity, and age.
> *(Easteal, 1993: 91)*

While there is complexity in these narratives, at the core most demonstrate a willingness of males to employ violence as a way of controlling the life of the woman. There is, for example, the following case in which the male used homicide as the device for discarding a partner who was no longer wanted:

> The homicide of Rose M. (age 30, home duties) is unusual in many respects. For one, the death was a result of strychnine poisoning, the only poisoning homicide that is found in these files. Rose was found dead at her suburban Bayswater home, seated in a chair in the kitchen, after a call from her husband, Ken M. (age 33) had alerted a neighbour that something might be wrong since Rose was not answering her telephone. The attending police noted that there 'were no signs of violence. There are no suspicious circumstances ...'

So the matter stood for three months, until the toxicology report revealed that the cause of death was strychnine poisoning. The obvious suspect, Ken, denied any responsibility for the death. There are several signs that point to his being responsible. For one, he had in recent weeks established a close relationship with another woman which had been observed by many witnesses (and the woman, in fact, moved in with him after the death of the wife). Rose had complained to her friends that her husband had been noticeably cool towards her, and had cut off all sexual relations with her. Witnesses also established that Ken had said he would not pursue another divorce (Rose was his second wife), since his first divorce 'had cost him $94 000.'

There were, as well, several suspicious inconsistencies in his statements to the police. Finding no other person with motive or opportunity, and rejecting the notion of suicide, the police eventually charged the husband with the homicide of his wife.   (Case No. 21–86)

So, in this little house in Bayswater we encounter one of the few true mysteries in these files. One obvious factor which emerges from this is that the reality of criminal justice procedure is far removed from what one reads in mystery novels. It is difficult to trace the trail of a suspected homicide when it has taken three months to determine the key fact that the victim was, in fact, murdered. The case demonstrates, however, that jealousy or the threat of separation is not always the motivation which drives males to take the lives of their spouses. The case might be made, of course, that in the eyes of the husband his wife was a disposable possession, to be cast away when a new love entered his life. In such a scenario, the wife is still viewed as property, but property which can be cast off when so willed by the male, and thus the killing is an ultimate expression of control.

In another case, the issue was the attempt to exert sexual control. A young woman (age 18) had been friendly with a male co-worker. The male become progressively more eager to press his attention on the girl, who became increasingly concerned with his advances. One night he convinced her that he could give her a ride home. What happened at the point is not clear, since the male tells a story that the girl attacked him, which the police and courts chose not to believe. What seems most likely is that the male pressed his attentions too vigorously, the two fought, and somehow the male lost his head and stabbed the girl to death (Case No. 1041–85). While technically this is not a case where a relationship had been established, the two had known each other, the early moves toward a sexual relationship had been made, and it appears that it was the young woman's resistance to the male's sexual advances which resulted in her death.

What this does is to underscore again the fact that there are diverse threads running through this material, and there are many ways sexual bonds can result in homicide. In another of these different cases, the victim was a child with whom the male had struck up a sexual relationship, and the homicide was a crude attempt on the part of the male to fend off the consequences of public disclosure of the relationship:

R.L. (age 46, unemployed) had not had great luck in his life. A police report described him as having: 'a long criminal history including offences relating to violence and dishonesty ... He appears to be a person of little education, with an alcohol abuse problem extending over a long period of time.' From 1983 to 1985 he served a term in prison.

Over recent years R.L. had formed a friendship with the C. family (both of the parents of the C. household had lengthy criminal histories themselves). Upon his release from prison, the attachment with the C.'s was close enough that for a period of time R.L. rented a bungalow located at the back of their residence.

Isolated from other kinds of contacts with women, R.L. over the months and years developed a close relationship with a daughter of the household, Tammy C. (age 12). This had developed into what the police in their subsequent report described as an 'unhealthy relationship', that is, the two became sexually involved.

This was a dangerous game to play because of its potential consequences, and perhaps to protect himself, R.L. moved away from the C. household. He continued to see the family, including Tammy, however.

The peril was increased when Tammy became pregnant, a fact which was discovered when she suffered a miscarriage. Tammy refused to reveal the identity of the father to her mother. She did, however, tell two of her young friends that R.L. was the father, and further, that he had threatened to kill her if she revealed that he had been involved with her sexually.

Apparently becoming apprehensive that the whole affair was coming unstuck, R.L. called Tammy while she was having her birthday party. He asked Tammy to come over later because he had an additional present. When Tammy arrived, he produced a shot gun and shot her once in the head, killing her instantly. R.L. then called Tammy's mother, and asked her to come over as well. Upon her arrival, he held the gun to her head, threatening to shoot her and the rest of the family as well. R.L. then attempted to choke Tammy's mother to death, but she was able to break away and alert the police.   *(Case No. 1199–86)*

This narrative not only indicates the diverse threads by which sexual intimacy can be tied to homicide, but as well the problems of developing adequate schemes of classification. In this account there is sexual intimacy which links the male with his female child victim, but also it could be seen as a form of homicide which is the outgrowth of another crime (in this case, the illegal sexual relationship with a child), or even a form of conflict resolution (involving the silencing of a witness), both of which shall be covered in later sections of this book. It is included within the present scenario because it was the sexual intimacy which provided the essential link between offender and victim, and became the cause of the behaviour which followed. It also serves to emphasise the difficulties in presuming that only jealousy, the threat of separation, or even depression are the driving factors in masculine homicides arising out of such intimacy. Instead, this killing appears to constitute a last, desperate bid on the part of this socially incompetent male to control the young person and to prevent disclosure of the relationship which had come to pose a great threat to him.

A further illustration of the diversity of motives in settings of sexual intimacy is found in the following case:

A.B., a retired bank manager, and his wife Nancy B. (age 56, retired school teacher) were having difficulty adjusting to retirement. Previously, their lives had been busy, and by all accounts the marriage was a stable and comfortable one. The children report that to their knowledge, there were no instances of violence in the marriage.

With the retirement, however, the two seemed to get on each other's nerves. A.B. in particular, seemed especially edgy. To complicate matters, he had constructed an elaborate delusion that he had contracted AIDS as a result of an incident some four years previously involving one of the young women working at the bank. The woman expressed amazement when asked about this later, denying emphatically that there had been any sexual contact between them (there was an age differential between them of over forty years). She did note that at a bank outing there had been one occasion where there took place something which she took to be a 'sexual advance' on A.B.'s part, but it consisted of no more than 'him pushing his body against me'.

One afternoon, the married couple were driving back to their suburban home from Melbourne. A.B. became especially agitated. He had convinced himself that one of his daughters had discovered the secret of his AIDS, and that she was going to confront him when they arrived home. He felt he had to discuss the matter with Nancy before they returned to their home.

By the husband's account, he then stopped the car so they could 'have a talk'. The problem was that his wife didn't want to engage in any such discussion. A heated argument broke out. What happened then can be taken from the later transcript of the police interview:

Q: 'What made you upset?'
A.B.: 'It was a build-up of things during the day, and the fact that I thought there was going to be a confrontation with the family. I knew they weren't happy ... '
Q: 'When you say you got upset, do you mean emotionally or otherwise?'
A.B.: 'Yes, emotional ... always emotional. I suppose I was a bit wild, too. I possibly got upset with Nancy, and then it was the end of Nancy.'
Q: 'The end of Nancy?'
A.B.: 'Yes, you know, in all those years of marriage I'd never hurt Nancy.'
Q: 'And, did you strangle Nancy?'
A.B.: 'Yes, I could see myself losing her, you know ... '
Q: 'Well, do you recall actually grabbing Nancy around the neck?'
A.B.: 'I've thought about that quite a few times. I recall putting my hand over her mouth to stop her crying out.'
Q: 'Do you remember why she cried out?'

A.B.: 'Because I had my hand on her throat. I mean, I'm not a killer, I've never even killed a dog or a cat . . . '
Q: 'Why did you kill Nancy?'
A.B.: 'I thought there was going to be a big discussion when we got home that night.'
Q: 'Did you go to that area with the view of strangling Nancy?'
A.B.: 'No, I was going to talk to her . . . '
Q: 'Was there any premeditation on your part in Nancy's death?'
A.B.: 'No . . . no . . . but, normally she would listen to me . . . but, she wouldn't listen . . . she was saying no, no, no, we better not.'

After killing his wife, A.B. picked up a piece of glass and slashed himself on the throat and wrists. When after some time it became clear to him that this attempt at taking his life was unsuccessful, he then deliberately collided with another car. While unsuccessful in bringing about his death, A.B. was injured. During the course of treatment in the hospital, A.B. developed severe psychotic symptoms. *(Case No. 3999–86)*

There is in this tale no consuming anger, fuelled by jealousy, nor profound depression pushing the male toward suicide. There are no warning symptoms in terms of any prior violence. There is agitation on the part of the male, there is an argument (over whether or not there should be a discussion), and it could be said that the woman has resisted the will of the male. It was, to be sure, the male who killed, and probably at the core was the resistance of the woman to allow the male to control the situation.

Some of these cases approach the bizarre. In one, the female victim and her husband first attended a party with friends, where the woman consumed a large quantity of both beer and wine. She became so drunk that she had to be helped to the car for the return home. After arriving at home, she consumed more wine (her blood alcohol level was established at autopsy to be 0.27). Apparently the woman and the man began to engage in sex, and the woman requested bondage. Her husband handcuffed her wrists, tied her feet with rope, then gagged her with pantyhose, then proceeded to engage in sexual intercourse, first administering several blows to her body. The woman died some time during the encounter. (Case No. 5261–87)

In another of these cases, the woman victim and her husband became involved in an argument (apparently provoked by the male's drinking) on their patio. Blows were struck, dishes and food thrown at each other, and then the two grappled, became entangled, and fell, with the heavier male falling on top of his wife. The woman died from injuries sustained from this fall (Case No. 5436–87). A further case involved a woman whose aggression and abuse had been a persistent problem to family and neighbours (the police had been called to the house because of her behaviour on a number of occasions) who apparently was killed when she became involved in yet another abusive argument with her husband, when she placed a belt around her neck and taunted her husband to pull it tight. The two then fought, and the woman died from the injuries sustained. (Case No. 1034–89)

Some caution, then, is essential in terms of examining the scenarios of masculine violence when men kill when influenced by themes of sexual intimacy. While some scenarios predominate, notably those deriving either from jealousy/possessiveness or depression/suicide, there are some killings in situations of sexual intimacy where it is not easy to trace and categorise the male's motivation. These eight cases constitute the group of such cases, with most of the remaining fitting into patterns where the homicide arose out of classic themes of jealousy, possessiveness and control. Even in the few cases which differ from the general pattern, the violence is masculine, and the death is of a female sexual intimate, and to some degree the violence has been a mechanism for controlling the behaviour of the woman.

Masculine control/jealousy violence which reaches other victims

While the major and obvious target for violence generated by jealousy or control will be the female sexual partner, in some instances others in the scene become victims either as well as, or instead of, the woman. There were, in all, twelve cases where the violence of the male reached out to the sexual rival of the male, and represents one form of what Daly and Wilson (1988) refer to as 'killing the competition':

> R.L. had been living with V.L. (age 46) for some twelve years. In recent months, R.L. had become progressively more violent toward V. so she decided to leave.
>
> Eddie K. (age 56, pensioner) had been a close friend of both for a number of years, and V. decided to move in with him. V. was uncertain how to proceed, since she still felt some warmth toward R.L. In fact, one week after moving in with Eddie, V. returned to R.L., but, as she said later, 'it didn't work out' and she went back to Eddie.
>
> After a few weeks, however, R.L. could take the state of affairs no longer. He wrote to V. stating that if she did not return he would do something 'he did not want to do.'
>
> A few days later these words were translated into action. During the day one weekend, R.L. entered Eddie's house and punched him several times, finally being restrained by onlookers. R.L. left, but as he did so he screamed at Eddie: 'I will get you, I will kill you.'
>
> At 6 pm that night R.L. returned with a shotgun, but was seen 'sneaking around the house'. The police were called, and when they couldn't find him around Eddie's house, they went to R.L.'s house. They questioned R.L. but he denied possessing a gun or being near the house. Meanwhile, Eddie filed assault charges against R.L. with the police.

Early the next morning R.L. surprised Eddie as he left the house, shooting him with the shotgun. Eddie ran into the house, pursued by R.L. who fired a second and fatal shot to the head. He also shot V., although she survived. Shortly after, R.L. committed suicide by driving his car into a tree.

(Case No. 4169–86)

As has often been true in these accounts, there were clear warnings of the lethal violence to come. Police were alerted that violence with a gun had been threatened, but the response proved ineffective in averting the use of that weapon in the homicide which followed. The themes of the case are similar to others involving jealousy. The woman, his possession, was not just slipping out from under his control, but even worse she was taking up with a new sexual partner. In this instance, the offender selects as the target for his jealous rage his sexual rival, and then takes his own life afterwards. The male did attempt to take the life of his woman partner, but the wounding did not prove fatal. In a comparable case previously discussed, a male took the lives of both his sexual partner and a male friend who had been sought out to help protect the woman. The female victim was worried, correctly, that the restraining order she had obtained from the police would not be sufficient to guard against further and more intense violence. (Case No. 2997–88)

The next of these cases displayed the same element of jealousy, but differs both in that the male offender showed no prior signs of violence either toward his estranged wife or towards her new lover who became his victim in the homicide, and further, he confined his violence to his sexual rival:

Debbie had been married to A.P. (age 39) for some seven years. She had previously been married, and the 12-year-old son from that marriage lived with the married couple (and had, in fact, been legally adopted by A.P.). While A.P. was from all accounts a quiet man with few friends and a limited social life, he enjoyed a close relationship with his adopted son.

After six years in which the marriage from all accounts went reasonably well, the relationship between Debbie and A.P. deteriorated. The two had begun to live separate lives, and Debbie initiated an affair with Bob F. (age 39) whom she had met at work. Shortly after, Debbie announced her intention of leaving the marital household to live with Bob. Since it was the Christmas season, Debbie agreed to put off her departure for a few weeks.

This period was a frustrating one for A.P. Debbie was spending most of her nights away with Bob, while A.P. would remain at home with the son. Responding to A.P.'s pleas for reconciliation, the couple went off for an island holiday, but the attempt failed and the couple returned to Melbourne.

Upon arrival, Debbie immediately telephoned Bob, then left to spend the night with him at his flat. Somehow, the next day A.P. was able to lure Bob to his house. He apparently first sat with him and had a drink or two (Bob's

blood alcohol level was found to be 0.016), and then came up behind him
and shot him once in the back.

The police found a note at the scene written by A.P. intended for his wife.
In it he claimed that Bob had destroyed all of their lives, and argued that it
was necessary for him to kill Bob in order to save his wife and son. In
particular, he stated that Bob would neglect the son and soon tire of Debbie.
A close friend of A.P.'s claimed that A.P. had told him that Bob 'was a con
man, shifty, and wouldn't look after [the son] properly and end up using
Debbie and dumping her'. He also commented on the jealousy, saying that
A.P. 'couldn't stand being at home while his wife was out with this other
person', and, ominously, that 'This guy will be fixed up.' A.P.'s car was found
abandoned on the Great Ocean Road but no trace of A.P. has been found. It
was presumed that A.P had committed suicide.   *(Case No. 3969–86)*

While the jealousy of this male is shared with many of the other male
killers reviewed here, what is different about this case is that the anger
is aimed exclusively at his sexual rival. Clearly, in playing the delaying
game wavering between the two households, the wife had underestimated enormously the capacity of her husband for violence.

Conclusion

The use of lethal violence arising out of sexual relationships, for whatever reason, is distinctly a masculine matter. Of the 102 homicides that
involved a sexual bond, only 16 involved women offenders. In a typical
year roughly one in five homicides will involve male offenders whose
victim is linked to them in one way or another by virtue of a sexual
bond. The overriding theme that runs through these killings is masculine control, where women become viewed as possessions of men, and
the violence reflects steps taken by males either to assert their domi-
nation over 'their' women, or to repel males who they feel are attempting to take control of their sexual partner.

Daly and Wilson have observed that in looking at many of these cases
it is important that the conception of the problem be wider than the
obvious sexual jealousy that is often found, observing that:

> a better label might be *male sexual proprietariness*. It is manifested in the
> dogged inclination of men to control the activities of women, and in the
> male perspective according to which sexual access and woman's reproductive
> capacity are *commodities* that men can 'own' and exchange. This proprietary
> point of view is furthermore inextricably bound up with the use or threat of
> violence in order to maintain sexual exclusivity and control.
>
> *(Daly and Wilson, 1988: 182)*

What has been found in the present scenarios, of course, is that there
are actually two dominant forms of sexual ownership. One is the form

that Daly and Wilson identify, where violence, and rage fuelling that violence, is aimed at generally younger women and is in response to the attempt of the male to control the reproductive capacities of the woman. These data are consistent with the pungent observations of Bean: 'Murder is the final irrevocable step, the ultimate expression of men's control over women. For some men, the need for control is not satisfied until this irrevocable step is taken.' (Bean, 1992: 43) In a common variant of this scenario of jealousy, the action shifts to encompass the male competition in the sexual triangle.

The second scenario is no less proprietary, since in many of the accounts where the homicide is part of the male suicide plan the woman is clearly seen as a possession, or commodity, which the man must dispose of prior to his own death. In these cases as well, the killing represents the ultimate control of the man over the woman (there were no cases where a depressed woman killed her male partner as part of her suicide plan).

Across these scenarios, the final act of violence in a large proportion of the case studies has not occurred as a result of a domestic argument which has spontaneously overheated (although this happened in some of the cases). Instead, in a majority of cases these reflect a calculated and planned homicide in which males exacted their final and terrible price of violence on the women they once loved, or on the males they deemed to be sexual rivals.

CHAPTER 4

Confrontational homicide

While it is generally well known that males typically account for over 80 per cent of homicide offenders (for example, Wolfgang, 1958; Voss and Hepburn, 1968; Wallace, 1986; Falk, 1990; Strang, 1992), it is less well known that at least half of all homicides involve incidents where males play the role of both victim and offender. Consistently, empirical studies such as that carried out in New South Wales by Wallace (1986) show that a slight majority of all homicides (53 per cent in Wallace's research) involve male offenders taking the lives of male victims.

Classifying these male-to-male homicides has always provided something of a problem. Whereas an overwhelming proportion of male offender-female victim homicides take place within some bond of intimacy, male-on-male homicides tend to be spread across a range of relational categories, including 'strangers', 'acquaintances', 'friends'. Rarely are they found in relationship bonds of family intimacy (an exception would be a stepfather killing his infant son). Put another way, the existing groupings of 'relationship to victim' in homicide research are unlikely to provide much in the way of insights regarding the social dynamics that have brought these actors to the point when a killing results where both victim and offender are male.

Since such killings account for over half of all homicides, it seems appropriate that we begin to seek ways of grouping such homicides that are both descriptive and theoretically helpful in accounting for the 'behavioural transactions' (to use Luckenbill's, 1977, term) that result in homicide. Our method, once again, is to read through the individual accounts of homicide in order to identify the dominant scenarios which describe this masculine violence.

What is immediately striking in the analysis of these accounts is the role of what seem to be spontaneous arguments between males in lethal encounters. In appearance, these are similar to what Wallace (1986: 155) described as 'interpersonal disputes':

> Interpersonal disputes formed the basis of the majority of killings outside the domestic sphere. A large number of these quarrels were unpremeditated events that erupted between strangers or acquaintances, usually while socializing in or around a club or hotel, or in the home of either victim or offender. The content of the disputes in these circumstances may be less important than the male context in which they occurred. *(Wallace, 1986: 155)*

Such disputes are comparable to some degree to what Wolfgang (1958: 191) classified as an 'altercation of relatively trivial origin, insult, curse, jostling, etc.', this category making up the largest in volume of the 'motives' of homicides in Philadelphia (accounting for 35 per cent of all killings). Observing the importance of 'altercations' in the general picture of homicide, Daly and Wilson comment on the kinds of typical homicides that are found in American statistics:

> Most of the victims were men, and almost all were killed by men. Most of the victims, like most of the offenders, were nobodies: unpropertied and unmarried, little educated, often unemployed. Most of the homicides were not committed in the course of robbery, but instead arose out of arguments or insults or rivalries. Most of the victims were acquainted with their killers. Only a handful were related to them.   *(Daly and Wilson, 1988: 124)*

It is the anatomy of these masculine disputes that will be the focus of the present chapter. There were, in all, 84 of these confrontational homicides (this scenario accounting for 22 per cent of all homicides). Daly and Wilson underscore the point that in these killings, the underlying issue is 'honour'. Yet, honour among these men often is triggered, if previous accounts are correct, by what may appear to the outsider to be the most 'trivial' of altercations. What is it that provokes males in these circumstances to the point where they kill? Understanding how these events, which often seem to proceed from what appear to be relatively minor starting points, but then flare into lethal violence, is fundamental to the development of any theoretical understanding of the nature of homicide. To seek that understanding, and to identify the basic interactional dynamics of such killings, we now return to our case studies.

Some case studies of confrontational homicide

In the first of these accounts, it can be seen how conflict can build spontaneously to the events which result in a killing:

Gabe W. (32, soldier) boarded a train at Flinders Street Station (the main city commuter railway station) after an evening of drinking with his friends (his blood alcohol level was subsequently established to be 0.224). When Gabe attempted to take a seat, Mike M. ordered him, 'offensively,' to move on to another seat. Challenged, Gabe refused, and attempted to force his way on to the seat. Mike leaped up and struck Gabe, and the two fought. Although Gabe received a number of blows, and was kneed in the face, he finally managed to pin Mike down.

Witnesses relate that at this point Gabe said: 'If you don't stop now, I'll break your neck.' Then, believing that Mike would stop, Gabe released him. Mike instead produced a knife, stabbing Gabe three times in the chest. One of the blows penetrated the heart. Gabe collapsed and died in the aisle.

(Case No. 4714–86)

In many respects, this is a classic form of confrontation. The violence evolved quickly between males who had never met previously. We cannot know what the initial non-verbal cues were that flowed between the protagonists. The two males, however, knew that this was a contest of honour. In essence, Mike was saying this is my space, and you challenge my claims at your peril. For Gabe, the public nature of the confrontation could not be ignored. The altercation took place in a definitively public arena in front of a social audience whose presence would have to be felt by the combatants. In this case, the whole set of events, from start to finish, occurred within a few minutes. As is characteristic of such skirmishes, the combatants did not anticipate at the onset that a death would result. Their intent as they entered into the exchange was to defend their honour by means of the fight.

In the next account similar features are found, except that the direct role of peers is more obvious in the confrontation:

Late one Saturday night, Anthony N. (age 19, unemployed) was walking back with friends towards their home after attending a local 'Octoberfest.' They had enjoyed a pleasant evening of drinking at that event (Anthony's blood alcohol level was later established at 0.08). In a small park, they met up with another group, including Don B. (age 18, unemployed) and Peter. T. (unbeknown to Anthony and his group, this second group had armed itself in advance with broken billiard cues and knives).

One of the young women in Anthony's group was part of the triggering of the confrontation between the two groups when she asked if she could ride Peter's bike. He replied: 'You can have a ride if I can ride you.' Insults and challenges began to flow back and forth between the two groups. At one point, Anthony is recorded as having said to Don: 'You're a bit young to be going to Octoberfest, aren't you?' Don responded with: 'Don't call me a kid.'

The exchanges escalated into pushing and shoving. Anthony said: 'If you want to have a go, I'll have a go back.' Don then threw a punch at Anthony, and the fight was on. At first it was a general group scuffle, and at one point Anthony broke a beer stein (obtained at Octoberfest) over the head of a member of Don's group.

The main group conflict began to simmer down, but Anthony and Don sought each other out and continued their personal dispute. At first Don was armed with the broken pool cue, but Anthony was able to take it off him. Peter then handed Don a knife. Witnesses agree that at this point, Anthony kept repeating to Don: 'I'll kill you, I'll kill you.' Don was able to come in close to Anthony, however, and slashed out with his knife, stabbing Anthony in the left thigh, right hand, and finally the left side of his chest. By now all eyes of the groups were on the two. They saw Anthony stagger, and he began to bleed profusely. The two groups broke off the fight, each going their separate ways.

One of Anthony's friends asked if he was feeling all right, to which he replied: 'I think I have been stabbed.' The friends helped him to a nearby house and called an ambulance, but Anthony died before medical help arrived. Don had no idea of the seriousness of the injuries he had caused, and was said by his friends to be 'shocked' when he was informed the next day of Anthony's death. *(Case No. 3661–85)*

Here, again, the males were quick to take up violence in defence of their honour. In this account, one of the provoking comments ('You're a bit young') would fit into the pattern that Wolfgang (1958) termed 'trivial altercation', where the nature of the provocation would hardly warrant setting off a scuffle which would have lethal consequences. A fundamental characteristic of such confrontations is that initially the intent is to defend masculine honour by means first of words, then the fight. The killing is not a planned event, but flows out of the more spontaneously developing fight.

As before, it is a public setting (in this account a park), and in this case the friends of both of the principals play an important supportive role in the conflict (including providing the weapon at a crucial point in the encounter). Peers here provided more than a passive social backdrop to the encounter, as the combat widened to include what had initially been an audience. The intent at the onset was to fight, and even afterwards the parties, including the offender, were unaware of the extreme consequences of their conflict. As in the first instance, alcohol lurks in the background as a feature of such events.

In some incidents, the spark which provokes male aggression consists of actions toward women friends:

One weekend night, Tommy F. (age 29, unemployed) and his friend Charlie began their round of drinking, first at the Crab Cooker restaurant, then gravitated to the Bowling Green Hotel where they remained, drinking, for several hours. Another group came in much later in the evening, including Mike D. (age 26, assembly worker), Pete, and Rog, who was a boyfriend of Jennie (a waitress at the pub).

At closing time, as Tommy and Charlie were leaving, they passed Rog and Jennie in the hallway. In passing, Tommy made a comment to Jennie which Rog took to be an insult. An argument developed between Rog and Tommy which led to a fight between them on the sidewalk outside. Tommy was punched to the ground, and the fight broke up with Tommy and Charlie withdrawing to their car which was parked nearby.

Shortly afterwards, Rog, Jennie, Mike and Pete came out of the hotel to head for home. Tommy and Charlie had waited for them, and the two once again approached and proceeded to confront and challenge Rog. When the other males joined in, Tommy pulled a knife and backed away to his car.

Mike and Pete gave chase to the car. Mike picked up a piece of timber, and began to hit the car repeatedly. Tommy suddenly leaped out of the car, and stabbed Mike with his knife. Badly hurt, Mike fell to the ground. Tommy kicked him several times in the head, then jumped back into the car and drove off. The knife had penetrated Mike's heart, and he was dead when the ambulance arrived (his blood alcohol level was 0.05).   *(Case No. 3264–86)*

In addition to the initial impetus being provided by an incident involving a woman friend of one of the males, this narrative shows how confused the roles may become, since when groups are involved the person killed may have been peripheral to the initial events which led to the fight. The fatal events involved, in other words, a member of the initial social audience who became swept up in the fight, from background to foreground of the action, and died as a consequence. The scene of the initial conflict is a pub. The combatants were previously unknown to each other.

All of the previous events occurred relatively quickly, proceeding from initial insult to the fatal wounding within a matter of minutes. In other cases, the time dimension is more extended:

Keith R. (age 27) and his close friend Stan J. had been drinking through the late evening hours of Friday and on into the early hours of Saturday morning. Somewhere along the way, they had managed to insult the sister of a bouncer in one of the clubs they attended, Gabby R. As the two friends, very drunk, were leaving their local football club at 5 am, Gabby decided to settle the score of the insult to his sister, and picked a fight with Stan.

Being a bouncer, Gabby was very fit, and Stan was drunk. In no time Stan was down and receiving a severe beating. Keith attempted to intervene to pull Gabby off his friend. At this point, Gabby's friend, and another bouncer, Sam B. turned on Keith. Witnesses say that he not only punched Keith, but after Keith was down he was kicked repeatedly and savagely in the lower back.

Keith seemed winded and shaken by the beating he had taken. He took a taxi home. A few hours later, his wife found him moaning with pain, and took him to the hospital. His condition worsened steadily over the three days he was in the hospital. Doctors decided finally to operate, and found that his kidney had been severely damaged by the beating he had received. After the operation, Keith's condition suddenly deteriorated, and he died some six hours afterward. Despite the evidence of a brutal beating, and testimony regarding the kicks by the bouncer, the Coroner found in this case that the killer was 'acting in self defence'.   *(Case No. 446–85)*

As in the previous accounts, there is in this narrative a mix of masculinity and alcohol. Unlike the previous cases, rather than moving rapidly from insult to fatal injury, the event was extended over several hours. The first altercation had taken place in a pub, then some hours afterwards the affair was concluded outside a football club.

The pub looms as a recurring locale for masculine violence. In a few instances, the fight, and killing, take place in the pub:

Dennis (age 23, unemployed) and a group of three friends had been celebrating the birthday of one of the group when they stopped in the Doutta Galla pub at 9.30 in the evening. Fred (age 31) was there drinking alone. The initial provocation for a fight was the challenging eye contact between Fred and one of Dennis's friends. The friend said: 'I don't like this arsehole Turk [Fred was born in Turkey] ... he looks sleazy.' Fred then approached the friend and said: 'What are you staring at?' To which the friend replied: 'What are you on about?' Fred then claimed: 'You're staring at me', to which the friend replied 'Get out of here.' One of the other members of the group attempted to intervene at this point, and Fred told him: 'Fucking keep your head out of it.' In reply, the one who had attempted to intervene said: 'Well, fuckin' cop this', and punched Fred in the head.

An all-out bar room brawl developed. Fred produced a knife, and slashed his attacker across the stomach, and followed this by stabbing his opponent of the staring contest in the leg. Dennis and his friends, and other patrons in the bar, armed themselves with billiard cues and surrounded Fred, who then sought shelter behind the bar. When Dennis reached over to pull him from behind the bar, Fred stabbed him in the chest. One of Dennis's friends, known in the pub as 'Dogsbody', pummelled Fred several times over the head with a cue. Fred twisted around and was able to stab his attacker twice in the body. Patrons then started shouting: 'Let's kill him, he's stabbed Dogsbody, let's kill him.' Fred attempted then to seek shelter in the pub office behind the bar, where the barman was counting the night's takings. Fred locked the door, and pleaded: 'Don't let them get me, they're going to kill me.' Several men kicked at the door until they were able to break it down. Fred then grabbed the barman, and held a knife to his throat, threatening to kill the barman if the group approached any closer. Someone yelled 'The Turkish cunt has got him', and the group started throwing bottles at Fred to make him release the barman. When the barman was able to break free, Fred was showered with an avalanche of bottles. The police entered at this point, and the fight subsided. Dennis was found, dead, on the floor (his blood alcohol was 0.309). Fred denied the stabbing, but acknowledged that he 'was running for my fuckin' life, I was, mate'. Fred's blood alcohol level was found later to be 0.047. (Case No. 3631–87)

In another illustration of the minor provocation that can set these events in motion, the initial invitation to fight in this account came in the form of the non-verbal 'eyeing off' between two males. In this case, the whole event takes place in the pub itself, rather than having the final confrontation spill out into the nearby streets. There is, as well, a hint that ethnicity played some role in the conflict, as the aggressor in the precipitating events, and the eventual killer, was Turkish and epithets thrown referred to his origins.

It is probably more common for the lethal violence to occur outside the pub:

> Leonard (age 23, labourer) and John finished work and went to the nearby Shamrock and Thistle pub, arriving at 5.30 and drinking heavily through the evening (Leonard was later found to have a blood alcohol level of 0.227). In the course of the evening the two exchanged insults with a number of the bar patrons, and one of them later alleged that Leonard had made a sexual pass at his girlfriend.
>
> At one point, John went off to the toilet. Another patron came roaring out of the pub later, alleging that John 'was a poof, he put the hard word on me'. He then approached Leonard, and a fight broke out between Leonard and this patron, who broke a billiard cue in half and hit Leonard several times over the head with it. At about this point, Leonard and John were told: 'You don't even drink here, it's not your pub, get out.' The two were asked by the barman to leave, and they did.
>
> Another of the patrons alleged that at this point he went outside and found Leonard vandalising a car, including pulling off the radio aerial, which he used to strike the patron (although the police could find nothing to verify this part of the story). This patron then went inside and sought the help of a friend. The two of them then carried out a vicious assault on Leonard and John, first holding each and punching them until they fell to the ground, then kicking each of them alternately in the body. For good measure, they jumped up and down on Leonard several times. The two then went back inside to continue their drinking. Leonard died from the effects of a lacerated liver.   *(Case No. 4795–87)*

This illustrates what is probably the more common scenario of a confrontation which begins in the pub or disco, with the final lethal violence occurring in the street immediately outside. In this case, the two were seen as outsiders to the others who were in their 'local'. Further, as has been seen in other of these accounts, a fight which begins by one person, may be finished off by somebody else.

A similar case of violence starting in the drinking establishment, and finishing in the streets is found in the following account where the confrontation began in a nightclub.

> Daniel (age 34, sales representative) went into a well-known King Street nightclub, and began drinking with a female friend (who was a member of the Victoria Police). The friend asked Daniel to hold on to some of her things for the night, including her police badge. Somewhat later, another patron, Les (age 23) was observed causing trouble for other patrons. Daniel went over to the bouncer, produced the police identification, stated he was a policeman, and asked that Les be thrown out because of the trouble he was causing. The bouncer, having no reason to doubt Daniel's legitimacy as a policeman, asked Les to leave.

When Les found out that a police officer was responsible for having him ejected, he became enraged. He was overheard to say: 'Are you going to let a cop tell you how to run fucking security? ... Bring him out, I'll punch the shit out of him.' He also stated: 'It's a cop who's been trying to con my girl.' Les nearly got into a fight with the bouncer, but was dissuaded from that. He then got into a taxi with four other people, and offered to pay $10 if he could use the cab and cruise around looking for Daniel. A short time later the search proved successful, and Les leaped out of the taxi, chasing after Daniel shouting: 'Keep running, you cunt! I'm going to bash your brains in.' When he caught up with Daniel, he began to 'pile drive' punch him, and then when Daniel fell to the ground, kicked him viciously, again and again, yelling: 'You bastard, you bastard, you don't do that.' Les then returned to the nightclub, where he was heard to say: 'That guy copped it, I knew I'd get him ...' Daniel died from the head wounds received during the kicking (his blood alcohol level at autopsy was found to be 0.178).   *(Case No. 4024–88)*

While having many of the central elements of other confrontations, one of the unusual features of this account is that the victim was in occupational and lifestyle terms, clearly of middle-class background (this is one of the very few cases where either victim or offender are from middle or higher class social positions). It shows, again, how an initial dispute begins in a bar where the offence to masculine honour is laid down, with the actual violence taking place in the public space outside the drinking establishment. In this, and the following account, the potential of exceptional violence in these encounters is demonstrated:

On the night of Boxing Day, Martin O. (age 33, cleaner and maintenance worker) decided to go out for a few drinks with his sister and other family. They went first to the Bricklayers Hotel, and then after it closed, to Regines Disco. At about 2 am the rest of the group decided to head for home, but Martin decided to stay on 'for a while'.

Martin stayed until the disco closed at 4.30, and began to walk home. By this time, Martin had consumed a considerable quantity of alcohol (his blood alcohol level was found later to be 0.232). At the same time, Jamie T. and Paul B. also left the disco and headed up the same street. Martin and the other two exchanged insults and taunts. Then, Paul and Martin started to fight. Without warning, suddenly Jamie entered into the fight, giving Martin a savage kick which knocked him over. Jamie followed this with several more kicks to head and body while Martin was down. At one point, Jamie reached down and ripped open Martin's pockets and wallet, taking what money he could.

Paul alleges that he ran off at this point, since he felt that Jamie was out of control. As he was walking away, he saw Jamie pick up a large rock, and drop it several times on Martin's head. When police arrived on the scene a few minutes later, they found Martin dead of what the autopsy determined was traumatic brain damage resulting from massive fracturing of the skull.

(Case No. 4995–86)

From available records, it is hard to fathom what provoked the extreme viciousness of this attack. In this narrative a sub-theme of 'other crime' enters in, given the theft of the wallet. Since the events leading to the death appear to fit the general pattern of masculine conflict and confrontation, this has been considered here rather than Chapter 5. The theft here seemed to be an afterthought, rather than the major motivation on the part of the offenders. Unlike some of the previous accounts, it appears that while both victim and the offenders had been drinking in the pub, the precipitating events seemed to occur in the streets themselves. There was no evidence that the conflict in the streets was a continuation of some earlier dispute in the disco.

This pattern of confrontations taking place in the streets after leaving a pub is not uncommon:

> Alfredo (age 66, pensioner) was known to the police as one who occasionally would 'partake in alcohol' and as a result had developed what police records referred to as a 'minor police history'. On this summer's day, he had spent many hours in the local pubs of Northcote where he was well known (his blood alcohol was later established to be 0.164). He set off for home, first taking a tram to the bus terminus in Queens Parade to wait for the Hoddle Street bus. Apparently his foreignness (he was speaking at times in his native Italian) and his tipsy state annoyed a young man at the stop. The young man began an argument, which was broken up by others waiting at the stop. The bus arrived, and Alfredo and the young man both climbed aboard, with Alfredo taking a seat toward the front. As the bus was nearing his home, Alfredo got up and moved to the rear exit of the bus. At this point, the argument with the young man was renewed. When the bus came to a stop, the young man flung Alfredo backwards out of the bus, with the result that he hit his head on the curb, resulting in fatal head injuries.
>
> *(Case No. 433–88)*

As in the previous case, the whole of the confrontational events occurred after the victim had left the pub (and there is no indication that the offender had been drinking, although this cannot be stated with certainty since the young man was never identified). There is, as well, a mix of the ethnic conflict theme that has been seen in some of the previous cases.

At times, the violence in or around pubs involves bouncers:

> It was a long day of drinking for Paul (age 30, a construction labourer) who began early in the afternoon at the Morwell Hotel. He continued to drink there until 10, becoming along the way both drunk and abusive to other patrons. Around 10 pm Paul then shifted to a local club, and continued his earlier behaviour. After about an hour one of the waitresses complained to the manager about Paul's abusiveness. In turn, the manager asked Jim (known as 'The Gentle Giant') to keep an eye on Paul. Jim stated that he told Paul to 'Stop swearing or I will throw you out.' Jim had to speak to him two or

three more times, and finally told him that 'he had had enough to drink and he had better go home'. Jim then went into the kitchen for a cup of coffee, to allow Paul to cool off a bit and hopefully leave of his own accord, which he did.

The doorman, who knew Paul, reported that about 12.30 Paul 'walked past me and straight into a wall next to the entrance door to the hotel'. He heaved himself up, and weaved his way away from the hotel. Apparently still angry, Paul started kicking cars along the street. Jim was called out to the scene, along with another bouncer and the manager.

Paul apparently was convinced that someone had stolen his car (he had, in fact, come to the club in a taxi), and was yelling out things like: 'I'll kill the cunt who stole me car.' When the group from the club was unable to pacify Paul, or to convince him that he had left his car at home, the manager went back to his office to call the police.

Paul, however, continued to yell and kick cars. Jim again tried to calm Paul, but then Paul made the mistake of attempting to throw a punch at Jim. As a reflex, Jim stated, he countered with a left hand to Paul's jaw. Although it did not have great force, Paul's head snapped back, his knees buckled, and he fell backwards hitting his head with great force on the roadway. Paul died later in hospital as a result of traumatic brain damage.   *(Case No. 1458–87)*

Through account after account, the role of pubs and alcohol in confrontation is found. It is consistent with what has been observed elsewhere regarding the role of violence in and around licensed premises. (Homel and Tomsen, 1993: 61)

At times, in fact, the scenes are so clouded by the excessive intake that it isn't possible to trace with any accuracy what happened:

One Friday afternoon, Gary F. (age 43, labourer) collected his pay packet and set off for a night of drinking. People who knew him well said that Gary often drank a lot, but that generally drink made him quiet and friendly. That night, he spent most of the evening in the Railway Hotel. During the course of the evening, he met up with Calvin T. (age 26, railway labourer) and the two had several drinks together. They were, in fact, the last to leave the pub at closing time.

By then, both had consumed a large quantity of alcohol (Gary's blood alcohol was established later to be 0.296). They had walked only a short distance when an argument broke out between them (Calvin later was unable to remember what the dispute was about). The argument led to a fight. Calvin quickly was able to get the better of Gary, and when Gary was down, he was kicked and beaten ferociously about both head and body. Calvin finally stopped, then wandered off and continued his drinking, giving various accounts of the fight to people he met. He also was spending freely, and it was later suspected that it was Gary's money he was spending, since Gary's empty wallet was found beside him when police arrived to investigate.

An ambulance was called when a passer-by found Gary unconscious by the footpath, and Gary was taken to hospital where he died early next morning as a result of the beating he had received.   *(Case No. 1121–86)*

No amount of further investigation was able to penetrate the alcoholic confusion of these events to piece together what precisely had triggered the violence which resulted in Gary's death. It is not always possible to trace the fine details of these events if they end late at night, in deserted laneways, after a long night of drinking. What can be known is that the death resulted from a fight between two males, who before they set off from the pub had apparently been getting on well. Whatever set them off, it happened quickly.

There is through many of these accounts the persistent report of alcohol use by one or more parties involved. In fact, alcohol or drug use is reported in just under 90 per cent (76 of the 84) of the confrontational homicides. A similar finding of a high level of alcohol involvement in 'expressive' homicides involving 'confrontational competitions' in male-to-male violence was reported in Chicago by Block and Block (1992). There is, of course, a frequent link reported between violence and the use of alcohol (Gerson, 1978; Gibbs, 1986; Tomsen, Homel and Thommeny, 1991; Strang, 1992; Victorian Community Council Against Violence, 1992), although the nature of that connection is not easy to untangle. Obviously, there is some possibility that alcohol has a direct effect in terms of increasing aggression among some men (Boyatzis, 1974). Of greater relevance to the encounters observed here, however, is the nature of social settings in which large amounts of alcohol are consumed.

These scenes, including pubs, parties, barbecues (and the public venues available immediately afterwards, such as streets, public transport locales, parks, etc.) provide the open and leisure settings where working or lower-class males come together, most often for simple relaxation and recreation. Alcohol use tends to be a feature of such settings, obviously in pubs, but also at parties, barbecues and similar locations. But these are also contexts where males can 'eye each other off', where insults can be exchanged, where an audience provides an important social backdrop, increasing the importance of defending one's masculinity and honour (in a similar way Toch, 1969: 149–51, refers to the role of the 'chorus' in violent encounters). It is suggested here, then, that the major significance of drinking lies in what it tells us about the settings in which masculine contests of honour are initiated and sustained. Thus, while there may be some contribution of a physiological effect of alcohol on aggression, it could be hypothesised that at least of equal importance is the social context of leisure, where males flow in and out, which encourages and supports the taking up of violence in support of masculine honour.

Breaking from the scene to fetch a weapon

One feature which has been found in a few of these accounts is that one or another of the parties breaks off the immediate conflict, to bring a weapon into the scene:

> Mick F. (age 36, unemployed) started his drinking at the house of a friend late in the afternoon, and then the two of them moved off to their local, the Victoria Hotel. They continued drinking 'shout for shout' for some time (Mick's blood alcohol was later found to be 0.147).
>
> In the middle of the evening, the group was approached by Jimmy S. (age 53), another of the pub regulars. Jimmy, also feeling the effects of alcohol (some hours later, his blood alcohol was still found to be 0.197), upbraided Mick for some insulting comments he had made toward his 'missus' (observers commented that a trivial exchange had occurred between the two earlier in the day, or at least in their view the comments were trivial). There were mutual insults and challenges, and finally Mick hauled back and struck Jimmy, a short fight ensued, with Jimmy being rather badly beaten. Hurt as well as drunk, Jimmy needed help from bystanders to make his way out of the pub.
>
> Mick and his group settled back to their drinking, when they were interrupted by Jimmy's de facto wife, who proceeded to abuse Mick for his beating of Jimmy. Then, Jimmy himself re-entered the bar. Without a word he walked up to Mick, pulled out a knife, and stabbed him once in the chest. As before, Jimmy was set upon, this time by the friends of Mick. Jimmy was assisted out of the pub by his de facto spouse. Help was summoned for Mick, but the knife had penetrated his heart and he died before he could reach hospital.   *(Case No. 3778–85)*

This narrative pulls together many of the themes seen in earlier cases. The action takes place in a pub, the major protagonists had been drinking heavily, and the encounter takes on special meaning when the challenge to masculine honour takes places in front of peers. One difference is that there was a break in the action when the offender left the scene to search out the murder weapon. A further element that is somewhat different here is that the initial violence is taken up by the ultimate victim of that violence, this fitting the pattern which Wolfgang (1958) has termed 'victim precipitated' homicide.

In some accounts, the break to fetch a weapon is short when the weapon is close at hand:

> It was a pleasant spring afternoon, and a group of mostly teenagers gathered at the home of Mel B. (age 17, unemployed) for a barbecue. By 5 pm the party had run out of beer, so Mel, as host, gathered up a couple of friends and they went to a local pub to replenish the supply of drink.
>
> When they returned, Mel noted that Avery B. (age 17, unemployed) had consumed two cans of beer from the private stock of Mel's father. Mel had

explicitly instructed Avery not to touch that beer, and an argument developed. Witnesses stated that the two had been at each other earlier in the day, and on previous occasions as well. By then, both had consumed a fair quantity of alcohol (Avery's blood alcohol level was later found to be 0.133).

Fed up with Avery's attitude, Mel ordered Avery to '... get out'. Avery then punched Mel with a fist to the face, and the two began a minor scuffle which was broken up by friends.

The friends managed to calm the two down a bit, and Avery moved off a short distance, then again threw some taunts Mel's way. Mel went into the house, picked up a knife, and returned outside. Mel then lunged at Avery, stabbing him in the abdomen. Avery staggered a few steps, then collapsed. His friends took him by car to a nearby hospital, where he died a few hours later (from massive blood loss).

When approached in the evening by police, who indicated that they were trying to clarify the circumstances of the stabbing, Mel said (according to the police report): 'So what? I was stabbed once and the police didn't do anything about it.' When pressed further by the police who informed him that Avery was in a 'serious condition' (this was before the report came through that Avery had died), Mel became irate, repeating: 'The police didn't do anything when I got stabbed. I don't know why you are here now.'

(Case No. 3211–85)

In this case, the interruption of the confrontation was brief as the weapon was close at hand. This constitutes, as well, another of the accounts where the offender, after the termination of the encounter, remained quite unaware of the seriousness of his attack. When the weapon is a gun, the effects are more immediately apparent:

Jim M. (age 52) and Mrs S. had been neighbours for some years. In recent months, there had been several disputes between them over problems that took place when Mrs S. watered her garden. As she watered, apparently she would wet the side of the house of Jim. This angered him, and he finally started watering her house in retaliation. Mrs S. alleged that the two had heated exchanges over this, and that Jim had previously assaulted her over the matter (Jim denied the allegation).

On the evening of the Melbourne Cup, Mrs S. was working in her yard when Jim returned home after several hours of drinking in a few local pubs. Mrs S. stated that as he turned up his walkway, he kicked at the fence between their properties, and then spat at her. An argument between them ensued, as it heated up Jim leaped over the fence and assaulted her.

Hearing the argument, her male friend, Paul T. (age 59) came out of the house to come to her defence, holding a small axe in his hand. The two males scuffled, with Jim wrestling Paul to the ground. Mrs S. then came into the fray, hitting Jim over the head with rocks and the axe. This brought the fight to an end, with Jim subsequently returning to his own house.

He reappeared moments later with a shotgun, and fired a shot which severely wounded Paul. Jim went back into his house, but as Mrs S. was summoning the police, he came out of his house again and fired yet another shot into Paul. The second shot was fatal. Afterwards, Jim claimed that he was affected by alcohol to such an extent that he recalls little of what happened.

While Jim's blood alcohol level could not be established, Paul, the victim, was found to have a blood alcohol level of 0.16. *(Case No. 3459–85)*

Again the weapon was close at hand, although this offender was unlikely to decamp the scene unaware of the severity of the injuries. In another case, what started out as a fight at a party became, in a similar fashion, a homicide when the male who was defeated in front of an audience broke out of the scene to go to his home to fetch a gun, and then return to use the gun to restore his honour:

It was the beginning of summer, and George W. had an 18th birthday party at the back of his parents' home in a bush area of country Victoria. There were about fifteen to twenty young people in attendance, mostly drinking, talking and doing a bit of dancing.

Late in the evening a fight broke out between Billy E. (age 17) and Darren L., apparently over Darren's advance to a girlfriend of Billy's. The two had gone off into the bush for their fight. Richard B. (age 23) waded in and stopped the fight. In the process, he and Billy first exchanged heated words, then Richard punched him a couple of times to make sure the fight stopped. Despite feeling the effects of alcohol (Richard's blood alcohol was later determined to be 0.12), Richard had no trouble getting the best of Billy.

Billy was humiliated and angry, and left the party. Richard returned to the party, saying that: 'Billy reckons he's gonna shoot me ... he's gone home to get a gun.' It was established later that the two had a feud which had lasted for over two months, that started when Richard had also broken up a fight, punching up Billy in the process. The two had argued several times since.

A few minutes later Billy returned with a shotgun, hollering: 'Dinger, where are you?' When Richard walked out of the group towards Billy, Billy fired, killing Richard instantly with a shot to the head. Billy then turned the gun on himself. *(Case No. 4476–86)*

While it is not unusual for a weapon to be brought back into the scene, in these confrontational homicides in this Australian setting there are only a handful of cases where the weapon is a gun, and in none of these confrontational cases is there an instance where the weapon is a hand gun (in contrast to these kinds of altercations in the United States, as described in the case studies assembled by Lundsgaarde, 1977). This previous case is distinctive further in that it is the only case of confrontational homicide where the offender kills himself after killing his victim.

The male who has brought the gun into the scene may, of course, have that weapon taken from him, and he can become a victim of the violence which he has precipitated:

Gregor B. (age 24, machine operator) and his friend Ned set out one evening for a pub crawl. After many drinks, and while they were at their third hotel, Gregor went to the toilet. When coming out of the toilet, Gregor became involved in an argument with a woman who, like him, had had too much to drink (Gregor's blood alcohol level was found later to be 0.120). The nephew of the woman, Albert S. (age 18), intervened, shoving Gregor away. The two pushed at each other, arguing heatedly. The pub bouncer came over, and ordered Gregor to leave the pub.

When Ned came out, he found Gregor waiting in his car. Gregor was furious, explaining that he had been bashed up and 'called a "wog"' (Gregor was a recent migrant from Yugoslavia, and 'wog' is a general epithet applied to persons perceived to be ethnically different). Gregor then asked to be driven home so he could fetch his shotgun and bring it back in order to force his attackers to apologise. They went to Gregor's house to pick up the weapon. Gregor's wife pleaded with him to either stay home, or leave the gun behind, but he replied that this was 'something he simply had to do'.

Gregor and Ned returned to the pub just on closing time. As Albert and his group came out, Gregor threatened them with the shotgun, insisting that they all line up along the wall. They all stood quietly until Gregor turned to say a word to Ned, who was still in his car. At that moment Albert rushed Gregor, knocking him down and taking control of the gun. Three of Albert's friends began to beat and kick Gregor. Albert ordered Ned out of the car, and when Ned refused, smashed one of the car windows. Ned sped off. Albert then added his bit to the beating of Gregor, hitting him with the butt of the shotgun. He then pointed the gun at Gregor, and fired a shot which hit him in the neck, killing him instantly.

When apprehended a few minutes later, Albert said: 'He was going to shoot me ... I acted in self-defence. I know I acted rashly. Is the bloke all right, the bloke I shot? ... I wanted to shoot the tyres out ... When I first got the gun, I tried to shoot it in the air but it wouldn't go off ... I thought he wouldn't be hit ...' Circumstances suggest that Albert may not have intended to shoot when he did. Forensic tests revealed that the gun had a sensitive trigger. Further, Albert very nearly shot his own friends as well, one of them, in fact, receiving a burn mark on his jeans because he was close to the line of fire when Gregor was shot.   *(Case No. 2069–86)*

There is much here that fits the general pattern of this form of masculine violence. Gregor's sense of honour was offended by the argument (which started in a pub), the insult of being called a 'wog', and then by being thrown out of the pub. The fetching of the weapon in this case was explicitly about restoring Gregor's wounded masculinity since he at the time stated that it was his intent to use the gun to force his attackers to 'apologise'.

Race and ethnicity as elements of masculine conflict

Given the multicultural makeup of Victoria, with its large communities of migrants from Italy, Greece, Turkey, Lebanon, Serbia, Croatia, Vietnam and Southeast Asia (among others), it is not surprising that racial and ethnic identities provide dimensions along which masculine conflict can emerge, as in the previous case and some of the others

reviewed previously. There are several narratives of homicide in which
the thread of racism winds through the encounter:

V. (age 27, unemployed) was originally from Vietnam but had lived in
Melbourne for some time. He was planning to move to Queensland in a few
days to accept a job offer. A group of his friends (all Vietnamese) decided to
throw a party in his honour.

The group went along Racecourse Road to the local shops and pub to
obtain the supplies for the party. While part of the group went into the
Palace Hotel to buy beer, V. and a friend went across the road to buy some
pizza. As they crossed the road, a battered green sedan pulled up with what
the Vietnamese could only describe as 'western' males inside. These men
alighted from their car and started verbally to abuse the two Vietnamese,
following this with threats to use a chopping knife that one of the group
produced. V. remained alone briefly while his friend went to summon help
from their friends in the pub.

At the same time as the group of Vietnamese arrived on the scene, a
further group of 'western' males poured out of the pub. A general melee
developed, in which the Vietnamese group apparently threw beer bottles at
their attackers in an attempt to defend themselves. Surrounded now by the
original group augmented by those that had come from the pub, the
outnumbered Vietnamese broke ranks and began to run to the safety of their
flats further along Racecourse Road.

The green car followed in pursuit, grabbing and beating whatever
stragglers they could reach. One of these was V., who was viciously beaten,
including receiving a severe blow to his head. Found shortly later unconscious in the street, V. was taken to Royal Melbourne Hospital where he died
three days later of brain damage from the head injuries. *(Case No. 666–85)*

As is true of other confrontational homicides, there does not appear
to be any element of planning in this homicide. One group was walking
along the street, the other driving by in a car when the car stopped and
words were exchanged the pressure built quickly to its lethal outcome.
What is central in this account is that it was the simmering ethnic
tensions which provided the focal point of the conflict. As well, this is
another instance of how the audience of males can become thrust
directly into the scene as participants in the violence.

In a similar case of group conflict between 'Old Australians' and
Vietnamese, the victim in the end is in the 'Old Australian' group:

The dispute broke out between a group of 'Old Australian' and Vietnamese
youths on St Kilda beach, just behind Luna Park. It had started, according to
observers, when Donnie (age 16) and his friend Sam were walking up and
down the beach 'looking for a fight'. They approached one young person
and said: 'You fucking fat shit ... do you want a fight?' The two apparently
moved on after this boy backed off saying he didn't want to fight. Donnie
and Sam as they moved away from the one encounter, found themselves
amongst a crowd of Vietnamese young people.

In the jostling, the conflict shifted to the Vietnamese. Taunted, one of the Vietnamese boys kicked Sam 'in the guts'. The two Anglo boys drew out their knives and threatened the Vietnamese youths. This initial confrontation was broken by the girls in the Vietnamese group, and the two clusters separated. The Vietnamese group moved off some distance, while the Anglo boys stood around, playing with their knives, and showing off. One of the smaller Vietnamese lads walked over and offered his hand, trying to smooth things over. The Anglo boys responded by telling him to 'piss off', saying 'we'll keep on fighting'.

The Vietnamese group decided to leave. The boys went to the nearby changing rooms. Donnie moved up and challenged the Vietnamese youth who had kicked his friend, again pulling out his knife. The Vietnamese boy pulled out an even bigger knife. At this point, apparently, Donnie put his knife down with the intent of engaging in a fist fight to even things up. As he was doing so, Tan V. (age 14) slipped up from behind and stabbed Donnie once with his knife, then quickly dashed away. Donnie collapsed and died before medical help could be summoned.   (*Case No. 4189–86*)

This case had many elements that some would identify with 'pub violence', yet it took place in a public park area. In both this and the previous case, the initial provocation centres around racism of 'Old Australians' aimed at the recently arrived Vietnamese. Both involved conflict between loosely formed groups. Donnie's death, of course, provides another illustration of victim-precipitated homicide.

At times, the conflict which occurs takes place between two ethnic identities, as in the following narrative of a fight between Chinese and Vietnamese youths:

As was his usual custom, Edgar L. (age 19) left his suburban home to go into the China Town section of the city in order to take Kung Fu lessons. He met his friend Keith L. in Little Bourke Street, where they played some of the machines in the 'Tunza Fun' amusement parlour for a few minutes, then went off to their Kung Fu lessons.

Their class finished at 2.30 pm, and the two first had coffee with friends, then returned to the Tunza Fun at about 3.30, and started playing the Kung Fu Master machine which was their particular favourite. Suddenly, six Vietnamese youths approached and started to strike both Edgar and his friend. Edward then turned and challenged the group, saying (according to one witness): 'Come on, I'll do ya.' One of the Vietnamese groups came in close, produced a knife, and stabbed Edgar once in the chest. The Vietnamese group then quickly slipped away. Edgar staggered outside, and collapsed on the sidewalk, where he died a few minutes later (the knife had penetrated his heart).

The police investigation was able to pull together only scanty details of this homicide. They were unable to identify or locate any of the six Vietnamese young people involved. One of Edgar's friends recalled seeing the Vietnamese group sitting outside a Little Bourke Street restaurant earlier in the afternoon, and commented that this group had previously caused trouble for Chinese young people in the street. Further, there was some provocation on

Edgar's part, since earlier he and his friends had been yelling out anti-Vietnamese insults in Chinese as they had been walking down the street on their way back from their lessons. *(Case No. 1047–85)*

In this narrative a distinction can be drawn between the victim providing some provocation for violence, and the more specific term of victim precipitation of violence. Edgar at no point challenged his attackers with deadly violence, but on the other hand his earlier behaviour served as the catalyst for the aggressive behaviour of his attackers. Ethnic differences, again, provide the source of the friction. The main setting where the acts of this homicide were played out were the city streets, with the final stages taking place in the amusement parlour.

Groups, gangs and violence

Several of the previous encounters involve groups of males which come close in appearance to what some might refer to as 'gangs', as in the following homicide:

The feud between a group of young men predominantly of Italian origin (but including some Greek and 'Old Australian' members) and a group of 'Skips' (Old Australians—from 'Skippy the Kangaroo') had been going on in Werribee (an outer Melbourne suburb) for some time. Months before, a group of Skips had crashed a party at the local Italian Social Club, insulting and taunting various young males in attendance until a fight broke out. One of the ringleaders of the Skips on this occasion immediately left town to search for work. When he returned months later, as far as he was concerned he was ready to pick up where he had left off.

Soon afterwards, there was another encounter between the two groups outside a local convenience store. In the confrontation, mostly verbal, one of the Skips produced a gun, and threatened the other group with it. This incident was reported to the police by the Non-Skips, but no action was taken.

The night after, the migrant group decided to take steps to settle the matter once and for all. Word went out, and a large group of them gathered together (about twenty in all), and set off for a local school hall where they knew the Skips would be gathered.

At the hall, when the Skips saw the large group outside, they became apprehensive since they numbered a bare half dozen. They quickly locked all the doors, but one of the migrant group managed to sneak in through an open toilet window. He threw open the door, the large group poured in, and a general brawl broke out.

At first, it went very badly for the small group of Skips. Suddenly, however, one of the band leaped into the brawl holding a rifle. He managed to fire several shots. Unarmed and unprepared for an attack with a gun, the invading group quickly melted away. The shots were not warning shots (witnesses commented later that the gunman had struck a Rambo-like pose as he fired). One of the attacking group (Barry S., age 19, bouncer) was struck in the heart and died before he could reach hospital. One other was badly wounded, but survived his injuries. *(Case No. 3641-86)*

This has many common features with earlier accounts, but differs in the important respect that there were two groups involved whose conflict extended over time. The initial events, as best as these can be traced back to the confrontation in the Italian Social Club, involved some combination of masculinity and racism, a combination which took on lethal overtones in the final encounter.

There are examples of recognisable lifestyles that differentiate between groups of young people which then may provide the grounds for collective conflict, as in the following narrative:

> Colin (age 17) was a member of a loosely organised group known as 'Bogans', while Charles (age 19) was identified as a 'Headbanger'. Both were at a disco in a local tennis centre when a group of the Bogan males became involved in an argument with a group of girls who were hanging out with the Headbangers. After a brief exchange of taunts and insults, one of the girls punched Colin, who retaliated with a punch in return. Charles came over and attempted to pull the girl away. Colin called Charles a coward and a wimp, and began to throw punches at Charles. At this point, a general fight began between the two groups, involving ten to twelve people. Charles then pulled out a knife, and stabbed Colin several times in the chest and abdomen. Colin died shortly after (his blood alcohol level was found to be 0.079).   *(Case No. 1931–87)*

In this narrative, the disco provides an open, public setting in which groups of males circulate, thereby opening up the possibility of conflict. Both groups involved are distinctively working-class, but set off from each other rather clearly in terms of such behaviour as clothing and hair styles. One issue seen in these events was the active role played by the female Headbanger, since it was her punching of the Bogan male that initiated the physical violence.

Given the group nature of the conflict found in these last accounts, a natural question which follows concerns the extent to which these findings indicate the presence of gang behaviour in Victoria. Assessing whether there is a 'gang problem' requires some clarity and agreement regarding the use of the term 'gang'. There is nothing new, obviously, about collective forms of trouble in Australia. Newspapers in Melbourne and Sydney complained of the 'larrikin' problem over a century ago, and somewhat before that there was the 'Kelly gang'.

In the United States, however, gangs and gang violence tend to be given a more specific meaning. One concise definition offered in the United States was:

> A youth gang is a self-formed association of peers, bound together by mutual interests, with identifiable leadership, well-developed lines of authority, and other organisational features, who act in concert to achieve a specific

purpose or purposes which generally include the conduct of illegal activity and control over a particular territory, facility, or type of enterprise.

(*Miller, 1980: 121*)

While other writers have disagreed about the particulars of this definition (for example, see Spergel, 1984: 201; or Sanchez-Jankowski, 1991: 28–9), it would seem that in the American scene the term 'gang' is likely to refer to a group that has a relatively high degree of organisation, with an explicit leadership structure, a defined territory which is part of the gang identity, and clear colours or other insignia which set them apart. Using these rough guidelines, it would appear that such formalised gangs are rarely encountered in Australian communities.

There are instances, as seen above, of collective violence among young males. What seems characteristic of the violence in Australia is that much of the conflict between groups seems to result from what can be seen as the 'social friction' that occurs as groups flow past each other in public space. When conflict between two groups took place which led to a homicide, it often happened outside the neighbourhood of both groups.

Walmsley (1986) has observed a similar form of group movement, friction, and confrontations over honour in the UK, which took place in a 'troublespot' in Newcastle in a small area where there were twelve pubs:

Groups of young people moved from pub to pub during the evening and this led, towards closing time, to friction between groups suddenly arriving at a pub ... Such situations produce violent incidents whether inside or outside the pub. Again violence sometimes occurs when large numbers of people leave rival establishments (eg. dance halls) at about the same time.

(*Walmsley, 1986: 17–18*)

This writer went on to describe violent incidents which had taken place late at night at burger stalls, where it was observed that: 'In each case "individual worth and identity were at stake, in front of other bystanders, in an impersonal setting". Provocative remarks were made, or something was seen by one party as provocative and the incidents escalated into violence.' (Walmsley, 1986: 18)

Such accounts are virtually identical with those described in the present case studies. It should be noted that the friction which occurs in the social space is probably highly concentrated in terms of the times when violence is likely to result. The space is often occupied in the daylight and early evening hours by groups of other conventional citizens, whose separate claims to the social character of the setting are likely to exert a dampening effect on violence. One is likely to fight in front of an audience of masculine 'mates', and is inclined in other directions if in the audience is mixed aunties, younger sisters, grandfathers, or strangers occupying disparate age and gender roles.

What this also suggests is a different relationship involving space, violence and young males in Australia than in the United States. In the US it has been suggested that territoriality is one of the 'most important defining characteristics' of street gang behaviour, and this in turn is reflected in the way homicides are clustered in space (Block, 1993). In Australia, as perhaps is true in the UK as well, given the observations of Walmsley (1986), it is to be expected that there will be a much wider spread of the violence, although it must be emphasised again that when these group conflicts occur in Australia they are likely to occur in distinctly public settings.

Where group identities exist in Victoria (at least in the period being studied), such as 'Bogans', 'Headbangers', 'Wogs', or 'Skips', these are loosely defined and derive more from general and widely spread lifestyles, rather than membership in territorially based gangs. As indicated in the accounts above, group identities can nourish collective violence in Victoria, as seen in the pub encounter between the Bogans and Headbangers, or in the street clash between the Chinese and Vietnamese groups also previsouly described. The nature of that collective violence, however, seems tied more to issues having to do with the uses of public spaces, rather than to protection of home territory. As groups move through such public scenes as pubs, parties, streets, parks, or similar spaces, the frictional contact may result in contests of honour between males. The conflict, as can be seen in the case studies, may involve individuals or perhaps even groups. Without question, the collectivity of males is a central feature of the conflict, with group members on both sides providing both participants and social audience for the contest as it emerges and erupts into violence. In this, it is suspected that there is much in common with a large proportion of male violence in the United States, including homicides which become identified as 'gang violence' in American cities.

At the same time, while there is group violence, what is not present in the current Australian scene are formally organised and structured gangs. These Australian groups do not have a formal leadership structure, they do not wear insignia which sets them apart from other gangs, and there is not a clear identification with, and protection of, their local territory. Homicide in Australia can be seen to be an occasional consequence of group activity, but not as a feature of the ritualised and formalised gang conflict found in the larger cities of the United States.

Confrontational violence with innocent victims

In most confrontational events, the ultimate victim will be a major actor either in the initial dispute itself, or the social audience that provides the setting for the conflict. In some situations which are clearly confrontational in their character, the victim is a bystander whom ill fate casts in the role of participant in the events:

Elton C. (age 28, builder) had been drinking heavily for some time at the Bayswater Hotel. He was buying for himself and others a drink that consisted of a mixture of vodka, bourbon and tequila. After of a few of these, Elton became increasingly argumentative and difficult to control. Finally, after making unsolicited and unwelcome advances to a group of women in the pub, Elton was ejected by the bouncer. Elton was furious. He climbed into the van he used in his building business, and decided to use the vehicle as his instrument to 'get even'. He drove the van at high speed around the parking lot, weaving in and out, menacing pub customers as they left the hotel. One of the bystanders was Bob T. (age 29). Elton sped his van towards Bob at a high rate of speed, then swerved away at the last minute. The rapid swerving caused a ladder and some copper tubing attached to the roof of the van to shake loose, and Bob T. was struck with great force in the neck and chest by the copper tubing. The tubing caused deep cuts, causing rapid blood loss, which proved fatal.

Being quite unaware of the serious consequences of his earlier behaviour, after having first left the hotel, Elton returned a few minutes later to have another go at pub patrons in the parking lot, and he consequently was arrested by police who by then were at the scene. Elton's blood alcohol level was established to be 0.245, while that of his victim was found to be 0.211.

(Case No. 662–85)

The precipitating events for this homicide are to be found in what happened in the pub, the confrontation between Elton and the bouncers, and then Elton's reaction to the humiliation of being ejected. Elton's car then becomes the weapon of revenge, and Bob became the unfortunate victim of Elton's sense of being wronged.

This use of a car as a weapon is found in the following case as well:

It was early on New Year's morning, and two groups of teenagers were doing 'wheelies' and otherwise causing trouble with their cars in a car park near the Barwon River. Three men approached the cars, and 'told off' the teenagers, who allege that in addition the men had damaged their cars by breaking off their external mirrors. The men then walked off down the road in the direction of a nearby caravan park.

The youths decided that they wouldn't 'let them get away with that'. With a cry of 'let's show them', the two cars took off in pursuit. The two cars made a pass at the men, and insults were hurled back and forth. The cars went past, then turned for a second run at the men at very high speed. The three men were able to leap out of the way, but the leading car swerved on to the shoulder and the driver lost control. As the car spun well off the road,

Charles (age 17, student), who was walking home from a party with friends (and who had not been a party to any of the events which precipitated his death), was struck and killed instantly.   *(Case No. 35–87)*

Again, this is a scene of confrontation and honour. The teenagers were at first intimidated (one of the older males had claimed, falsely, that he was a 'narc'), but given some time to talk up their courage, responded to the challenge laid down by the older men. As in the previous case, it was ill fortune that put Charles in the scene of a masculine conflict in which he played no active part, other than to become the ultimate victim. Confrontational violence, then, may reach out to claim victims who have played no part in the escalating steps which produce a death in the final stages of the encounter. Nonetheless, the violence which produces the fatal injuries emerges out of a challenge to masculine honour, and the setting is one of confrontation, with the victim suffering the misfortune of having wandered close enough to the scene to be caught up in the violence.

Confrontations involving friends

While in the main these confrontations are likely to occur in public settings such as a pub, party or in streets, and as a result involve participants who are either strangers or at best acquaintances, at times the rapid flaring up of argument and violence can involve persons who are well known to each other, as is found in the following case:

Murkha G. (age 46, unemployed on worker's compensation) and Eddy C. (age 48) had been close friends for fifteen years. They had been neighbours for ten of those years, and visited each other's house frequently. Both were unemployed on worker's compensation. Eddy had been involved in a car accident the previous week, and according to his wife, was 'rather depressed'. One day, both of the families went to a traditional Turkish religious ceremony attended by roughly 300 guests. It was an event associated with joy and celebration, and there was much drinking. The two friends had managed to consume virtually a whole bottle of raki (a powerful form of spirit alcohol) between them, and a new bottle was placed on their table. While both had been drinking heavily (Murkha's blood alcohol level was later established to be 0.05), Eddy was visibly intoxicated. His friend decided that to protect him, he would keep the bottle away from him for the rest of the party.

Throughout the night, Murkha would keep repeating when his friend asked him for more to drink: 'You've had enough', to which his friend would reply: 'I can take it.' Later on, when once again Eddy asked for a drink, Murkha suggested that he: 'have some lemonade, you've had enough to drink'.

Eddy took this as an affront to his honour. He was enraged, and according to witnesses he 'turned white'. He threatened Murkha with the lemonade bottle, then 'stormed' out of the hall.

He was followed by both his wife and Murkha. His friend caught up with Eddy just after he had opened the boot of his car. The wife saw the two 'grab' at each other, went up and pulled Eddy away to break up the fight. In fact, Eddy had stabbed Murkha in the neck. Murkha collapsed on the road outside the hall. An ambulance was summoned, but Murkha died before he could receive medical attention.

Questioned at the station afterwards, Eddy said: 'It must be me, but I can't remember. I was drunk ... [regarding the knife] I don't remember getting it out ... I remember we fight, that is all ... Things are mixed up. Murkha was laying down. I thought I pushed him ... I remember pushing him, but I don't know why.' *(Case No. 3128–86)*

This has much in common with other of the confrontational encounters. It involves two males, both of whom were under the influence of alcohol, caught in an honour contest in front of what is for them an important social audience. While the initial spark that set off the confrontation might appear trivial when placed alongside its eventual consequences, for the males involved it was serious enough to set in motion the steps which escalated to the killing. A similar encounter involved a group of Chileans who were members of a soccer club:

A group of club members sat around drinking for several hours after one of the regular Saturday matches, including the club secretary, Sal (age 48), the club president Max, and a supporter Julio. It seems that over recent months Sal and Max had had several disagreements over the running of the club. On top of this there were political disagreements, which surfaced on this particular day as Max and Sal began to argue. As the dispute heated up, Sal became agitated and punched Max. Max did not retaliate, telling Sal not 'to be stupid', and Sal backed off and apologised. Later, another argument developed, this time between Sal and Julio over the use of a telephone, blows were struck, and Julio then grabbed a billiard cue and hit Sal over the head with it. Sal then said he was leaving, and was followed outside by Julio. Julio returned after a short time, and continued to drink with the others in the room (starting another fight in the process).

When the group finally closed the club and left, they discovered Sal lying unconscious on the footpath. The group took Sal home, where his wife cleaned him up and put him to bed. When he did not regain consciousness in the morning, an ambulance was called and he was taken to a hospital where he died a few days later as a result of complications which developed from the severe beating he had endured. *(Case No. 3864–87)*

This account is similar in many ways with the previous one. The scene was one where heavy drinking was taking place, involving persons well known to each other. One distinctive feature in this set of events was that the initial fight involved two persons well known to each other, with the eventual deadly assault pulling in a third party who was more peripheral to these initial persons and their relationship.

Among men, when these quarrels occur, the setting can be a pub which has provided the focal point for their meeting:

David (age 46, builders labourer) and Richie were part of a group who drank regularly at the Junction Hotel. David, who was described as a 'happy-go-lucky type of guy' by his friends, had been drinking for several hours prior to joining his regular group at the Junction (his blood alcohol was later found to be 0.390). He was sitting with the group at a large table, when after having a few more drinks, he called over to a woman friend at the other end of the table, saying: 'Come down and have a drink with me.' Richie, it transpired, had just left the woman friend to go to the bar to buy some more drinks (a barmaid estimated she must have served Richie over a dozen rum and cokes). After a few minutes, Richie came over to the two of them, put both hands on the table and said to David: 'I'm telling you, you'll never do that again.' David mumbled some reply, provoking a challenge by Richie: 'Come out the front and I'll show you ... I'll teach you a lesson.' When David got up, the woman friend said: 'Come on, Davie, sit down and don't be stupid. You are full.' David replied: 'I'm all right, leave me alone, just watch me jacket.'

Richie's account of what happened outside was that David threw a punch at him, and that he then hit David once, and then David fell backwards and hit his head on the road. When Richie tried to lift David, David fell back and hit his head again. Another friend came over (also drunk), and tried to help, but the two of them continued to have trouble managing to keep David up. A third observer to these events noted that: 'His head would have been probably four or five feet off the ground when he fell back. I think he would have done that about three times.' An ambulance was called and took David to the hospital where he died a short time later of the serious head injuries he had sustained.   *(Case No. 3465–88)*

This pattern of exceptional drunkenness, and then a lashing out at a person with whom the offender had previously been friendly, is repeated in several other accounts. There were, in all, thirteen homicides (15 per cent of the 84 confrontational homicides, in other words) where the victim and offender knew each other reasonably well prior to the killing. While the nature and intensity of these friendships varies considerably, it is obvious that the friendship bond by itself does not serve as a barrier to prevent individuals (nearly always males) from becoming caught up in a contest over honour or reputation.

Some deviant cases: confrontations involving women

While this analysis has proceeded with the presumption that confrontational homicides are definitively male behaviour, there were among these cases some in which the central actors were female:

Carol (age 31, single mother) was walking to the local supermarket near the council flats where she lived, when she became involved in an argument with

Donna (age 21) and Tricia. The two women apparently felt that Carol had insulted them, and was responsible for graffiti alluding to their lesbian relationship. As the argument heated up, Donna suddenly punched Carol, grabbed her by the hair, and threw her on the ground. Since Carol had her 6-month-old baby with her, she thought that a defensive response was called for, and she managed to break off the conflict and run with her child back to her own flat.

Carol then armed herself with a small wooden baton, and had two male friends drive her so that she could 'go down there to get them two bitches.' The men stood by the car while Carol went to the front door of Donna and Tricia's flat, calling out: 'Now, come on out and fight me.' Tricia came to the door, and alleged that Carol hit her across the face with the baton. Tricia then woke Donna who had been napping. Donna grabbed a knife and went outside. When she saw the weapon, Carol said: 'Hey, you don't have to use the knife.' Carol then backed off, and started running for the car. Donna followed, shouting 'I'm going to fuckin' kill you.' Donna lunged forward, and stabbed Carol in the chest. Carol's right pulmonary artery was cut, and she bled to death at the scene. It was later established that Donna had a long history of violence, and had previously stabbed Tricia during one of their domestic disputes. *(Case No. 4202–88)*

There is much in common with the other conflicts which have fatal outcomes. Insults are exchanged, a fight breaks out, the action breaks off and one of the parties leaves to fetch a weapon, and then returns to a scene where the final violence takes place. It differs, and remarkably so, in that it involves women. In another case, an argument at a barbecue breaks out, and a killing follows:

Ruth (age 42) is an Aboriginal woman with a long history of physical abuse by males and alcoholism, and had previous arrests for assaultive behaviour. She had begun the day of these events consuming two bottles of methylated spirits in the morning, followed by considerable wine in the afternoon (even five hours after the fatal injuries, she still had a blood alcohol level of 0.17). In the afternoon, a group assembled around the barbecue, where Ruth was preparing sausages and other meat. Apparently an argument broke out between Ruth and one of the males. Ruth picked up a knife and began to lunge at her antagonist. A mutual friend, Billy, moved in between them in an attempt to smooth things over. Trying to continue the fight, Ruth swung the knife wildly, trying to get around Billy. Instead, she struck Billy once in the arm, and once in the chest. Billy collapsed shortly after, and died before help could arrive. *(Case No. 1234–88)*

In this narrative we can see the pattern of extensive alcohol use so common in other confrontational homicides: a provocative exchange (lost now in the confusion of alcohol) and then sudden resort to violence. A distinctive feature of this account is that while the offender was female, the victim was male. This case provides another illustration, as well, of how once violence is set in motion its effects may touch actors

not central to its precipitation. In another case, similar in the sense that
the individuals had known each other and had been drinking heavily, a
woman and a man sitting around a bush campfire began an argument
over some stolen cigarettes. The woman started beating the man, who
pleaded with another male for protection. The woman became even
more enraged, and finally picked up a knife and stabbed the male in
the back. (Case No. 3200–89)

The final case involves women both as offender and victim:

> Kylie (age 29, unemployed) and Sally (age 26) had been friends for many
> years, both growing up in the Broadmeadows area, and both had just
> recently been in Fairlea (the prison for women in Victoria). Kylie was living
> with her sister in her sister's flat. While in prison, Kylie had started a corre-
> spondence with Larry, which she stopped after leaving prison. Sally, whose
> sentence continued for some time, then took up and continued this letter-
> writing to Larry (Kylie was unaware of this).
>
> One afternoon the three were sitting around after sharing drugs (Kylie
> was later found to have traces of diazepam, nordiazepam, oxazepam and
> morphine in her body), when Kylie looked through some of Sally's letters
> and found the letters from Larry. An argument developed between the two.
> After hurling abuse back and forth the two began to scuffle (Kylie's sister
> stated later that Sally was 'off her head on drugs'). Sally then went into the
> kitchen, brought back a knife, screamed 'You reckon I'm a cunt do you?' and
> stabbed Kylie twice in the chest.   *(Case No. 2174–87)*

The precipitating events for the fatal injuries in this account consist
of the same kinds of provocative insults that account for many masculine confrontations. The violence follows in a sudden burst, and a
friendship of long standing is in a matter of an instant torn apart by the
death of one (and a further stay in prison for the other).

While there are too few cases to begin to make anything approaching
firm conclusions, it is distinctive that in all four of these events involving women, while the basic interactional dynamics were similar to the
male confrontational homicides, the women knew their victim reasonably well. Thus, when this form of spontaneous swelling up of provocation, rage and violence occurs involving women in the offender role, it
is not likely to occur in those kinds of settings where the potential
victim would be unknown. These four deaths, at least, are not the sort
that occur in the 'social friction' of movement through public space
that is part of so many of the male-on-male homicides.

These handful of cases require, of course, that we be clear about what
we mean when we refer to this pattern as a masculine scenario. Virtually
all (80 of the 84, or 95 per cent) of the confrontational homicides involve
males as both offender and victim. The handful of female offenders
represent a small proportion both of confrontational homicides, and the

homicides where women are involved as offenders. There are 43 of these homicides in all where women are offenders, so that the four confrontational offenders represent just under 10 per cent of the homicides accounted for by women offenders (most women killers restrict their violence to a close circle involving either sexual partners or their children, see Chapter 7). The script of confrontation is one which can be read and played out by women, but this is a rare event, especially when placed up against the greater frequency of males to become involved in this form of violent behaviour. Over 95 per cent of confrontation homicides involve males as both victims and offenders. The dynamics of confrontational violence, in other words, are overwhelmingly masculine in character.

Luckenbill's six-stage model of conflict

Luckenbill (1977) argued that homicide can be viewed as the outcome of a dynamic interaction involving a victim, an offender and the audience in front of whom these actors play. He observed that such interactions can be seen as moving through six stages. The first stage consists of an 'opening move' performed by the victim and defined by the offender as an offence to 'face'. This opening move could be a direct, verbal expression by the victim, it might consist of the refusal of the victim to cooperate or comply with the requests of the offender, or it might consist of some physical or non-verbal gesture which the offender subsequently defines as offensive.

The second stage where murder was involved resulted when the offender interpreted the victim's opening move as offensive. Luckenbill makes clear that it may not be the victim's intention to be offensive. What is at issue is the interpretation on the part of the offender.

In the third stage the offender, rather than excusing or ignoring the provocation, or leaving the scene, responds with a 'retaliatory move aimed at restoring face and demonstrating strong character' (Luckenbill, 1977: 181). In most cases, this consisted of a verbal or physical challenge being issued to the victim. In a small number of cases, the interaction ends at this stage, since the offender in issuing the challenge actually kills the victim.

In the fourth stage, the victim has been placed in a problematic position by the challenge laid down by the offender. A range of options potentially are available at this juncture. An apology might be extended, the behaviour perceived by the offender as offensive might be discontinued, or the victim might leave the scene. Instead, when a killing took place the victim stood up to the challenge, and entered into a working 'agreement with the proffered definition of the situation as one suited for violence'. (Luckenbill, 1977: 183)

In the fifth stage, the offender and victim are committed to battle. Fearful of 'displaying weakness in character and consequent loss of face', the two evolved a 'working agreement that violence was appropriate' (Luckenbill, 1977: 184). In some cases, the parties sought out and secured weapons to support their verbal threats and challenges.

In the sixth stage, after the victim had fallen, there were three ways that the situation was terminated. In over half of the cases reviewed by Luckenbill (1977) the offender fled the scene, while in the remaining cases the offender either voluntarily remained or was held for the police by members of the social audience.

There are many of the male-to-male homicides, especially the brief confrontational killings, which seem to fit particularly well with the model of conflict posed by Luckenbill. It is in these encounters that it is possible to trace the movement from the initial move by one of the actors, through the stages which result in the lethal violence. Toch (1969: 131), noting a similar phenomenon, has commented on how violent encounters can be 'cumulatively created' by the individuals involved. Consider the initial case study of this section, in which a soldier and a young male begin an argument in a railway carriage, which results in a fight, and then the death of the soldier from a knife wound. In this account, the opening move (in our terms, the challenge to masculine honour), is made when the young man, Mike, tells the soldier, Gabe, to find another seat. Stage Two follows when Gabe interprets the move as offensive, and then Stage Three occurs when Gabe, rather than looking for a seat elsewhere, challenges Mike by attempting to take the seat. Mike in moving to Stage Four then 'must stand up to the challenge' which he does by springing up, fists ready, which then leads to the actual fight (Stage Five), and then Gabe's fatal stabbing. Mike then left the scene, and was apprehended later by police (Stage Six).

While the escalating steps in the confrontation of this narrative correspond to those specified in the model, it became clear as an attempt was made to apply the six-stage model to other homicides that there were apparently some differences in the Victorian data and those available to Luckenbill. Despite the fact that the records were reasonably extensive, at times it simply was not possible to trace all of the stages, even in confrontational homicides. The data simply are not available in some instances to trace through the steps from some initial provocation, the various stages leading up to the killing itself.

One persistent problem was that posed by the homicides whose events were extended in time. There was one account, for example, where the only information available was that P.C., a male, walked up to P.K., another male, who was drinking in pub, and shot him with a rifle

(Stages Four and Five of the model). P.C. then fled, and was apprehended later by the police (Stage Six). While P.C. alleged that P.K. and some of his friends had 'set him up' some time in the past, the specific form of Stages One, Two and Three, the opening moves, could not be determined from the Coroner's files. In another account, reviewed above under the section on collective violence, two groups of young males had been feuding for many months. The death resulted when one group finally decided to corner a small number of members of the other group at a meeting hall where they were practising martial arts. When the group broke into the hall, a collective fight began. One of the members of the group being attacked broke out a rifle, firing a number of shots which wounded several members of the attacking group, one of whom was fatally hurt. Here the problems with the model are multiple. For one, the origins of the feud (the initial Stages One, Two, Three) have been lost in time. For another, given the group character of the conflict, whatever the original stages were, they may not have involved those who played major roles in the final stages of the drama. While the groups could be seen as moving through a series of stages in building up to the lethal encounter, the specific individuals who became victim and offender may have had limited roles in the stages prior to the final lethal encounter.

There were other cases which moved through developmental phases, but the ultimate victim played no part in the evolving interactions. There were two cases reviewed above where the ultimate victim had little to do with the escalation through the steps of violence, other than to become the victim. In the case of the man who became the victim of Elton's wild driving of his car in the parking lot of the pub where he had just been ejected, there were initial stages to the event, and it is certainly possible to trace the steps that resulted in Elton's rage and consequent behaviour. In a manner well outside that of the model posed by Luckenbill, however, the victim played no role in these early stages.

Finally, there is the claim by Luckenbill that these six stages characterised all homicide cases regardless of such factors as 'age, sex, race, time and place, use of alcohol, and proffered motive' (Luckenbill, 1977: 186). In the present study the greatest applicability seems to be in the forms of masculine violence which are the focus here. While possibly relevant in some accounts of intimate violence, these stages would not be found in cases involving sexual intimates where the extremely depressed male plans suicide, to be preceded by the homicide of his female partner. Nor would it apply to cases of infanticide, where the offender is engaged in a complicated denial of the existence of the victim.

It is the present general conclusion, therefore, that while of some heuristic value, the observation of Luckenbill that his model fits all homicides cannot be confirmed. Despite the extensive data in the present case studies, there are a number of narratives where it simply is not possible to identify each of the six stages in the model. Furthermore, in several of the patterns of homicide found here, the dynamics clearly do not unfold in the stages laid down by Luckenbill.

In many of the killings, however, especially those confrontations which move quickly to the point where it becomes lethal in its consequences, it is possible to identify a developing dynamic that has some correspondence to Luckenbill's model. In these situations, we can agree with Luckenbill when he asserts:

> homicide does not appear as a one-sided event with an unwitting victim assuming a passive, non-contributory role. Rather, murder is the outcome of a dynamic interchange between an offender, victim, and, in many cases, bystanders.   *(Luckenbill, 1977: 185)*

The issue of class, gender and economic marginality

Perhaps the most important failing of Luckenbill is that while he describes an important pattern of interaction, and points out that both victim and offender may play significant roles in that interaction, the model does not provide any clues as to why the offender and victim become involved in what proves to be a homicide. Luckenbill (1977: 186) comes close when he underscores the importance of the role of 'maintaining face and reputation and demonstrating character', language which implies a masculine motivation for the violence. As his description stands, however, it provides a potentially helpful description of the interactive dynamics that make up a confrontational encounter, but it does not address either the gender characteristics or the economic marginality that feature so strongly in male-to-male violence.

It is the present contention that it is important to see confrontations as 'contests of honour' in which the maintenance of 'face' or reputation is a central matter. Further, these are seen as quintessential masculine matters. This agrees, then, with Daly and Wilson (1988) who have argued that it is males who become involved in violence around the issue of reputation:

> A seemingly minor affront is not merely a 'stimulus' to action, isolated in time and space. It must be understood within a larger social context of reputations, face, relative social status, and enduring relationships. Men are known by their fellows as 'the sort who can be pushed around' or 'the sort that won't take any shit', as people whose word means action and people who

are full of hot air, as guys whose girlfriends you can chat up with impunity or guys you don't want to mess with. In most social milieus, a man's reputation depends in part upon the maintenance of a credible threat of violence.

(Daly and Wilson, 1988: 128)

The theoretical account provided by Daly and Wilson is one of the few that recognises the diverse forms of masculine violence that make up contemporary homicide patterns. It is their argument that the general thread of masculinity that runs through homicide reflects forms of male aggressiveness which can be accounted for by evolutionary processes of adaptation. While their formulation is helpful in moving us towards an understanding of the masculine character of violence, in its present form it needs some expansion to encompass the class elements of this form of homicide. The lethal violence being examined here is defined both by its class and gender characteristics. It is predominantly male and working/under-class behaviour. How is it that we can account for these two features of confrontational homicide?

It is the defence of honour that makes what some might consider a 'trivial' provocation become the grounds for a confrontation which builds to a homicide. Wolfgang was one of the early observers of the phenomenon of the apparent triviality of the events which provoke some homicides:

> Despite diligent efforts to discern the exact and precise factors involved in an altercation or domestic quarrel, police officers are often unable to acquire information other than the fact that a trivial argument developed, or an insult was suffered by one or both of the parties. *(Wolfgang, 1958: 188)*

It seems clear, however, that what is trivial to a firmly respectable observer may be quite central to the marginal actor's sense of masculinity. Daly and Wilson (1988) have argued along similar lines, that for some men it is important that to maintain their sense of honour they not allow themselves to be 'pushed around', that they maintain a 'credible threat of violence' (Daly and Wilson, 1988: 128). Such perceptions are actually consistent with Wolfgang's observations. After the sentence noting the apparently 'trivial' character in some of the disputes leading to homicide, Wolfgang went on to observe:

> Intensive reading of the police files and of verbatim reports of interrogations ... suggest that the significance of a jostle, a slight derogatory remark, or the appearance of a weapon ... are stimuli differentially perceived and interpreted ... Quick resort to physical combat as a measure of daring, courage, or defense of status appears to be a cultural expectation, especially for lower class males ... *(Wolfgang, 1958: 189)*

Further, Wolfgang (1958: 189) is explicit in his statement that it is the observers in the criminal justice system who, drawing upon middle and upper-class values which have influenced the shaping of legal norms, have seen the disputes which lead to homicide as trivial in origin. For the lower-class players in the homicide drama, the challenge to manhood is far from a trivial matter.

Putting it together: the structure of confrontational homicide

In the common schemes for classifying relationships between victims and offenders, these confrontational clashes between males would be split pretty evenly between homicides involving 'strangers' or 'friends/ acquaintances'. In terms of the common 'motives' for homicide, many would fit into the grouping of 'altercation of relatively trivial origin' (Wolfgang, 1958). Certainly, there are many of these killings where the precipitating incidents seem negligible when placed alongside the final outcome. A case can be made that in both his substantive text and in the presentation of case studies, many of the homicides described by Wolfgang correspond to the present grouping of confrontational homicides (for example, see Wolfgang, 1958: 226–7).

What is at issue here is how best to capture the social dynamics of the relationship between the victim and offender in these circumstances. Obviously, the statement either that the parties were 'strangers' or 'friends-acquaintances' which would come from common classifications of such 'relationships' would be empirically correct, but would be useless in terms of actually describing the nature of what has transpired. In some accounts the individuals have not known each other, while in others they have a passing acquaintance (as in some confrontations that begin in pubs). The form of the confrontation is the same, regardless of these circumstances. Accordingly, groupings such as 'stranger' or 'acquaintance' are inadequate to express the nature of the interactional dynamic occurring between these males.

What is fundamental to the confrontation scenario is that it is the altercation itself which defines the relationship between the parties. The two have come together, and become known to each other, through the fight itself. Whether they are friends, acquaintances or strangers, the dynamics of male confrontation are played out within a set of mutually recognised expectations regarding how the encounter is to proceed. In these accounts (except those few where the ultimate victim truly was an innocent bystander) the victim as well as the offender was actively involved in the encounter. In many the victim actually initiated the violence. In most of the remainder, the victim was a willing participant in the encounter.

This form of homicide has been identified in the work of Daly and Wilson where they refer specifically to 'confrontational disputes' arising in a 'field of honour', arguing that homicides arising out of 'trivial altercations' are essentially affairs of honour bearing a strong resemblance to honour contests observed in other cultures:

> The precipitating insult may appear petty, but is usually a deliberate provocation (or is perceived to be), and hence constitutes a public challenge that cannot be shrugged off. It often takes the form of disparagement of the challenged party's manhood: his nerve, strength or savvy, or the virtue of his wife, girlfriend or female relatives.   *(Wilson and Daly, 1985: 69)*

It is, of course, the essential masculinity of this form of homicide that is of central theoretical interest, both in the present case and the works of Daly and Wilson. This is the most common of the scenarios of violence observed in the present data where, in the main, the principals are male, although it has been noted that four cases (5 per cent of the confrontational homicides) did involve women. The script defining the various moves which make up this pattern is one which is drawn upon nearly always by men, but is on rare occasion followed out by women.

To summarise, this form of homicide involves behaviour which is essentially a contest of honour between males. In the initial stages of the encounter, what the participants in a confrontational killing intend is first to argue, then to fight. The argument which produces that fight is spontaneous, as are the events which follow. These conflicts typically occur in leisure scenes, especially scenes where males predominate. The venue most often is a public setting, including in and around pubs, in streets or laneways, in public parks or reserves, parties or barbecues, and in public transport settings such as bus stops, railway stations, or even on the train carriages or buses themselves. In most such settings, an active role is played by the social audience, particularly male peers. The social nature of such scenes is reinforced by the role of alcohol, whose use has been found to be a feature of a great majority of these homicides.

The lethal violence is not premeditated, at least at the starting point of the conflict. Some confrontation scenes move rapidly to the point where deadly violence is employed, as where the parties begin with a fist fight, then raise the stakes by pulling knives. Others are more complex, however, and may involve one of the parties leaving the immediate scene to return a short time later with a weapon. In some instances the conflict may become elaborated into a feud which simmers for weeks, or months before the lethal violence results.

Through it all resound the joint themes of masculinity and lower social class position. Extreme violence in defence of honour is definitively masculine and lower or underclass in its makeup. But, not all such males feel compelled to defend their reputation or status with violence. Why it is that some males pursue violence to secure their reputation or status, while others avoid such challenges, constitutes a major question for further research and theoretical discussion.

CHAPTER 5

Taking exceptional risks:
homicide in the course of other crime

There are some circumstances where a person will carefully plot the taking of another person's life. In many situations, however, the killing results from events which initially are about something else. One such situation, as we have seen, is that where two males begin an argument, and their words lead to blows and then a death. Upon setting themselves out to fight, the males in confrontation are knowingly exposing themselves to some risk, since there is always the known danger of losing a fight and being physically beaten. What most are not likely to know is that the fight will lead to the death of one of them.

In the next scenario, however, the individuals are thrusting themselves typically into a much greater risk situation, either in terms of the threat to the lives of potential victims, or ultimately to their own lives. When individuals set out to commit a serious crime such as armed robbery, they do so recognising that the threat of violence employed may, in fact, become real violence. And, that this threat is real is demonstrated in the accounts which follow.

Homicide which occurs in the course of other crime contributes a significant proportion to the total amount of homicide observed in the present research. In the five-year period, there were a total of 61 such homicides (16 per cent of all homicides). Four distinct sub-themes were identified within this general homicide scenario.

The first variation: double victims

The first major variation on this theme is made up of those cases where the victim in the initial crime becomes the victim in the homicide as well (31 of the 61). Most often, the offence where this double

victimisation occurs is armed robbery. In some cases since the offender
was not apprehended the details of the event are scanty:

> D.Z. (age 24, night watchman) was employed by Metropolitan Security
> Services as a night patrolman. On Saturday 2 March, between 12.30 and 1 am
> he was seen in the vicinity of Salty Street, Altona, in his marked company car.
> Shortly after, people in the vicinity of the nearby K-Mart Store in the Altona
> Gate Shopping Centre heard the sound of a shot. D.Z. failed to answer his
> car radio after 12.30 am. At 3.30 am his car was found with its headlights on.
> His body was found a short distance away, near a time-clock checkpoint at the
> west end of the store. He had been shot with a .22 rifle. There was evidence
> of tampering with the door adjacent to the time clock. No offender has been
> identified in this death.   *(Case No. 599–85)*

Despite the sparse nature of this account, there is enough information to make the reasonable guess that the victim had been killed
during the course of an armed robbery. Little more can be known
about what happened between victim and offender to provoke the
killing in the course of that robbery. Even less is known in the case of
A.S.:

> Shortly after 8 pm, an unknown person (or persons) entered and robbed the
> service station where A.S. (age 24) worked. At 8.10 pm, A.S. was found,
> unconscious, on the floor with a gunshot wound to the head. He was taken to
> hospital where he died ten days later without regaining consciousness. No
> other details have been uncovered in this case.   *(Case No. 1837–86)*

Again, the specific dynamics of provocation are unknowable in cases
such as this where a person has been victimised in a situation where all
that is known is that either a robbery or a burglary has also taken place.
Some of these unsolved, double-victim crimes involve elderly victims:

> There had been three attempted break-ins to houses in Drummond Street,
> Ballarat, on that New Year's Eve. At midday on the following day, relatives
> who had come to visit Karen S. (age 70, pensioner) became alarmed when
> she did not answer her door. Finding the door unlocked, they entered only
> to find the woman dead in her bed. She had been struck over the head
> several times with a ceramic jug. The house had been ransacked.
> *(Case No. 11–88)*

In some of these double-victim cases more is known, as in one where
the offenders were drug users in search for money to support their
habits:

> Paul and Amy, both heavy users of heroin, decided to travel to Reservoir (a
> Melbourne suburb) to do a burglary. At the time, Paul was using 3 to 4 grams
> of heroin a day, and since he was unemployed relied on burglaries to support

his use of drugs. They first approached the house of Samuel (age 88, retired) and when they told him they had forgotten an address, he invited them in to check the telephone book. They then left his house, and tried unsuccessfully to break into two other homes. By this time it was dark, and Paul decided to break into Samuel's house. He first knocked on the door. When there was no answer, he then went around the back, and broke a window to gain access through the back door. According to Mark, at that point Samuel jumped him from behind. Mark punched Samuel several times, then tied him up and put him on a bed. Paul then ransacked the house, finding $200 in cash and a $300 watch. When Samuel's son came the next day, he found that Samuel had died during the night of complications resulting from the beating he had sustained.   *(Case No. 1885–88)*

In another case, because the victim lived for a short time, somewhat more detail is available although the offenders have not yet been identified:

After a work accident, S.G. (age 44, unemployed), a recent migrant from Rumania, moved to a block of land in the country. One night, a neighbour observed S.G.'s house on fire. Driving up to the house, the neighbour saw S.G., suffering from severe burns, attempting to climb into his car. The friend put him in his own car, and drove him to the nearest hospital which was in Ballarat. S.G. told the neighbour during the drive that two men had tried to steal money from him. Failing to find any money, the two poured petrol over him, then lit a match and set him alight. S.G. was first treated in Ballarat, then transferred to the Burns Unit of the Royal Melbourne Hospital where he died two days later. His murder remains unsolved.

(Case No. 2353–85)

In other cases where the homicide was solved, it is possible to sketch out more details of what took place:

It had been a long day for J.R. (age 43, mechanic, part-time taxi driver). He had left home for work at 5 am, and had told his previous taxi customers at around 11 pm that he intended to go home. Shortly after 11 pm, S.D. (age 22) climbed into his taxi while it was parked at a service station in Hampton. S.D. first asked to be driven to a street in Brunswick were he dropped a Christmas present off for his son. He then asked to be driven north along Sydney Road, then into a deserted area near Campbellfield.

S.D. then asked J.R. to stop. He produced a .22 sawn-off rifle which he had concealed in a bag, and ordered J.R. out of the car. After taking about $150 from J.R., S.D. forced him into the boot of the car, closing the lid firmly. After a few minutes, he opened the boot again, and shot J.R. several times with the rifle. S.D. then drove off in the taxi, stopping to dispose of the body outside the country town of Finley, and to throw the gun out somewhere north of Shepparton. He then drove until the taxi ran out of fuel just north of Jerilderie. S.D. then fled to Queensland where he was apprehended one month later.

S.D. was unable to provide any motive for the killing. His family regarded him as a violent individual with a short temper. He had threatened to kill his ex-wife, and had previously been involved in a stabbing incident. He had a previous record with the police, including offences of violence.

(Case No. 5036–86)

Even with the information that is available, it is difficult in this narrative to account for why the offender felt he had to kill his victim. In another case, the armed robbery led to a death which occurred some time after the initial crime:

M.H. and K.H. were unemployed and addicted to heroin. One of the methods they employed to obtain money for drugs was armed robbery (although they later stated that it was never their intent to harm anybody).

One night the two armed themselves with knives and entered a milk bar at Templestowe (a Melbourne suburb). The proprietor, H.H. (age 65), came out from the residential portion of the premises to serve them. Seeing them armed and masked, H.H. put up minor resistance, which stopped when one of the robbers cut him on the hand.

The two took the money out of the till, then forced H.H. back into the residential quarters, insisting that H.H. tell them where the rest of the money was hidden. Fearing for their lives, H.H.'s wife told their attackers where they could find the rest of the money (about $1300). The intruders grabbed the money and ran out of the milk bar.

A few days later H.H., who had a history of lung and heart problems, collapsed and died. Drawing upon medical testimony, the Coroner concluded that 'the stress suffered by the deceased in the armed robbery resulted in prolonged emotional disturbance and physiological change ... resulting in heart failure ... ' finding that the death 'was substantially caused by the unlawful, dangerous and intentional acts' of M.H. and K.H.

(Case No. 2732–85)

The lethal effects of taking exceptional risks, as found in this account, may take a form quite unanticipated by the criminal offenders. Two of the cases where armed robbery leads to murder involve attacks on homosexuals:

J.S. (age 55, part-time cleaner) was known to be a practising homosexual who frequented Footscray Park (which had a reputation as a homosexual meeting place, particularly at night). One night when he was in the park, R.H. (age 36), who had just had an argument with his girlfriend, came into the park and sat down on one of the benches to simmer down. While on the bench, R.H. overheard a conversation in which he believed that J.S. had $1500 in his possession.

R.H. decided to take the money from J.S. He went back to his car and took from it a sawn-off .22 rifle. In order to frighten off others who were in the park, R.H. went up to them, first attempting to frighten them by shouts and insults, finally firing his gun into the air.

When the others had dispersed, R.H. began to stalk J.S. J.S. apparently attempted to run away, R.H. was able to catch him. A witness who remained said that J.S. attempted to push the gun away from his head, and R.H. then fired the weapon at J.S. J.S. screamed and limped a couple of steps away, then fell. R.H. then fired another shot into his body.

R.H. then took his victim's wallet and fled. A little while later, he inspected the wallet and found that it contained only $40. R.H. then returned to the scene and searched his victim's body for the money. Finding none, he took his car keys and then searched his victim's car. There was no further money to be found. Immediately after, R.H. left the state, and was arrested some three weeks later in New South Wales.   *(Case No. 3925–85)*

In this case, the homosexuality of the victim was peripheral to the decision first to rob, then kill his victim (although it might have contributed to the level of violence in the encounter). In another case, the armed robbery was part of a group's harassment of homosexuals:

> The Lagoon Pier Changing Rooms in Beaconsfield Parade, Port Melbourne, had developed a reputation as a meeting place for homosexuals, especially in the early hours of the morning. This reputation reached the homophobic community as well, attracting the attention of a group of young men who engaged in the attacks on homosexuals known as 'poofter bashing', although they also intended to rob their victims as well.
>
> After first spending the late hours of the night in various pubs, the group then went to the changing rooms to beat up homosexuals. At 3.30 in the morning they jumped on their first victim, but after being grabbed and beaten he was able to squirm out of their grasp and flee.
>
> A short time later, B.C. (age 30) arrived. There is no evidence that B.C. was a homosexual. He had been out with his wife and friends to dinner earlier that evening. Afterwards, he and his wife had an argument, resulting in B.C. packing a bag and leaving. He left home at 2.30, and stopped by the changing rooms at 3.30. When he walked into the men's toilet, he was jumped on by the waiting group of young men. He was beaten and kicked savagely, and afterward robbed by his attackers. When police were called to the scene at 5.15, they found B.C. dead on the floor of the changing room. Severe head injuries were the cause of death.   *(Case No. 920–86)*

In this incident involving 'gay bashing' there tends to be combined dual motivation of robbery as well as a homophobic dispensing of punishment aimed at the gay lifestyle.

In the following case, the 'other crime' is a combination involving drug dealing, robbery, and possibly revenge for a previous robbery:

> Jenny D. (age 32, pensioner) frequently had obtained heroin from D.K. ('American Dave') for the past four years. On 3 December 1986 Jenny called American Dave to arrange a drug deal at a suburban railway station. The real purpose of the meet was to lure American Dave out of his house, which a boyfriend of Jenny's successfully robbed while American Dave was away. Jenny received a share of the $1000 that was taken.
>
> Two days later, Jenny needed more heroin and once again arranged to meet American Dave. Her friend who had conducted the robbery warned

her that American Dave would 'know you set him up'. Jenny replied that there was no problem, since '... I have got him once or twice before'. The friend gave her an extra $100 for her to buy him some heroin as well.

Jenny left and did not return. Jenny's boyfriend and two women went to American Dave's house, and inquired what had happened to Jenny. He denied seeing Jenny, abused and hit the women, and then chased them from his house with a pistol.

Jenny's body was found later that same day in the gutter of a country road. She had head injuries consistent with being beaten with a pistol, as well as bruising to the face and arms. American Dave was charged with Jenny's murder. While on remand he confessed to another prisoner that he had killed Jenny, stating that she had owed him 'a lot of money'.

(Case No. 4677–86)

Here is a complex situation where a deviant lifestyle, and the participation in a cluster of criminal offences (robbery, drug use, fraud), become part of the lethal violence.

A similar mix of drug dealing and robbery is found in the following narrative:

Police received a call to attend at 65 Hoddle Street (in inner Melbourne) at 2.17 one morning, arriving within ten minutes to find the body of T.P. (age 29, unemployed) on the floor near the rear door with a knife buried in his stomach. Death was caused by multiple stab wounds.

The police investigation pieced together the following observations. T.P. for some time had been making his living dealing in drugs, especially heroin. One of his regular customers was D.P. (age 23, unemployed). Although T.P. was his regular lifeline for drugs, D.P. had become antagonistic towards him, with D.P. making several threatening telephone calls to T.P. Because of his dependence on drugs, D.P.'s life had become increasingly chaotic. Lacking a job he had no source of regular income to support his drug habit. His lack of money had forced him to move from place to place because of his non-payment of rent.

On the night of the murder, T.P. and some of his friends were drinking and chatting in T.P.'s home. D.P. came by and joined the group. At the time, several thousand dollars were spread over the table along with a large supply of drugs. T.P. offered a free shot of heroin to D.P., which he accepted. About half an hour before the police received the call summoning them to the scene, the friends left to go to a nearby disco for drinks, leaving T.P. alone in the house with D.P.

D.P. claims that the killing was done by two masked men who broke into the house in order to rob T.P. However, this does not explain where D.P. suddenly had the money to pay cash for several days of expensive hotel accommodation and restaurant meals. Further, he had arranged with some friends to give him an alibi for crucial times (when the friends found out that a murder was involved, they provided full details to the police). The police concluded that D.P., having a history of discord with T.P. anyway, murdered T.P. to obtain both the money and a supply of drugs.   *(Case No. 273–85)*

One characteristic of the previous two events is that the victim and offender were known to each other. That is, unlike many of the other of these killings which flow out of the commission of other crime, these were not 'stranger killings'. This situation, where the victim and offender are known to each other, was found in the following case as well:

Alice (age 42, nurse) had employed Mark (age 30) to paint her house several months previously. Being short of money one late November day, Mark first went to the house of another previous customer who owed him $3000, and when he found no one at home, broke in and vandalised some of the furniture. He then went to a nearby pub and had several drinks. Afterwards, he decided to burgle Alice's house, because by his accounting she owed him $200 for the work he had done on her house. When he arrived at the house, he knocked at the front door, and was surprised when Alice answered (she had been on a late shift the previous night).

As he told the story, Mark then pushed his way into the house, demanding his $200. When she refused to pay, he tied her up and gagged her, then proceeded to rummage through the house for items to steal. At one point he had observed that the gag had caused Alice to collapse, so he loosened both the gag and the bindings. At that, Alice then started screaming and hitting him. Mark then subdued her, tied her up again, and then stabbed her to death (she was stabbed a total of eleven times). He then left (taking a few items of jewellery), locking the door behind him.

Later that afternoon, Mark called the police and informed them of the murder. Mark became upset at the reports distributed to the media by the police which indicated that Alice had been sexually assaulted (which Mark denied). Mark then called a local television station, and arranged to meet them at the Jolimont rail footbridge so that he could tell his side of the story. When he arrived for the interview, he was arrested by the police, with the proceedings being filmed by a television crew.   (Case No. 5156–87)

In the most common situation it might be presumed that, most often where an offender sets out to commit a crime such as robbery, it would involve an unknown person, but in some instances the knowledge of the person and perhaps the presence of money is an important feature of the crime, and also likely to be tied to the thought processes that lead to the killing.

A rather different set of circumstances involving persons known to each other can occur when the crime is attempted sexual assault, as is found in the following case:

W.J. (age 33, unemployed) and his girlfriend R.M had come to Victoria seeking work. One day, they met up with a circle of amiable friends in Melton (an outer Melbourne suburb), and began to arrange and plan for work. The group had a pleasant afternoon, drinking at a local pub and shooting pool. As it became evening, the group retired to the house of G.M., continuing to drink and also to smoke marijuana.

They continued this well into the evening. By all accounts everyone was getting along. When it became late, it was clear that W.J. was too far gone on drugs and alcohol to drive. G.M. offered to let W.J. and his girlfriend use the extra bedroom in his house. The offer was accepted and the couple retired to bed.

Later, R.M. was awakened when she felt that someone was in the room, touching her arm. It was G.M., who was naked. R.M. pleaded with him to leave, to which he replied: 'Are you going to do it? ... or I'm going to, you know, start a drama or something like that.' When she refused, G.M. then upped the ante, saying: 'Are you going to do it? ... or I'll get the gun and shoot both of you.'

R.M. again refused. G.M. then left the room, returning with his shotgun. He pointed it first at R.M., then W.J., repeating what he had said. R.M., terrified, attempted to waken W.J. who had slept through these events. Finally, he woke up, saw G.M. with the gun, saying: 'What are you doing? Leave us alone.' G.M. replied: 'Take that', and shot him. *(Case No. 4580–86)*

This was the only case in this five-year period involving a double victim where rape(or the intent to rape) was the initial offence. It is to be anticipated that with a longer time span, or a large set of data, cases would emerge in which there are women victims who are first sexually assaulted, then killed, but none such are found within the present case studies.

In another case, again involving offenders known to each other, the offender argued that the homicide was a result of what was originally intended as an assault:

Lynne C. (age 25) made her living as a prostitute. She had managed to arouse a deep anger in Kylie S., allegedly because Lynne had both 'dobbed in' her brother to the police, and also set him up for a bashing. She arranged to pay Lynne for services provided to a male friend to whom Kylie owed some money.

It was arranged for her to meet her client at a suburban motel. After the two had been in the room for a few minutes, Kylie and a male friend broke in. They bound and gagged Lynne, and started to beat her. During the course of the beating, Lynne died of asphyxiation because her mouth was tightly sealed and she was unable to breathe through her nose. Kylie and her two friends then took the body and dumped it several kilometres away in some vacant bushland. *(Case No. 1264–86)*

An unusual feature of this case is that it is one of the few where the original offender involved was a female. There is another case in these files where the death apparently resulted from an assault:

Len C. (age 21) had accumulated a total of seventeen offences prior to the events which resulted in the death of Arnie B. (age 72). Earlier that day, he had knocked at a door, and assaulted two young men, totally unknown to him, because he believed that they had assaulted his brother (it turned out that a previous occupant at the address was responsible).

The facts of the death are difficult to establish. All of the physical evidence suggested that Arnie had been struck several times with a blunt instrument while seated, watching television. Len's story was that Arnie had approached him in the toilet of a nearby pub. Len alleged that in the toilet Arnie had come up to him and attempted to touch his penis, which Len says he 'brushed off'. Len states that he then followed Arnie through a fence and up the back stairs to Arnie's council flat. As he was climbing the stairs, Len stated that Arnie set his small dog on to him. Len then punched Arnie, and pushed him into his flat. Len was apparently surprised when he was informed that Arnie was mute and deaf. *(Case No. 2919–85)*

This case is murky in terms of what transpired and how it should be classified. On the basis of the information available, it appeared that the offender had a history of exceptional violence, and that in all probability the above events were part of a pattern of assaultive violence, perhaps with the intent to rob.

A number of factors stand out in these and other case studies of double victims. First, most of these cases involve offenders who are highly marginal and willing to take great risks with their own lives and the lives of their victims. Second, where known, most of the offenders are male. There were five cases where females were involved in the offence, two involving women only in the homicide (prostitutes who turned on their clients), and three involving women as accomplices in the killing. Men offenders accounted, putting it in other terms, for 25 of the 31 double-victim homicides.

The second variation: the offender as victim

There are times when the tables turn suddenly on criminal offenders. One of the hazards of serious crime, in other words, is that the offender may find himself (in most cases) the victim of lethal violence (becoming what has been called a 'reverse victim', Maxfield, 1990). There were, in all, 18 such reverse victims found in these files. In some of these cases, the victim of the initial crime turns the tables and becomes the offender in the homicide (7 of these 18 reverse victims were where the killer was a civilian victim of the initial crime):

Late one night, two intruders, M.F. (age 25) and P.E. (age 22) broke into the house shared by the brothers N.T. and T.T. According to the story the brothers told the police, their attackers carried a gun and attempted an armed robbery. The brothers managed to divert the robber with the gun, there was a general struggle, and the brothers killed both robbers with knives (the autopsy established that both of the intruders had died of multiple stab wounds, and that they had both been drinking heavily). The Coroner found at the inquest that the 'wounds were justifiably inflicted' while the brothers 'were acting in self defence.' *(Case Nos. 2083–85 and 2084–85)*

In a similar account, the initial crime consists of attempted theft of a motor car:

> For most of the evening, D.A. (age 28, car driver) had been drinking in a suburban hotel a few kilometres from his home. Without a car, perhaps short of money, he attempted to solve his transportation problem by breaking into a car. As D.A. was in the process of hot-wiring the car, the car owner, R.T., came on to the scene. D.A. then made his second mistake of the night by taking a swing at R.T. R.T. had the advantage of not being intoxicated, and was further exceptionally fit. It was a short fight. While D.A. was able to land at least one blow which caused a slight cut to R.T.'s face, R.T. quickly got the best of him, hitting him several times to the face and body. D.A. suffered severe injuries to his face, including facial fractures.
>
> While serious, these wounds by themselves were not fatal. Five days later, D.A. underwent surgery for treatment of the fractures under general anaesthetic. Upon completion of the surgical procedures, the drug Naloxone was administered. The consequences were rapid and fatal. D.A. developed acute pulmonary oedema, and died shortly thereafter. The Coroner found that the Naloxone was 'reasonably and properly administered', and the observed fatal effects in D.A.'s case are 'extremely rare though documented in medical literature.'
>
> Further, with respect to R.T., the Coroner found that during the fight he had continued to strike D.A. 'where a reasonable person with comparable high fitness and strength ... would have known or ought to have known that to continue striking the deceased after the second strike could or would result in serious injury'. Nonetheless, it was held that the sequence of events were such that R.T. could not 'reasonably be held responsible either in causation or degree of proximity', and the death, therefore, was declared to be 'accidental'. Although clearly marginal, the case has been kept in these files because the initial chain of events was set in motion by the attempted auto theft, and the fatality itself was an outcome, even if indirect, of the beating sustained in the course of that theft.   *(Case No. 2017–85)*

In these cases, the original offender has taken the risk of engaging in a serious crime, creating a scene in which the stakes run high. Citizens may fight back, and at times the result may be the death of the original offender. In a slightly large number of cases (11 of the 18), it was police who were responsible for the killing. Among such cases are those in which the death results from police intervention in the course of an armed robbery:

> C.B. (age 27, unemployed) had first met his partner-in-crime, F.H., in prison. C.B. was a regular user of drugs, especially opiates. After release, C.B. and F.H., in order to obtain money, had been engaging in a series of armed robberies of small chemist shops, focusing on those which were sub-agencies of the State Bank of Victoria.
>
> These robberies had been frequent enough, and concentrated in a small enough area, to allow the Armed Robbery Squad of the police to make reasonable guesses regarding where they might strike next. Several such

shops were staked out, including one in Huntingdale Road, Chadstone (a Melbourne suburb).

This was the shop that the two had selected for the next robbery. At 9.30 one morning, the two, armed with cut-down .22 rifles and wearing cut-up jumpers for hoods, entered the shop. Witnesses inside said that the pair were 'very polite' and kept repeating that everyone should 'stay quiet and nothing will happen'. Another reported them as saying: 'Do as you're told and nobody will get hurt'.

After taking money and drugs from the shop, the two ran to their car. The waiting police identified themselves and called out for them to stop. An instant later, several shots were fired, wounding F.H. and killing C.B. The Coroner found that under the circumstances, the death of C.B. was 'justifiable homicide'.   *(Case No. 242–85)*

Several of the persons who can be classified as 'offender victims' were killed by police in the course of making an arrest. Some of these involved shoot-outs, where the victim as well as the police fired a weapon during the encounter:

Milton M. (age 22) had been under police surveillance for some time as a suspect in several robberies which had been at gunpoint (including discharging of the gun). Based on information they had obtained, the police stepped up their watch on Milton, since they anticipated that another robbery was about to occur. Milton was observed leaving his house, with 'what appeared to be a firearm tucked down the front of his pants.' He drove to a nearby car sales yard, where he switched cars.

Apparently Milton became aware that the police were following him, since he pulled an abrupt U-turn, and headed directly for the police car, veering away at the last minute. The police then pursued Milton, turning on their lights and siren. The car was intercepted, and the police jumped out of their car with their weapons drawn. Observing that Milton had drawn his weapon, the police fired a number of shots at the car. Milton appeared to slump on the passenger side of the car. The police then called out: 'Police: get out of the car', and fired a further warning shot into the air.

Milton decided to make a run for it, opening the passenger side door, and fleeing down the street. As he was running, he half-turned and pointed his revolver at the police over his left shoulder. The police then fired more shots, one of them hitting Milton in the back of the head, killing him instantly.

(Case No. 1269–87)

Another of these cases where police were confronted with an armed suspect involved a person suspected of killing one of the security guards who also is found in these files as a 'double victim':

George (age 33) had a long history of criminal offences. Police had located him and made an attempt to arrest him for suspected murder in the car park of a shopping centre. As they approached his car, police allege that George produced a firearm, and pointed it at police as he attempted to drive away. Police fired three shots at him as he sped away. When his car crashed into a

pole a short distance down the road, it was found that one of the shots had
gone through the car's rear window, and into the back of his head.

(Case No. 4364–88)

In some circumstances, the offender was killed in the course of an
armed robbery when he was not, in fact, carrying a lethal weapon
himself:

> Over thirty armed robberies had been committed on service stations and
> convenience stores in the bayside suburbs of Melbourne, provoking the
> police to saturate the area with a large number of police, including assigning
> police officers to surveillance duty at specific stations. After several fruitless
> days, the more experienced Armed Robbery Squad officers at the Beach
> Road Solo service stations were replaced by two young constables from the
> local East Bentleigh uniform branch.
>
> Just after 9.30, Arnold G. (age 25) entered the station wearing a full
> balaclava and overalls. He went over to the counter, grabbed the attendant by
> the throat, and thrust his hand into the till. The attendant then fell to the
> floor. Coming up from behind Arnold, the two constables were unable to see
> that Arnold was not armed. One of the constables called out: 'Police here ...
> stop.' When Arnold turned to face the officers, both opened fire, and Arnold
> was killed.   *(Case No. 4394–87)*

There were as well in these years, some other cases which were less
clear-cut in terms of the dynamics of the police behaviour:

> Glen A. (age 24) had been suspected by police of being involved in the kill-
> ing of two police in what became known as the 'Walsh Street Killing.' Fearing
> for his safety (and knowing that he was a suspect), Glen, in the company of
> his solicitor, surrendered himself to police. He was formally charged over a
> previous arson, but not detained regarding the police shooting.
>
> Glen was granted bail on the arson charge on the conditions that he
> report to the Coburg police every week, and that he live with his parents.
> While Glen was careful to report regularly, he was violating the bail condi-
> tions by continuing to live in his Carlton flat. Police discovered this location,
> and as part of the massive effort to locate the police killers, placed his flat
> under 24-hour supervision.
>
> The listening post established for the flat was abandoned on the day that it
> was determined that Glen was going to move from the flat. As Glen was
> driving his car, he was stopped and questioned on another matter (con-
> cerning a hit-and-run involving the son of a policeman). For some reason, at
> this point the police took Glen back to his flat for further questions. When
> they entered, Glen stood by, according to the police account, as they
> searched the ground floor of the flat. The group then went upstairs, where
> Glen was alleged to have gone over to a pile of clothes and pulled out an
> imitation pistol. One of the police then pulled his gun, telling Glen to drop
> the pistol. When Glen did not drop the gun, it was said, the officer then fired
> six shots from his pistol into Glen. His gun being empty, the officer then took
> another gun from a fellow officer, and fired another shot (into the back of

Glen's head). Glen died later in hospital from the effects of the bullet wounds.   *(Case No. 2060–89)*

This case has provoked considerable controversy, and ultimately led to the prosecution of the police officer on a charge of murder, but the jury returned a verdict of not guilty. In a similar case:

Gary S. (age 36) was a known criminal and drug user, currently out on bail for the murder of a drug trafficker. Police decided to raid his house having been tipped off that he was dealing in heroin and that he was in possession of a firearm. When they approached the house, they apparently made enough noise to alert Gary that someone was approaching. Since Gary was apparently fearful of reprisal for the previous murder, he armed himself with a baseball bat and went to the back door. The police stated later that when they burst into the house, they thought he was armed with a gun, rather than a bat. Police fired several shots at Gary, following him into the house, with the final shot being fired into the back of Gary's head. Gary died at the scene.
(Case No. 695–88)

In the five-year period of this study, there were in all ten homicides where the police were responsible for the killing. The circumstances of some of these cases has been a source of public concern, and a special inquest has been carried out by the Coroner on some of these events (a report was released in December 1993). In July 1993, in fact, several police were charged with murder over the deaths in two of these accounts (Case Nos 4364–88 and 2060–89).

Even more clearly than in the previous variation, there is a strong theme of masculinity in these cases where the offenders in the original crime become the victim of the homicide. Further, all of these reverse victims are exceptionally marginal in both an economic and social sense. It takes extreme conditions to push persons to the point where their own lives become exposed as a consequence of their criminal activity.

The third variation: professional killings

One further and rather specialised variation consists of professional or contract killings. While these contain elements distinct enough to occupy, perhaps, a theme by themselves they are included here because, as is true of the rest of such accounts, the link that ties the victim and the offender goes backward to other crimes. The rationale which leads to the killing, in other words, is to be found in the connection of the victim with his or her earlier criminal activity (often difficult to piece together). There were five such cases in these files. The first of these cases, involving two victims, involves alleged contacts within the criminal underworld:

It was the routine of Mrs B.P. to clean the Lygon Street flat in Carlton every Friday morning. When she arrived at the flat on 31 May 1985, she found its two occupants on the floor, dead. Both had been shot in the head in 'execution' style. As is typical in professional killings, which the police concluded this was, the story could be only partially pieced together.

One of the victims, A.C. (age 24, student) was an innocent victim who had the misfortune of becoming the flatmate of a person involved in the drug trade. The other victim, B.W. (age 23) was known to police as a result of his drug dealing, and his involvement with escort services. The limited information that the police could assemble suggests the possibility that 'hit men' from New Zealand were hired to 'damage' B.W. (that is, beat him up) as a warning because his behaviour had become erratic and threatening to the wider criminal organisation of which B.W. was a part. The police believe that when the two hit men went to the Carlton flat, they expected to find only one person. Upon finding two, the killers decided, according to the police report 'to kill both of them so there would be no witnesses.' The case remains unsolved.   (*Case Nos 1584–85 and 1585–85*)

In another case involving two victims, both were apparently involved in the complex set of criminal activities that ultimately led to their deaths:

Lynnette G. (age 29) was a heroin addict who formed a de facto relationship with Robert P. (age 30) in August 1986. Shortly afterwards, the two moved into a private hotel, Purnell's, that had become the front for a crime business involving importation of drugs, armed robbery and standover debt collection. Robert became involved in the dealing of drugs, while Lynnette's role most often was on the importation side as a courier.

Robert and Lynnette played relatively minor roles in the operations of the group, which was alleged to be bossed by Peter G., Gary M. and John F. It is not clear why, but over time Robert's role in the group became problematic. Some of the troubles hinged around the arrest of one of the other couriers in the group, with whom Robert had developed a close relationship (it was alleged that the arrest of the courier was, in fact, engineered by Gary). At any rate, the three leaders became apprehensive of Robert, especially when he went on his own to Pentridge to speak with the arrested courier.

As a result of his contacts with the courier, Robert arranged to go into a bush location with Lynnette to pick up a supply of heroin left there by the arrested courier. Peter, Gary and John suggested that they all go and make a day of the trip, including a picnic. When Robert told a friend about the new arrangements, the friend tried to warn him about the possible dangers involved. Robert indicated that he thought there was no cause to worry. Robert and Lynnette set off on the picnic, and have not been seen since. Their bodies have not been recovered, but police have alleged that Peter, Gary and John arranged for their deaths, and then were able to dispose of the bodies in a fashion so that they would not be discovered.
                                          (*Cases Nos 1325–88 and 1326–88*)

A common characteristic of these deaths is that it is impossible to state for certain what has happened. The victim has been known to be involved in criminal activity (or connected with someone who was), and the death gives every indication of being a 'contract' or professional killing. The scenario is brief, and the events seem to connect back to an earlier pattern of criminality which is presumed to account for the circumstances which provoked the death.

A fourth variation: prison killings

Included within this cluster are cases which involve killings which took place inside prison walls. These pose a particular problem for classification because of the scant information which tends to be available. The first of these is brief:

> M.A. (age 33) had a criminal history extending back to adolescence, and had experienced several stays in prison. One afternoon when the inmate count at Geelong Prison was one person short, during the resultant general search of the prison M. A. was found in a cell, dead as a result of multiple stab wounds to neck and chest. At inquest, the Coroner found that 'Despite continuing investigations the identity of the person or persons involved in the death has not been discovered.'   *(Case No. 2868–87)*

In common with such killings, no information could be obtained from other inmates which threw any light on the offenders in this homicide, let alone the social dynamics which resulted in the killing. This silence is found even where more of the specific circumstances are known, as in the following account:

> Allen T. (age 41) was serving his time in Pentridge Prison. As Allen and a prison officer were delivering meals in 'H' Division, upon entering a yard the officer observed one of the inmates holding a homemade knife. Following standard procedure, the officer retreated to the doorway, calling for help. The door was then slammed shut from the inside. From a vantage point on the wall, another prison officer observed C.H. (a prisoner) strike Allen several times over the head with what appeared to be a white bag (which had been filled with weights). As well, when the officers were able to reach the scene, Allen was found to have suffered stab wounds (his death, however, resulted from the head injuries).
>
> While Allen had earlier written to the State Ombudsman complaining that threats of violence on him were being ignored by the prison authorities, there was no indication of any motive or animosity involving C.H. (who was one of those convicted of the Russell Street bombing, in which a central police station was bombed, and one police constable killed, see Case No. 1133–86 below). None of the prisoners present in the yard provided information in the course of the investigation.   *(Case No. 3261–88)*

One of the common characteristics of the killings originating in the criminal culture is that little is actually known about the concrete circumstances of the deaths. The offenders, as is common with the general scenario, are all male. The available evidence suggests strongly that the deaths are related to the criminal activities in which the victims have been participants. The bonds of the criminal culture, however, make it difficult to assess in most of these the specific provocation that has resulted in the killing. Even when a conviction results, the story of the homicide itself will most often be unclear. Again, what is clear is that the two victims, and their attackers, were all male.

The final variation: police as victims

Police work can be risky, involving as it does the responsibility for apprehension and control of individuals who under the right circumstances may be willing to resort to lethal violence. In the five-year period there were four such police victims, the first of these involved a police officer who interrupted two persons as they were in the process of stealing a car.

> Policeman M.M. (age 34) was on night duty during the early hours of a Saturday night in a small country town. After returning from patrol, he drove the police vehicle alone to his house to fetch some milk for coffee. On the way home, he came across R.N. and M.L. who were attempting to steal a car. They had successfully broken into the car, but when they had hot-wired it they found the battery was flat. As M.M. came across them, they were trying to push-start the car.
>
> M.M. parked the police car and after talking with the two for a moment, radioed back to the police station for details about the car. R.N. was, in fact, well known to the police and had an extensive record. He also harboured considerable resentment toward the police because of his perception of their harassment.
>
> When M.M. returned to the car to continue his questioning of the two suspects, a struggle broke out between R.N. and the policeman. R.N. gained control of the policeman's gun. M.M. shouted: 'Don't, R., don't do it.' R.N. answered back: 'I'm going to kill you', and fired five shots into M.M.
> *(Case No. 3589–86)*

In this account, the circumstances are of a classic type where a police officer encounters offenders as they are engaging in criminal activity, and then becomes a further victim of the crime. Some of the cases in Victoria where police are killed, however, result from a deep antagonism between police and members of the criminal underworld. Included among these is the death which resulted from the 'Russell Street Bombing':

> At about 12.30 pm on 27 March, 1986, a two-tone Holden Commodore was seen being parked on the kerb at Russell Street just outside the door of

the Police Complex. At 1 pm a large explosive device that had been placed in the car exploded, destroying the car, causing heavy damage to the police building, and injuring a large number of persons. One of these, Constable Angela R. Taylor died later in hospital from burns received in the explosion.

This set off one of the most extensive and exhaustive investigations in the history of the Victoria Police. Forensic examination of the explosion scene was exacting, and was able to establish that the device consisted of: (1) a 'Diamond' brand alarm clock; (2) an 'Everready' battery; (3) a block of wood (which was later identified as having been sawn from a post at the property of one of the accused); (4) 50 mm flat-head nails (which were identified as coming from a box of nails in the possession of another of the accused); (5) a galvanised metal strap (which was identified as coming from the lid of a 'Willow' brand rubbish bin owned by one of the accused); and (6) wires. Other items identifiable at the scene and later linked up with various of the accused included fragments of a rug and tool fragments.

The various files on this case run into hundreds of pages. Five persons were ultimately charged with the bombing. The complex story of the bombing works its way through several other crimes, including armed robberies of banks, a burglary of a milk bar, several car thefts, and armed robbery and burglary of a dwelling, a brutal sexual assault, and other offences. All of these offences weave in a complex pattern toward the gradual escalation of the motivation for the bombing, and the accumulation of the various bits and pieces of paraphernalia which were brought together in the construction and concealing of the explosive device. The five charged were all known offenders, and had done time in prison. Numerous witnesses later were able to testify to the 'intense hatred' of police by two of these in particular, and their 'desire to kill as many police and court staff as possible'.

(Case No. 1133–86)

This was the first of two well-known cases involving deliberate and planned killing of Victoria police. The second became known as the 'Walsh Street Killings':

Constables S. Tynan (age 22) and D. Eyre were on patrol when they were called upon to investigate a report of an abandoned car in the middle of the road in Walsh Street, South Yarra. As the two constables left their divisional van to approach the vehicle, they were gunned down by a number of men who had been waiting in nearby bushes.

Shortly after the killings, the Victoria Police began to piece together the story. Their informers in the underworld of Melbourne indicated that the shootings were in response to the gunning down of their friend who was a suspect in a homicide connected with an armed robbery (Case No. 4364–88, above). Following their leads, the police were able to identify a number of potential suspects and accomplices. Two of the suspects were subsequently killed by police in the process of apprehension (see Case No. 2060–89, above). Two individuals close to the remaining suspects were placed in protective custody after agreeing with police to testify against the remaining four individuals who were alleged to have taken part in the killings, and who were placed under arrest.

The case of the Crown relied heavily upon testimony of the two persons held in protective custody, but the testimony of these two collapsed during the course of the trial. In this case, unlike the Russell Street bombing, the police were not able to assemble a large body of persuasive forensic evidence to substantiate their case. The four defendants were acquitted after a lengthy trial. After the finding of the court, the Victoria Police took the unusual step of formally closing the file on the case.   *(Case Nos 4369–88 and 4370–88)*

There are a number of features which stand out in this account. One is that it shows how interconnected criminal events can be, since the initiation of these was a first killing involving an armed guard, which apparently then led to the attempted apprehension and shooting of the suspect of this killing (described above in Case No. 4364–88). In retaliation, the two police constables in the previous account (Case Nos 4369–88 and 4370–88) were allegedly chosen at random by underworld killers attempting to 'even the score'. In turn, this was followed by the police killing of two of the suspects of these Walsh Street shootings (Case Nos 2060–89 and 4949–88, this last not included in the text). It is not certain at this point if we have seen the end of this tragic trail of death. Police resentment is deep over the murder of the two constables, and the unsuccessful prosecution of the case laid against their alleged killers. In turn, friends in the criminal world who were close to those killed by the police also feel frustrated by the failure of the case against the police officer tried for killing Glen A. (Case No. 2060–89), as well as antagonism aimed at those who became witnesses for the prosecution in the Walsh Street killings. This potent mix of anger and frustration could easily lead to further violence and bloodshed.

Homicide during the course of crime: concluding observations

Thousands of crimes are committed every year in Victoria. Only rarely do these lead to a death. In some cases, the fact that a death results requires a bizarre turn of fortune, as in the case of the unsuccessful and probably drunken car thief who died in hospital as a result of a reaction to a drug used to treat the injuries he received at the hands of the owner of the car he attempted to steal (Case No. 2017–85 above).

One observation that can be made in most of these cases is that exceptional risks are being taken by the offender of the initial crime. One indication of this is the common role that guns play in these crimes. These are offenders who, in engaging in the initial offence such as armed robbery, are committed to a more desperate course of action than others who contemplate serious crimes. Many of these offenders are either firmly caught up in an established criminal career, as in the cases of police killer M.M. (and those involved in the Russell Street bombing) or S.D. who shot a taxi driver, or they are enmeshed in heroin addiction, as in the cases of American Dave, or D.P. who killed his drug dealer. With their bonds to conventionality greatly attenuated, they are, thereby, on top of the risks taken in the commission of the initial crime, more ready to take desperate measures if something goes wrong during the course of that crime.

Closely related is the fact that this linkage of marginality and exceptional risk taking is to a large degree masculine behaviour. The offenders in 56 of the 61 cases where a death is attributable to the course of other crime are males. Women, like men, find themselves in desperate economic circumstances, and sometimes take risks as a result. When marginal women act, however, their actions are unlikely to place others, or themselves, at risk of violence, especially in terms of violence instrumental in the course of some criminal activity.

This form of homicide has been identified in most other studies of homicide. Wallace (1986: 160) in her Australian study found that 'instrumental' violence in the course of crime, or apprehension-intervention with respect to crime, accounted for 21 per cent of all homicides in New South Wales in the 1968–81 period. A slightly lower proportion was observed in the 1975–85 US data by Maxfield, who found that 16 per cent of homicides were in one way or another related to the commission of another crime (Maxfield, 1989: 675).

A feature of both of these studies is that they are based on very large numbers of cases. As a result, they provide some estimate of the levels of the specific types seen here. Both, for example, report that when the homicide is a situation of the 'double victim', that is, the victim of the homicide was also the victim of the other crime, robbery or theft account for a larger proportion than does sexual assault (these trends were more sharply pronounced in the United States, see Maxfield, 1989: 675, contrasted with Wallace, 1986: 159). Both researchers use the term 'instrumental' to highlight the link of these homicides with some other on-going criminal activity, and the same usage is suggested by Block and Block (1992) in their identification of instrumental killings as a form of 'homicide syndrome'. Maxfield (1989) uses the term 'reverse felony' to cover the situation where the criminal in the initial crime becomes the victim of the homicide, such events making up 3.3 per cent of all homicides in his US data. He reports that the police or citizens are found in roughly equal proportions as the killer in these events.

At a more theoretical level, Daly and Wilson (1988, and Wilson and Daly, 1985) have identified the general issue of masculine competitiveness, and employed the concept of 'risk taking' to cover the hazards posed when persons engage in behaviour such as serious criminality.

As such, they are able to place this specific pattern of homicide within a general theory which sees masculine proclivity for violence as part of more general strategies of coping with the competitive situation which exists between males.

A final observation of these cases is that in a large proportion of the cases the victim and the offender are unknown to each other (this is especially true in those involving double victims). In the more common classifications of homicide research, these would be considered 'stranger' homicides. Examination of data on 'stranger' homicides in other research, in fact, shows that a majority of these take place in the course of some other crime. In the national study of stranger homicide in Canada, for example, Langevin and Handy (1987) report just over three-fourths of all stranger homicide fit this pattern, with the largest proportion (44.4 per cent of all stranger homicides) taking place during a robbery, with a smaller proportion happening as a result of sexual assault (21.1 per cent), with the remaining taking place in a category described simply as 'during other crime' (10.3 per cent). Wallace (1986) turns the analysis around, reporting that in the case of homicides that occur in the course of robbery or theft, almost three-fourths (72 per cent) involved situations where the victim and offender were 'strangers'.

In the present research (using an approach similar to that of Wallace, 1986: 159, with respect to these forms of homicide), the fact that the parties are strangers to each other is deemed to be an ancillary feature of the dynamic which links offender and victim. The definitive feature of their relationship is the nature of the crime which is what brings them together, rather than the fact that they are strangers.

Putting the matter another way, it is suggested that in thinking about the 'relationship' between victim and offender in situations where the killing results from the course of other crime, the category that is developed should refer explicitly to that pattern of criminal activity. The relationship which produces the death is the crime itself. In some cases the individuals know each other, in other cases they do not. If they know each other, they may have been friends at one time, or it may just be a passing acquaintance. It is not the relationship of friend, acquaintance, or stranger which defines social dynamics that result in the killing. It is, in fact, the criminal behaviour. As such, that criminal behaviour should provide the central focus of attention in the way these homicides are classified, and in the theorising about this risk-taking behaviour.

CHAPTER 6

Homicide as a form of conflict resolution

Disagreements and conflicts are an inevitable feature of social life. What varies widely are the procedures employed to negotiate such discord. For many, the thought of violence, or even direct confrontation with others, is repugnant. Elaborate mechanisms are called upon to rationalise and drain away the tension of potentially threatening scenes. As an extreme measure, the civil law serves as an ultimate bureaucratic process of dispute resolution. In some circumstances, however, these non-violent alternatives are rejected, and more direct, and violent, methods are employed to settle the disagreement.

A review of the present case studies indicates that among the masculine scenarios of violence is found a persistent theme where violence is taken up as a planned device for the resolution of conflict. Such a tactic is not to be undertaken lightly. The risks are great, since in the course of the resulting conflict there will often be a fight involving deadly weapons, with the consequence that the initial perpetrator of the violence becomes its victim. Afterwards, the rational and premeditated character of the killing may expose the killer to the full weight of prosecution for a charge of murder. How it is that some males are willing to take such enormous risks is a puzzle that can be resolved only by review of the texts of several accounts of this form of homicide. There were, in all, 38 of these conflict-resolution homicides, these making up one in ten (10 per cent) of all homicides.

Cases of violent conflict resolution

Most of the accounts of conflict resolution involved individuals who at an earlier point in their relationship had been reasonably close, that

113

closeness indicated by a willingness to share such resources as money or living accommodation. What would then happen is that the very sharing of these resources provided the core of a dispute between the two which would not go away, but could not be ignored. Debts, in particular, can be difficult to negotiate:

> Gregory R. (age 25, unemployed) and Ken S. (age 24, also unemployed) had been close friends since primary school. Neither had regular full-time employment, and evidence suggests that they were well enmeshed in the local drug scene.
>
> A recent rift had developed between them, arising out of a $600 loan Ken owed Gregory (Gregory had lent the money as part of a drug deal, but Ken had used the money to buy drugs for himself). Ken also had reason to believe that Gregory had been informing on him to their motorcycle gang ('The Immortals').
>
> Deciding to bring the matter to some sort of a head, Ken obtained a gun and persuaded a friend to drive him around looking for Gregory. They tried a number of addresses, including a party where Gregory had been earlier. The two ultimately found Gregory back at his home. Ken went up to the door carrying his gun. Gregory, apparently having been forewarned that trouble was afoot, and met Ken at the door holding a sawn-off shotgun in his hands. An argument ensued, leading to a struggle in which glass panels of the door were broken. Ken's gun fired, striking Gregory in the head and killing him instantly.   *(Case No. 175–86)*

In many respects, this represents almost an ideal type of conflict-resolution homicide. Both of the individuals are enmeshed in a lifestyle of unemployment and drug use that places them well at the boundaries of ordinary community life. The dispute is about a matter, money lent over a drug deal, that cannot be brought within the boundaries of legitimate dispute-resolution procedures.

The two individuals have known each other for some time, and within some homicide-relationship typologies (for example, Wolfgang, 1958; Wallace, 1986) this would be considered as a homicide among 'friends'. There is a reasonable amount of planning in this particular account, such that the violence is a considered and intentional device for dealing with the conflict over the debt. It could be argued, of course, that Ken did not necessarily mean to kill Gregory. What is certain, however, is that a scene was created where the threat of what could be lethal violence was contemplated as a way of bringing a conflict to some end.

In the previous case, the issue was that of a debt, a matter that can easily set these forces in motion, as is illustrated by the next narrative as well:

> Ben was a well-known drug dealer in the country town of Bairnsdale, and Gary had been buying marijuana from him for years. Some months before,

Gary had made a $200 purchase from Ben, but had been unable to pay because money was tight. As time went on, Ben became increasingly insistent about repayment, and began to make threats of violence. The threats became increasingly abusive, and at one point led to a fight between the two. Ben followed this with telephone calls, threatening the life not only of Gary, but also his wife and children. Deciding that Ben was serious, one night Gary gathered up his shotgun, dressed himself in black, and went to Ben's house. Peering through the window, Gary saw that Ben was watching TV. Gary fired several shots at Ben, killing him on the spot. Gary then set the house on fire in an attempt to confuse the investigation, but the fire was put out before any serious damage was done.   *(Case No. 1127–87)*

One comes to know one's customers over time, in the drug world as in any other business. Conventional and unconventional transactions are based in part on the building up of trust between buyer and seller. For the person in a conventional business, however, there are a number of options open in the pursuit of a slow paying customer that are closed to one who trades in an illegal commodity. Pushed to the extreme, the grievance of this seller became progressively surrounded with violence, reaching a climax with the lethal outcome.

When thieves fall out: coping with friends who steal

The more heavily the participants are involved in criminal activity, the more difficult it becomes to settle disagreements within conventional frameworks, as indicated in the following:

The trouble between Del (age 33, plumber) and George came to a head over the Christmas holidays. The two had first become friends when Del was a customer of the shop where George worked as butcher. What was especially attractive to Del were the drug deals that George offered as a sideline to his regular fare. Del over time gradually became involved in the drug business with George, and for some period the drugs were kept at Del's house since it seemed safer to keep them there. At one point, George and Del together raided a competitor's marijuana crop, taking the spoils to Del's house where it was packaged and stored until it was sold.

Gradually, however, the friendship cooled, and George in particular came to distrust Del. At first George was apparently ill at ease with the control that Del started exerting over what he thought was his business, but he then became convinced that Del was stealing from him, this reaching the point where George became convinced that Del was responsible for a burglary to his house. Just before Christmas, George confided to a friend that he had purchased a hand gun, and was going to 'take care' of Del. Two days after Christmas, Del arranged to do a deal for drugs with George, giving George an advance of $2000 on a transaction that was to total $8000. Later that day, George called Del, telling him that he could come to the house to collect the drugs. When Del arrived, George stepped up behind him, and shot him several times, killing him on the spot.   *(Case No. 5447–89)*

If you are both a thief and a drug dealer, how do you handle the problem of a partner who is stealing from you? Bound tightly together because of business and friendship networks, it becomes progressively more difficult to ignore the perceived problem of the partner's dishonesty. George in his view found himself worked into a corner where in order to sever the working relationship, he had to take the step of killing the distrusted partner.

There is a similar account in which the individuals originally became involved with each other as a result of friendship forged in prison:

> The badly decomposed body of Mitch B. (age 32, unemployed) was under a heavy growth of weeds at the back of a block of flats in mid-1988. Three years later Harold M. and Jim M. were charged with the death on the basis of information supplied by a prison informer. The three had been close as a result of time spent together in gaol, but they fell out because of allegations that Mitch had been stealing from Harold's wife. Unable to deal with the matter any other way, Harold and Jim obtained a pistol and solved their problem by killing Mitch.   *(Case No. 1792–88)*

Again we see here the problem of persons enmeshed in the criminal subculture confronting the problem of theft. In a way similar to the previous account, the individuals in this narrative found that their options narrowed swiftly to the use of lethal violence. In a similar case study, the planned use of violence against one who was thought to be stealing from the group suddenly turned back on to those initiating the violence:

> Everett (age 32, unemployed) was a chronic alcoholic and user of amphetamines, with a history of violence. Michael (age 17) also was a heavy user of amphetamines, and used Everett as his source of supply. Since he was unemployed, Michael would steal goods and trade them with Everett for drugs.
>
> Everett and two of his friends were drinking at a hotel in an outer eastern suburb, and as they became more and more drunk (Everett's blood alcohol level was later established at 0.238), they decided that they would give Michael a 'hiding' because of his alleged theft of a camera from a neighbour and of some marijuana plants from Everett.
>
> When Michael arrived at the hotel later that afternoon, Everett and two of his friends offered to drive Michael to a place where he could sell the camera. They took Michael to a secluded area in the Dandenongs, and started to bash him up in the car, telling him that they were going to 'bash him up and cause serious injury'. and that 'This would be your last ride'. All the while, Michael (who had thought that Everett was a friend) kept asking what he had done wrong.
>
> Everett then ordered Michael out of the car, and was helped when one of his friends grabbed Michael by the hair and jerked him out of the car. At this point Michael produced a knife. When the attackers crowded around him, he slashed out, stabbing Everett in the neck, and another of the group in the

chest. Michael then took to his heels, and was able to make his escape. Everett died from his wounds before he could obtain medical aid. When questioned by police, Michael stated that he had acted in self-defence, arguing: 'What else could I do?'   (*Case No. 745–88*)

The turning of the tables on those who initiated the attack provides an illustration of how the odds can turn quickly in these events, and is another example of 'victim precipitated' homicide (Wolfgang, 1958). What it serves to underscore is the important point that the decision to use violence is one which involves great risks, including the possibility that equally or more extreme violence may be thrown back upon the person who initiates the violence. In this case, and in others as well, what is at issue in the scenario is the willingness of some involved to set themselves off on a course to use violence to settle a dispute. It is not always clear how that violence will be negotiated, and who becomes the ultimate victim.

Other matters: the problem of shared space

There are a number of sources for the conflicts which set the forces in motion. Another can be that these persons often share the same space, and out of that closeness disputes can arise which do more than erode the friendship:

Jimmy Z. (age 37) rented a house in Kensington (an inner Melbourne suburb). Since the house was close to their work, his two friends Tommy S. (age 21, factory labourer) and Daryl W. (age 22) settled into a routine of staying at his house. This continued for some weeks despite the fact that Jimmy and Tommy became more and more hostile to one another.

As Daryl tells the story, Jimmy woke him at 9 am one morning, asking: 'What am I going to do?' Since his friend was clearly distressed, Daryl agreed to walk up to the local shops with him to buy 'smokes and a drink'. On the way to the milk bar, Jimmy asked Daryl if he could obtain a gun. Daryl said that he wouldn't be able to, but then asked why Jimmy needed a gun. The reply was: 'To kill Tommy'.

Daryl states that at this point he argued that this seemed an extreme reaction. Jimmy indicated that he was fed up with Tommy, that he was tired of the constant niggling, and that they had had an argument the previous night in which Tommy had threatened him with a knife.

When they returned to the house, Jimmy asked Daryl to close a connecting door that would close off an area where a handyman was doing some house repairs. Jimmy then picked up a hammer, and walked over to where Tommy was sleeping, and began to hit Tommy repeatedly about the head. Not knowing what to do, Daryl ran out. When he returned an hour or so later, Jimmy was covered with blood, the hammer was broken, and Tommy was dead.   (*Case No. 1005–86*)

Unlike the previous accounts, in this narrative the violence was not provoked by debt or theft, but rather seemed to be an extreme response to gradually accumulating, mutually provocative acts between flatmates which had begun to include threats of violence. The question 'What am I going to do?' captures the problem faced by these individuals. In marginal groups, cut off from the protection represented by police and the law, the threat of violence may be especially disturbing. In their view, they may see little recourse but to take up even greater violence as a way of coping with the looming threat.

At the same time, one other rather odd case study indicates that the factors which cut people off are many, and can include cultural differences as well:

> Eduardo and Austin were both Africans who had been sharing a flat for several months. Their original friendship had deteriorated, and the two had been bickering for some time. Austin's complaints included the fact that Eduardo refused to pay his share of either rent or food, and in addition kept removing Austin's property (including TV and video). Eduardo was also, in Austin's view, continually making noise at inconvenient hours. The arguments became more heated, and reached the point where the two were challenging each other to fight. Austin told a friend of his that he was a 'commando' and that he was going to kill Eduardo.
>
> One morning, Eduardo got up early, and made his usual amount of noise while taking a shower. Austin was awakened, and again complained to Eduardo. Both decided, according to Austin's account, that the time had come to settle their differences. They both went to their rooms and dressed for the fight, which took place in the driveway outside. Austin quickly got the better of Eduardo, and after he had punched him several times, Eduardo fell to the ground. Austin then grabbed him by the hair and banged his head several times on the concrete. After a few minutes, when Eduardo did not regain consciousness, Austin threw a bucket of water on him, thinking that would revive him. When Eduardo did not respond, Austin went to a neighbour, who summoned an ambulance. Eduardo, however, died of massive brain injuries before medical assistance arrived.   (Case No. 2256–89)

Austin and Eduardo had been close enough at one point to be willing to share accommodation. As their mutual grievances accumulated, the two apparently had no way to vent the hostility, given their view of themselves as males, but to use their fists. While in other circumstances this might have led to a kind of mutual resolution of the problem, the exceptional violence of Austin assured a lethal end to this form of masculine dispute arbitration.

Violence as a counter to violence

With these groups caught outside the world of conventionality, one common feature of the accumulation of dispute and misunderstanding

is that escalation leads to threats and displays of violence, then provoking the use of violence as a form of protection, as in the case of Jimmy
seeking a way of dealing with Tommy in Case No. 1005–86 above. This
use of violence as a counter to threats is seen in the following narrative
as well:

In June 1988 two timber cutters exploring a mine shaft in country Victoria
discovered a badly decomposed, headless body. Documents on the body
established that it was that of Phil H. (age 35, unemployed), better known to
his friends as 'Rhino'. The story the police were able to piece together
indicated that for some time Rhino had been a source of trouble for his
friends.

On the day he was killed, Rhino had engaged in a heated argument with
Perry H. (age 20, unemployed). Partly the argument was because Rhino had
earlier broken into the house of Perry's sister, stealing a video and stereo.
Also, Perry was certain that Rhino had stolen some pills from one of the
rooms in his house. In response, Rhino was said to have threatened not only
Perry, but Perry's children, and was seen to have struck one of the children.

The group (several lived at the house) then calmed down a bit, and settled
into some serious drinking. After a few hours, most had gone to sleep. One
of the residents of the house stated that Perry then came up to him and said:
'Let's kill the scumbag.' The two then finished off about half a bottle of
whisky, and by then 'were in an aggro mood'. The two went out to Rhino's
truck, where Rhino slept. Perry went in through the passenger's door, his
friend went in on the driver's side. The friend stated that at this point Perry
said 'something like, how you goin'?' and Rhino turned to the friend and
said: 'G'day'. The friend states that at this point he told Perry to forget about
it, but that as he was turning away he heard a couple of 'thumps' and then
heard Rhino gurgle. The friend returned to the truck, and looking at Rhino
told Perry that he was dead, but Perry still stabbed Rhino two or three more
times in the chest.

The conspirators first disposed of the body by burying it in a shallow grave
in nearby bushland. Becoming apprehensive that it would be discovered,
they returned later to dig the body up and then dispose of it down the mine
shaft. At some later point one of the co-defendants returned to the scene and
cut the head off the body and buried it in isolated bushland some distance
away.

When questioned later, Perry said that: 'I wouldn't have done it if he
didn't threaten the people I love.'   *(Case No. 2329–88)*

What methods are available to handle personal threats within close
personal circles? For others caught more firmly in the conventional
world, such situations might be dealt with by a call to the police, perhaps some technique of avoidance, or calling on friends or neighbours
to help out in solving the problem in some non-violent fashion. These
males choose a violent path. The killing, further, is not a spontaneous
event, but comes after a period of reflection and planning, somewhat
abbreviated (and not notably astute). This combination of marginality,

the building up of violent exchanges, and then an ultimate intentioned homicide is found in the following account as well:

> Joe A. (age 28) was shot down early one morning just after he had started at his job as a cleaner in the local post-primary school. He had a prison record, and a history of violence combined with a reputation for a bad temper. He was known to be a good street fighter, and had worked as a bouncer at a number of local pubs and discos.
>
> He had previously been a close friend of Mike S. (they had met in an Office of Corrections Attendance Centre). According to police, in addition to socialising with Joe at parties and discos, Mike had also been involved with him in committing crimes. Mike also had a reputation for violence.
>
> The two tempers ultimately clashed, and a fight resulted in which Joe hit Mike with a spanner. Mike had become convinced that Joe had informed on him while he was in gaol, and that he also was responsible for firing shots at his house. When police were called as a result of the shots, Mike told them not to worry as he himself 'would fix things up'. Shortly afterwards, when Joe went out from the school where he was working to check on a report that someone was tampering with his car, he was fired at by a man the police believe to be Mike. Joe attempted to run, but was cut down by the bullets. His killer walked up to him and fired a final shot into his head before jogging off to a waiting car.   *(Case No. 291–86)*

In this account is found the interesting phenomenon of the coming together of the two worlds, one legitimate, the other illegitimate, when the police became involved over the shots which were fired just prior to the final episode. The informal rules of the culture in which many of these individuals live dictate, however, that conventional mechanisms for deflecting conflict away from a violent and deadly course were closed off. In the local language, one becomes a 'dog' if he 'dobs in' a fellow member of the culture. Here, police offered to help but Mike elected to 'fix' things himself, with a gun.

Dead men (or women) tell no tales: killing to silence

There are three cases where a friend has become a potential threat in terms of possible testimony to either police or courts. The offender then protected himself by killing the victim who is seen as posing the threat. The homicide in such cases, in other words, is motivated by the intent to destroy critical evidence. In the first of these cases, the victim had early on willingly agreed to participate in the cover-up of a crime, only to come under increasing pressure as the successive interrogations wore down the concocted story:

> Peter S. (age 15, student) had been present when his older brother and Don C. (age 26) were involved in stealing a car. When Peter's older brother fled to

Queensland, Peter became the key witness whose story would either convict or acquit Don. Don was greatly agitated by the prospect of going to prison, and offered to buy Peter a trail bike if he would change his story to protect him. This Peter apparently agreed to do, and Don bought him the trail bike.

As the investigation developed, however, Peter's story became unstuck when he realised that if he continued with his story he would be tripped up in its inconsistency and also throw the whole blame on to his brother. For a while, Peter wavered between two different stories, but finally broke down and told the true story which implicated Don.

Don was furious, telling his friend George E. that 'the little bastard dobbed me in'. Don and George decided the way that Don could avoid prison was to kill Peter. They approached a friend to borrow a dinghy which they would use to drown Peter, telling the friend what they intended to do. The friend refused the request.

Their next plan was to take Peter on a hunting trip, and to shoot him. This was easy to arrange since Peter thought of Don as a good friend, and enjoyed their hunting trips together. They planned the trip for a weekday, saying to one of their friends: 'Peter is going on a one-way trip on Thursday. It's all arranged because he is going to wag school and nobody will know where he went. His mother won't miss him because he's done it before.' The friend was unsuccessful in explaining that what was planned was 'stupid', and that Don would, at most, be at risk of a good behaviour bond since the alleged offence was his first, but Don's reaction was: '... yeah ... but this way I would be sure.'

Late on that Thursday, Don arrived back at his friend's house, saying: 'Well, I'm glad that's over.' He then recounted in detail how he and his friend had carried out the shooting. There seems to be a strange sense of unreality in this case, since Don told other friends the story as well. The friends thought that Don was simply telling tall tales, until the TV news broadcasts reported the finding of Peter's body.   (*Case No. 1606–86*)

In this case, other friends attempted to warn the offender away from the violent path he had set for himself, but he persisted. The successful removal of the certain threat of the former friend's testimony came only at the price of the graver peril posed by the charge of murder which was entered against him.

As odd as this trade-off may seem, this was not an isolated case. Another similar account involves a group of persons all of whom had been in prison:

Richard M. (age 21, unemployed) was a passenger in a car being driven by Paul R. (age 19) when there was an accident. Since Paul had a prison record, was drunk, and was not licensed to drive he prevailed upon Richard to claim that he was driving when the accident took place. Being 'good mates' Richard agreed.

Richard was not fully aware of the consequences of his act of friendship. Tension began to build between Richard and Paul as it became clear that Richard was going to face serious traffic charges in magistrates' court (where his prior prison record would spell trouble), as well as a bill for $5000 damages which Paul could not pay.

Paul became convinced that Richard was going to break under the pressure. About four weeks after the accident, Richard arrived home from work in the company of two friends. Paul and two others drove up. Richard went over and chatted for a couple of minutes, returning to his friends saying that if he did not return; 'they would know what to do.' Then one of Paul's friends came over to the two, saying: 'You haven't seen me here tonight, boys.'

Later that night, Paul woke up a friend asking if he could leave a car at his house overnight, saying that he would return the next day to 'clean the blood out of it.' The friend observed that Paul had blood on his hands and clothing. Paul returned the next day, and cleaned out the car, recounting to this friend in detail how he and his other two friends had carried out Richard's killing. Having left so many persons in possession of the knowledge of what the three had done, the Coroner had no trouble finding that Richard had died from wounds 'to the throat, chest and abdomen which were unlawfully and maliciously inflicted by . . . ' Paul and his two friends.

(Case No. 2951–85)

In this case, the cluster of individuals involved, including both victim and offender, had extensive criminal records including serving time in prison. Perhaps because of the common prison experiences, there was a heightened level of anger over what was perceived as the potential breach of loyalty in informing on a friend, this in part accounting for the brutality shown in the actual homicide. The final of these cases involved an individual who had just been released from prison:

Kenny I. (age 32) was released from prison at midday on a Tuesday, and immediately set about making plans for the elimination of Val W. Apparently Val, a prostitute who had, according to police testimony, 'a long criminal history', was a potential witness in a case against some of Kenny's friends in prison.

That evening, Kenny picked up his friend Lenny C. (age 26, unemployed and also with a recent prison record), and the two of them went by Val's flat to pick her up. While at the flat, Kenny, Lenny and Val 'shot up' some heroin. As Val went into the bathroom to inject herself, Kenny told her flatmate that Val had 'to be put off.' The two women, Kenny and Lenny then drove off.

The group were at the time in the northern suburbs of Melbourne, and drove along a deserted street close to the Campbellfield shopping centre. The flatmate in her testimony to the police alleged that at that point Kenny, Lenny and Val got out of the car, supposedly to 'do a drug deal' according to the story which they told the unsuspecting Val. A few minutes later, the woman stated that she 'heard a bang', and the two men then jumped in the car and said: 'Let's go', saying to her: 'You've seen nothing, heard nothing, and know nothing.'

The three then went to a nearby fast food outlet, and made themselves conspicuous to the attending staff. This was part of the tale they concocted which was to include them dropping Val off to do a drug deal, with them returning to find her killed by some unknown drug dealer. Unfortunately, the woman friend yielded under police interrogation, providing an account of the events which resulted in Kenny and Lenny being charged for the murder of Val. The woman disappeared prior to their trial, and it seems highly likely that she, too, fell victim to this form of protective violence.

(Case No. 4740–86)

If possible, this group of individuals appear to fall even farther beyond the boundaries of conventional life than the other groups we have examined. Deeply enmeshed in a criminal culture, which partly originated in prison, there was on the one hand scarce regard for informers, while on the other there was operating an equation which gave little value to the life of the victim in comparison to the threat of testimony which might send one of their mates to prison. Neither dead men, nor dead women, tell tales, and without such tales it is often impossible to mount a prosecution. In these last three accounts, the disagreement which is resolved through violence involves a triangular pull between the two parties (victim and offender) and the justice system.

Homicide and conflict resolution among more conventional males

While in general this pattern of conflict resolution appears to involve persons whose lifestyle is well removed from conventionality, there were a few whose patterns of living were, in fact, closer to mainstream existence:

Sam M. (age 46, property developer) and his wife were keen gamblers, travelling regularly to various casinos in Australia. On one of their visits to South Australia, they met Arnold through mutual friends. Sam and Arnold then started going to casinos together, often gambling against each other at backgammon. In late May 1989 Sam and Arnold played backgammon against each other at Adelaide, and Arnold ended up owing $17 000 to Sam.

Arnold was unable to pay the debt on the spot. A month later, in late June, Sam arranged for Arnold to come to Bendigo to bring at least some money to reduce the debt. Prior to leaving for Bendigo, Arnold obtained eight sticks of gelignite from a friend, telling the friend that he needed it to blow up a stump. The friend commented that Arnold seemed concerned at the noise and smoke made by a conventional burning fuse, and had asked for instructions on the obtaining and use of an electronic detonator.

Arnold then left for Bendigo, being met at the airport by Sam. The two men began playing backgammon that night, and were still playing late at night when Sam's wife went to bed. When the wife returned home from work the following day, she was surprised to find that Arnold was still there, and that he and Sam were continuing to play backgammon. The wife commented that she thought Arnold had planned to go home that day, and he replied that there had been a problem in transferring the money from his wife's account. Sam said that the money wasn't that important, and offered to drive Arnold to the airport if he wanted to go home. Arnold insisted that he would stay. At some point in the night she was told that Arnold had won back $5000 of the money he owed.

When Sam's wife arrived home the next night, she found once again that Arnold was still there, and that the two were continuing their backgammon game. The wife reported later that Sam seemed agitated, and assumed that this was because of the troubles that Arnold said he was having in transferring the money that was owed from the out-of-town account.

The wife went to bed at about 11 pm, and the men were still gambling. Before she went to bed she went downstairs to assure herself that all the locks were fixed on the security doors. She was unable to recall when her husband came to bed, noting only that it was quite late. Arnold later stated that the two had quit at about 2 am, and that he had then gone to his bed in a back bedroom.

Just after 6 in the morning, there was a large explosion in the couple's bedroom which was at the front of the apartment. The wife was able to stagger out on to a balcony, where she was rescued by a neighbour. When she had last seen her husband, he was unconscious and on fire. He died at the scene, with the cause of death being multiple injuries as a result of the explosion.

Arnold later stated that he had won back the money that he was owed, but Sam's wife disputed this claim, pointing out that the score sheet was not tallied in the manner that her husband used. The police became suspicious when Arnold's evidence became inconsistent over time, and when it did not fit with other witness accounts or with the forensic evidence. Arnold was charged by the police with both murder and attempted murder.

(Case No. 981–89)

This case represents a qualitatively different scenario from some of the other accounts. While the violence is clearly masculine, and it involves persons who could be considered friends, the principals are not deeply involved in a life of social marginality. The killing appears to be more an act of desperation by a person pushed to the wall by a large debt. A similar account is found in the following:

Ken P. (age 45, independent trucking contractor) was a hard-working 'truckie' who owned his own truck and was generally known to be a hard businessman where money was concerned. Three years previously he had formed a business partnership with John M. (age 40), but the partnership broke up after disagreements developed over money matters. Ken claimed that John owed him in the range of $35 000 from the proceeds of the partnership. Business and personal failure loomed over John. His wife left him, and his personal behaviour became noticeably erratic. It was his view that Ken was cheating him, and taking away trucking jobs that were rightfully his.

One night as Ken was loading his truck at a truck depot in country Orbost, a shot was heard, and upon investigation Ken was found on the ground beside his truck, with a bullet wound in his side. He died some three weeks later of complications from the wound which was established to be from a .303 rifle. John M. was later apprehended and charged with the homicide.

(Case No. 1314–85)

These last two narratives share with others the common theme of masculinity, friendship, and argument of debt, and violence, but differ in that the offenders cannot be seen to be deeply mired in a life of exceptional marginality. When pushed to extremes, it appears that some conventional males will call upon unconventional violence as a way of resolving what are seen to be desperate circumstances, as illustrated in the following as well:

> Ross D. (age 50, maintenance officer) had been working for a couple of years with the Ministry of Housing in Pascoe Vale. He had become progressively frustrated with his work situation. He had indicated to witnesses that he felt frustrated by what he saw as inadequate and inefficient work practices, and by his inability to change them. Over time, his resentment towards his workmates began to build, especially in relation to his supervisor, Graham S.
>
> Things reached a head when a tenant's dispute resulted in a complaint against Ross, which in turn led to Graham filing a report on Ross. In reply, Ross alleged that there were various incidents of corruption among his workmates.
>
> One evening late in August, Ross's parents (with whom he lived) reported that Ross appeared 'unresponsive and vacant'. He was 'abrupt and grumpy' toward his father, and spent much of the evening sitting at a table writing. After that, he appeared restless, and was, according to his mother 'like a caged lion, up and down.' He left the house at 10 pm, refusing to tell his parents where he was going, other than saying he was 'going for a drive'.
>
> Shortly afterwards, neighbours of Graham heard cries for help and moans, and saw a car fitting the description of Ross's car driving off down the road. A few minutes later, another neighbour found Graham unconscious in his driveway, covered with blood. From the forensic evidence, it was clear that Graham had been attacked in the loungeroom of his home, and had attempted to flee, travelling only as far as the driveway (where he died). Ross committed suicide by driving into a semi-trailer on the Goulburn Highway the following morning (there were five suicide notes left behind, which were what Ross had been writing the night before).   *(Case No. 3113–89)*

Conflicts at work can be vexing, but most find other ways of dealing with such situations that fall well short of violence, let alone lethal violence. On occasion, money matters can push conventional as well as unconventional individuals to exceptional action, as found in the following:

> Alex (age 52, farmer) and John were neighbours and farmers. Running into severe financial difficulty, John decided that the solution to his problems would be to subdivide his property. This required the submission of plans to local council for approval. That approval was not granted, primarily because of objections filed by neighbours, the principal of these being Alex.
>
> The pressures on John began to mount. In his view, it was the stress of their stretched financial circumstances which led to his mother's death from cancer. Finally, the bank informed John that unless the subdivision went ahead in the immediate future, they would be forced to foreclose.

John's story at this point was that he had heard gunshots coming from Alex's property. He had previously spoken to Alex's son about similar incidents. This time, John stated that he went to Alex's house to sort the matter out, taking with him a loaded .303 rifle. John stated that he knocked on Alex's back door, and that when Alex came out he ordered John off the property. According to this account, the two then began to wrestle over the weapon, and while he was unclear over the details, he admitted that Alex was shot while he was on the ground trying to rise from a prone position (Alex died from a 'close range gunshot wound to the head', according to the autopsy report). John then went home and changed and burned his clothing. He also went to a nearby jetty and dropped the rifle into Corio Bay (where it was later recovered by police). John was charged with murder by the police.   *(Case No. 2971–89)*

Of the total group of conflict-resolution homicides (41 in all), there were four of these cases where it could be said that the males involved were respectable in terms of their work and social lives. In these accounts, the violence as in other narratives is masculine and aimed at the resolution of a long-standing dispute. These four offenders could not be seen, however, as being tied to unconventional lifestyles or patterns. There are a few cases, in other words, when what appear to be relatively commonplace males are pushed to some extreme they call upon exceptional violence as a reasoned device for the resolution of personal friction. This was not common, however, since roughly only one in ten (4 of 41) of the conflict-resolution cases in these files involved individuals who could be seen as relatively conventional in terms of their lifestyles.

There was as well one further case where the violence represents a collision of conventional and unconventional worlds:

Rick was a self-taught, self-employed motor mechanic who made a living by reconditioning motor cars and engines. In May 1987 he advertised a V8 Valiant engine for sale in the *Melbourne Trading Post.* Phillip (age 35, unemployed) bought the engine from Rick and fitted it to his car. When he was unable to start the car, he called Rick to complain. Rick went to Phillip's house, and in order to attempt to start the car, supplied a starter motor at no cost. When the car still wouldn't start, Rick towed the car back to his garage and stripped the engine down. He found that the engine, which had been in perfect shape when he sold it, had twice the required amount of oil, and, as well, there was sand in the oil.

When Rick informed Phillip of the problem, Phillip began to show the first signs of aggression (Phillip had a long history of criminal offences, including arrests for assault). When Rick was unable to fix the car to Phillip's satisfaction, he began to make threats toward Rick, including threats of shooting up his house and 'blowing off his knee caps'.

When these threats became persistent, Rick's wife went to the police, returning to the police some five days later when the harassment continued (this time accompanied by Rick).

Drawing again upon the *Trading Post*, this time as a buyer, Rick purchased a .22 semi-automatic rifle, and taught his wife how to use it. The rifle was then kept stored, fully loaded, in the wardrobe of the couple's bedroom.

Phillip had decided it was time to take action regarding his threats. At about 5 one evening, Rick and his wife heard Phillip pounding on the back door. When they did not let him in, Phillip began to break down the back door. Rick called out several times telling Phillip to leave the house, but Phillip ignored these requests, and finally succeeded in forcing his way in through the broken back door. By then Rick had gathered up the rifle from the bedroom, and as Phillip entered the house, Rick shot him five times. Phillip staggered out of the house, and collapsed near the back gate. He was conveyed to the nearby Dandenong Hospital where he died three days later.

(Case No. 2622–87)

While the individuals in this account were far from friends, in many respects the account shares much in common with the earlier narratives of conflict resolution. Persons with greater resources and a different understanding of the legal system might pursue more conventional avenues to redress a problem arising out of what is perceived as a failure to live up to contractual obligations. On Phillip's side, his background of marginality and aggression provided him with a set of experiences such that the effective way to resolve conflict was direct physical violence. While Rick was perhaps less marginal, he, too, had a criminal history and as well was inclined to deal with Phillip's violence by the counter ploy of violence (although Rick and his wife had made at least an attempt to seek out conventional procedures to solve the problem). Ultimately, the two males were reduced to a situation where violence was met with violence, with fatal consequences.

Discussion

The categorisation of homicide found in previous research has not identified in explicit terms this particular pattern of killing as a mechanism of conflict resolution. In the most common of the 'social relationship' classification schemes based on relational distance, these conflict-resolution homicides never involve strangers, nor in the present instance are family members involved. The nature of the conflicts dictates that the parties involved have developed some amount of personal knowledge of each other (in order for the conflict to develop out of that relationship), so definitively most often these would fall within the boundaries of homicides between 'friends' or 'acquaintances'.

While such a classification is technically correct, by itself it tells us little about why the homicide occurs. In fact, in the first attempt to organise these themes (from the 1985–86 Victorian data), most of these homicides were placed within a grouping of killings occurring in a relationship of intimacy, that intimacy being friendship (see Polk and Ranson, 1991b). This classification changed as more data emerged from the second phase of the research (when the 1987–89 data were considered). What this form of internal replication showed was the inherent weakness of the traditional classification methods. People do not kill each other because they are friends. Something has to happen to push friends to the point where the previous bond of intimacy is transformed and violence becomes possible.

In the replication phase, it became clearer that there were two patterns by which persons who have been friends reach the point where extreme violence between them became possible. One, it was necessary to recognise that friends, as well as strangers and acquaintances, can find themselves in a situation where one lays down a threat to honour or reputation which is seen as requiring a violent response (for an exploration of why this might occur, see Polk, 1993). Two, under some conditions, persons who previously have been friends may reach the point where a disagreement between them festers over time and is seen by one or another of the parties as requiring violence in order to bring the matter to a conclusion. In any case, consideration of these themes allowed the development of ideas about how and why the homicide had occurred which is richer in information than the simple observation that the individuals involved had at some point been friends.

It is less clear where these homicides would be placed in the second vector of classification schemes concerned with either 'motives' or the 'circumstances' of the homicide. Wolfgang (1958) had as one of his motives of homicide 'altercation over money', which appears virtually identical to 'arguments over money' found in the Supplementary Homicide Reports of the Uniform Crime Reports (Maxfield, 1989), but such a term would describe only a portion of the homicides reviewed here, since many of the killings were generated by issues other than money. Falk (1990) reported as motives of homicide 'business dealings' and perhaps 'drug dealing' which similarly would mesh only partially with the grouping suggested here.

In the typology of homicide suggested by Wallace (1986), there is some overlap with what was referred to as homicides among 'people who shared home or work environment' or a special category provided for killings among 'criminal associates'. Regarding this last grouping, Wallace noted the same theme of premeditation observed in most of the conflict resolution homicides: 'These killings were always quite deliberate and premeditated; the victim's movements had been observed and he was usually shot in or around his house as he arrived at or emerged from his home.' (Wallace, 1986: 154) At the same time, the small number of this last category reported by Wallace (only 12 homicides out of a total of over 1300), and the fact that many of the events included in the first ('home and work') category are more confrontational, suggests that the present category is rather different in its makeup than what was intended by Wallace.

The general conclusion is that the particular grouping of homicide as a form of conflict resolution is quite different to that found in other classifications. This pattern of homicide is suggested for consideration in future classifications groupings since it constitutes a significant proportion of all homicides (roughly one in ten in the present investigation), and the nature of the terms describing the grouping provide a description which should mesh more neatly into theoretical frameworks attempting to account for homicide.

Only additional research will establish whether the scenario found here will bear up in other settings. This particular pattern was progressively refined as the investigation evolved. For purposes of replication, it is possible now to explicate the major defining features of this scenario. Conflict-resolution homicides are those where, first, the victim and offender have known each other for a considerable period, most often being friends in the early stages of their relationship. Second, conflict between the parties also begins to build over time, such that the dispute is clearly not a spontaneous outgrowth of an argument which suddenly flares up to the point of lethal violence. Third, one or another of the parties then reaches a point after the disagreement has built up where violence is elected as a method of resolving matters. As such, the case should show some evidence of planning regarding the use of violence to cope with the problem faced by one of those involved.

It may not be demonstrable that homicide was the intended outcome in each case, although it would be expected that the anticipated level of violence was extreme. In the present accounts of 'victim-precipitated homicide', for example, what the ultimate victim (who is the one who can be said to have planned the use of violence) intended may have been a high level of violence that fell short of homicide.

Given these three major criteria, it becomes relatively straightforward to make a distinction between most conflict-resolution homicides and those which occur within the confrontational scenario by virtue of the analysis of the themes which were found in the individual case studies. In the confrontational situation the precipitating events are spontaneous and involve a challenge to the honour of one of the parties, either in the form of a verbal insult, a gesture, or perhaps a jostle. The confrontation thereby lacks a history of a particular tension between victim and offender, particularly one which evolves out of what was previously a friendship. While most confrontations occur over a very short time span, even where there is a break in the action (most often for one of the actors to fetch a weapon), that break is relatively short, involving in most circumstances minutes or hours, rather than the weeks, months, or even years, for the dispute to emerge that leads to the conflict-resolution homicide.

Further, in most cases the conflict-resolution killings are readily differentiated from the other major male-on-male scenario, that involving homicides arising out of the course of other criminality. Thus, homicides where there is an ongoing robbery or armed burglary, where the initial victim of the robbery or burglary becomes a homicide victim (what can be termed 'double victims'), are easy to differentiate from the conflict-resolution homicides. Such a distinction is also straightforward in cases where the ultimate victim of the homicide is the initial offender (what can be termed 'reverse victims') in the crime that leads to the killing (as where police waylay an offender in the course of an armed robbery).

In the case of the present scenarios, employing the three criteria enabled a relatively direct determination if the case involved the commission of a crime such as armed robbery or burglary. Further, when the violence flared quickly, had no prior history, especially if it involved persons who knew little or nothing of each other prior to the encounter, it could be assigned readily to the confrontational scenario. While there was some possibility of difficulty in examining killings which occurred between males who had known each other for some time, in most instances it was relatively clear if the violence erupted suddenly (thereby being considered as a confrontational event), or whether the violence resulted from a previous set of disputes and displayed some evidence of planning on the part of some of the participants (thereby falling within the boundaries of the conflict resolution scenario).

At the same time, one of the characteristics of raw data is that, as schemes of classification begin to form, cases emerge which pose problems of 'fit'. Consider the following case:

Keith (age 26, unemployed) had met Charles while serving time in Sale Prison. After drifting around for a few weeks after his release from prison early in 1988, Keith met up with Roger, who was the brother of Charles, and from this meeting renewed his friendship with Charles. For some time, Keith had been seeing Roger, Charles and his de facto wife, and Dan, another friend of Charles.

The relationship between this group and Keith became somewhat tense, in part because of concerns expressed by Keith about the presence of stolen goods in Charles's house (Keith had voiced anxiety that discovery of the property might result in his return to prison). Insults began to flow between the various individuals, including Dan reporting to Charles that Keith had called him a 'dog' because of the time that Charles had spent in protective custody while in prison. Keith also alleged to Dan that Charles had 'lagged somebody in' while serving time.

Dan, as a result, argued to Charles that they ought to 'knock' Keith, but at first Charles said that he had replied: 'Look, don't worry about it, you're crazy, just don't do anything.' One evening shortly after, Charles, Dan, Keith and the de facto wife of Charles were in the car when an argument broke out between Keith and Dan. They pulled the car over, and the group tumbled out on to a nearby reserve, and a brawl began involving Dan and Charles fighting with Keith. A knife was produced and Keith was stabbed a few times in the thigh.

The group then got back into the car, with Keith being thrown into the back seat. They then drove to Roger's house, and when Roger came out to the car, he too, entered into the violence against Keith. At this time Roger said to the others: 'Well, we've just got to get rid of him.' Keith at this point said: 'No, come on, you know it's bullshit' and then, 'fair enough, all right, all right, I done it, I done it, fair enough.'

The group then drove the car out into the country. At this point, Keith began to scream and beg for his life, saying things like: 'I'm sorry, I apologise' and 'You're not going to kill me are you?' When the car stopped, Roger reached over and cut Keith in the throat. They pulled him out of the car by his hair, and Dan kicked and then stabbed him, calling him a 'dog'. Close to death, Keith started to moan. Roger then said 'Well, I'll finish it' and stabbed Keith one final time hard in the back of the neck. One of the party later commented that in order to retrieve the knife, Roger had to stand on Keith's neck. The offenders went to great lengths to conceal the crime, thoroughly cleaning the car, replacing the seat covers and seat belts, and throwing out their clothes.   *(Case No. 1193–88)*

In this account, the final acts of the drama began with the fight between the main players. The continuation of the violence, and carrying that violence to the lengths of the killing, on the other hand, were a result of the earlier base of arguments and tensions between Keith and the rest of the group. Thus, the group had been considering for some time the possibility of silencing the victim, and the fight provided the opportunity to accomplish this end.

This narrative suggests the possibility that in some cases there may be a blurring at the edges of the 'confrontational' scenario (which springs spontaneously out of masculine disputes over honour), and the conflict-resolution scenario (where there is an element of planning to the violence). In this case study, the death itself was the direct outgrowth of a fight which sprang up between the offenders and victim. At the same time, there had been a long-simmering dispute which had led some of the offending group to conclude well before the homicide that they should kill the victim.

Where does this homicide fit? Answering this question depends a bit on the direction of the research strategy. If a proposed system of grouping is to meet minimum standards of reliability, a set of rules should be present which allow the accurate classification of the case, that accuracy being gauged by the degree to which different coders produce the same judgments. With respect to the case study at hand, a problem is posed because it obviously contains some elements of two scenarios. If it is necessary to classify the case so that it fits either a confrontational or a conflict-resolution scenario, the rule might be proposed that homicides should be placed within the scenario where they fit most closely to the features on the checklist.

In this particular narrative, the individuals had known each other for some time, there had emerged a long-standing dispute such that killing the victim had been suggested earlier, but it would not appear that the actual killing was the result of a considered plan. At the same time, the triggering event for the killing was a fight which appeared to some degree to be a spontaneous event. A significant break in the action took place, however, after the initial fight when the victim was thrown in the car and taken back to the residence of one of the offenders. It was only then that the offenders took up the question regarding whether the victim should be killed, and they then made an explicit and considered decision to 'knock' him.

On the basis of a 'closest' rule, guidelines could be written so that this case, and others like it, would be placed in the conflict-resolution category, since on the one hand the participants knew each other, there was a long-standing dispute, and at a certain point the offenders explicitly decided to kill the victim. The reason for not inclining the case toward the confrontation scenario (despite the central role of a fight) is that in a large proportion of the confrontation scenarios there was no particular inclination on the part of the offender at any point explicitly to kill the victim. In fact, often offenders leave confrontational scenes convinced that they have only injured, perhaps not seriously, the victim.

There are of course other options, such as creating categories which explicitly recognise that scenarios may mix, as can happen where two males meet in a pub, they argue outside after leaving, a fight ensues, and then after the fight the offender robs the victim (this showing elements of scenarios involving confrontation and of occurring within the commission of another crime). Further, continual reading of additional cases in other jurisdictions could identify new themes in case studies which might require the specification of additional scenarios of violence. It is likely, for example, that if this work were extended to the United States it would be necessary to provide room for a scenario concerned with gang violence.

Emergent from the patterns found within these case narratives of homicide is a major scenario of violence that evolves around the readiness to use violence as a way of resolving some form of personal dispute. This pattern of violence, and its defining elements, emerged over the course of the investigation, with the shape changing between the first and second phase. In the initial 1985–86 analysis (Polk and Ranson, 1991a), these had been classified as homicides occurring within the relationship of friendship. In the second phase, which served much like a replication, a number of facts became clear. One was that some of the conflict-resolution killings involved people who had known each other for some time, but clearly could not be considered friends. The second was a problem that as long as friendship was the central matter, a handful of confrontational killings involving friends also had to be included in the grouping (these now have been shifted to the confrontational scenario since they fit that pattern more closely). As a logical matter, the further analysis indicated that the focal point of this scenario was not that the persons were well known to each other (although that is true for all of these cases), but that as a result of some matter evolving between them, a persistent dispute had emerged which one or both of the major actors felt had to be resolved through the use of violence. The emergent criteria, in other words, evolved around homicides where the parties had known each other well over a period of time, and where there was a demonstrable issue (often concerned with a debt, or similar matter) which the parties were unable to negotiate, which then became a matter to resolve through the planned use of violence.

Up to this point discussion has focused primarily on the form of the social dynamics that describe how conflicts emerge between victim and offender which become resolved through violence, but there were, as well, two dominant social variables that were found in most of these conflict resolution killings. The great majority (roughly 90 per cent), of these involve individuals who live close to the margins of conventional society. While the specific factors vary, in most of these killings the participants are likely to have criminal histories, often including spending time in prison, they are likely to be unemployed, and they may be involved in the use of illicit drugs.

It is a common observation that homicide in general is most likely to be predominantly a lower or under-class phenomenon (Wolfgang, 1958; Wallace, 1986). The findings here suggest at least a partial reason why this might be the case.

Persons tied more firmly to routine lifestyles, who possess financial and social resources, can be argued to be more likely to be able to confront such disputes by means other than violence. Obviously, even among the well-positioned, friends can become enemies as disputes emerge around such issues as money, property or even reputation.

Economic and social resources permit the well-positioned to cloak their disputes in the rational garb of legal or other arbitration systems, and thus vent disputes through channels that drain away the potential for violence.

If one's social position in the criminal community makes resort to the justice system a life-threatening matter, or if one is unable to pull together the large amounts of money that lawyers and other agents of arbitration may require, then alternative mechanisms must be sought. Put another way, one of the costs of extreme marginality is denial of access to the formalised system of justice. For the men in these case studies, the alternative has been the planned use of extreme violence. This pattern, as such, would appear to be close to what Black (1984: 1) referred to when he claimed that much of 'crime is moralistic and involves the pursuit of justice'. Black contended that crime can function as a form of social control, and is often provoked, as among these offenders, by the behaviour of someone else who is defined as 'deviant', although here it is acknowledged that the boundaries around the term are rather distinctively drawn. For these individuals, however, violence certainly becomes an ultimate form of exerting (or attempting to exert) social control.

A second common social thread that runs through all of the narratives reviewed here has been the distinctive *masculine* willingness to resolve disputes through the use of violence. There were some events, however, where women were involved. There were two cases where women were the victims in conflict-resolution scenes, including one of the cases where the victim was killed as a way of destroying evidence. There were two cases where women were peripheral participants in violence that primarily involved males (as in the case immediately above, where a woman was involved in the group that helped dispose of Keith's body). There was as well one case where a conflict developed between two prostitutes, one of whom thought the other had informed on her brother to the police, so with two male confederates she lured the victim to a motel room. There the victim was bound and her mouth gagged firmly, and then beaten. Since her nose was completely blocked, the woman died from suffocation (Case No. 1264–86).

These data require only a slight alteration of the observation regarding the masculinity of this scenario, since there was no case where a woman acting alone was the offender (although it is highly likely that the addition of more cases might produce such an occurrence). Women are involved in the social world of marginality and crime as sexual partners, friends, and participants. As such, they can be swept up in the events where violence becomes employed as a way of dealing with conflict. At the same time, their role tends to be either peripheral or passive, and it is exceptionally rare that women are the central, aggressive actors in this scenario. The use of violence as a device for conflict resolution is emphatically a masculine phenomenon.

It needs to be recognised that virtually all homicides involve some form of conflict, and thereby the killing can be seen as a resolution of that conflict. In the present analysis, a distinction is being made which flows roughly along the instrumental-expressive continuum. Some homicides are clearly events which are initially about something else, such as an exchange of insults, an unanticipated reaction during a robbery, or a heated domestic argument, which then boil over quickly and the consequent violence takes a lethal form. In other cases the violence is more instrumental in character, and there is evidence of some amount of thought given to the use of that violence as a solution to a dispute which has emerged. What is at issue here, then, is the question of why males are more likely to take the considered risks that are inherent in a tactic whereby violence is employed in a planned way to bring disputes to a conclusion.

Accounting for the masculine willingness to resort to violence in such circumstances becomes a more specific aspect of the general question posed by writers such as Daly and Wilson (1988) regarding why homicide generally is so distinctively male. To this can be added the further dimension that conflict resolution homicide involves males found at the outer boundaries of conventional life. Exactly why this scenario involves marginality and masculinity poses a conundrum which only further thinking, and more data, can answer.

CHAPTER 7

Rounding out the picture of homicide

Up to this point, this investigation has focused on major forms of homicide that are distinctly masculine. It is clear, however, that the four major scenarios do not exhaust either all forms of homicide, or even all forms of masculine homicide. The purpose of the present section is to take up the task of examining other forms of lethal violence, in part to round out the general description of homicide, but also thereby to make a case for the differentiation of the previously discussed scenarios of masculine violence.

Multiple homicides

Within any large set of homicide data, it is to be expected that there will be found two main forms of homicides where there are large numbers of multiple victims. In the five-year time period of this limited study, there were two dramatic examples of mass killings, the first of the two groups of multiple homicide. Mass homicide involves what Holmes and De Burger (1988) refer to as a 'murder spree', which they describe as follows:

> Victims of a murder spree typically are selected by chance; they tend to come into contact with their killer purely by accident ... A murder spree is characterised by the death of several victims over a rather short time span ... at the hands of a relatively reckless assailant who kills thoughtlessly upon impulse or expediency. *(Holmes and De Burger, 1988: 18)*

The first of the present case studies of this form of homicide consisted of what came to be known as the 'Hoddle Street Massacre':

After having a few beers at the Royal Hotel in Clifton Hill, Julian Knight left the pub at around 8.30 pm and walked home. He had been back in Melbourne for about a month after resigning from the Royal Military Collage, Duntroon. Arriving home, he went about gathering up two rifles, a shotgun, and ammunition. He crossed the railway line to gain access to a knoll where there were some trees. Knight knelt down, aimed one of the rifles at on-coming cars, and started his shooting spree. The criminologist Kapardis describes what followed: 'He pulled the trigger, then again, and again and again ... This was it – COMBAT; aiming at real targets, shooting at people and seeing them 'drop'. This was the real thing – killing people ... He was enjoying it, killing was giving him pleasure, and he kept on shooting, indiscriminately at people in passing cars ...' (Kapardis, 1989: 10–11). At the end a few minutes later, there were seven people fatally injured, and 19 others who had been less seriously wounded.

(Case Nos 3436–87, 3438–87, 3440-3443–87, and 3622–97)

This outburst of lethal violence put Knight in the record books as Australia's worst mass murderer, but he was not to remain there for long. Before the year was out, Melbourne reeled under the shock of another of these rampages:

Late in the afternoon of an early December day, Frank Vitkovic entered the Australia Post Building in Queen Street, Melbourne. He went to the fifth floor, and approached the counter where he asked to see his friend Tasos. The friend had not seen Vitkovic in months, and had no reason to think that there were not still on good terms. Vitkovic, on the other hand, had been through deep troughs of depression in recent weeks, and had come to blame others for his many personal difficulties, focusing blame especially on Tasos. When Tasos came up to Vitkovic, he pulled out a rifle, aimed it at Tasos, and pulled the trigger. Barely comprehending what was happening, but realising that Vitkovic was trying to shoot him, Tasos fled, crying out for other staff to call the police (which they did). Vitkovic then leaped the counter, and tried to stalk Tasos. Unable to find him, he then began to shoot other workers, first on the fifth, on the twelfth, then the eleventh floors. Finally, one of the office workers managed to grab him from behind, and the gun was finally taken from him. Vitkovic managed to shrug out of the grasp of his captors, and leaped out a window to his death on the footpath below. Eight people lost their lives in this killing spree.

(Case Nos 5346-53–87)

The two acts accounted for fifteen homicides, or 5 per cent of the total number of homicide victims found in the five-year period. It can be pointed out that in these cases, the victims were previously unknown to the offender. As such, these constitute a cluster of 'stranger' homicides. While this is a feature of these killings, it is the present argument that it is not as central as other matters to understanding the character of this homicide. There are a number of factors, not understood at this time, which trigger the horrific violence of these offenders (Lunde, 1975; Kapardis, 1989). The fact that victim and offender are strangers to each other is not particularly germane to the analysis of this, or even other, forms of homicide (see the next chapter).

Serial murder

A second major form of multiple homicide, serial killings, did not occur in Victoria to our knowledge within the five-year period. While mass homicide takes the form of a sudden outburst of killing which involves several victims, serial homicide involves the killing of separate individual victims with a time interval, most often weeks or months, between victims, often in a different geographic location (Egger, 1984, 1990). Holmes and De Burger (1988) have defined serial murder as consisting of repetitive killings, which are one-on-one killings with rare exceptions, where the relationship between victim and offender is that of stranger or slight acquaintance, where the killer is motivated to kill (these are not crimes of passion) and yet apparent or clear-cut motives are lacking.

It is exceptionally difficult to establish the rate of serial killing. Holmes and De Burger (1988) have estimated that in the United States there are between 3500 and 5000 serial killings a year. This is a large number indeed, and if accurate, it would mean that such killings account for up to 20 per cent of all homicides in that country in a given year, a number which others view as exaggerated (Egger, 1990; Kiger, 1990). The nature of serial killings, involving at times long time intervals between homicides, and different geographic locations (and therefore a record in a different place), and the fact that many of the bodies are successfully hidden, all combine to make it difficult to assess the size of the problem.

In the present study which covers a five-year period in Victoria, there were no known cases which fitted this pattern. There were relatively few homicides where the offender was unknown and the circumstances were unclear regarding the nature of the homicide. Among these, at most a handful could even conceivably fit common patterns of serial killing as identified in the literature (Holmes and De Burger, 1988; Egger, 1990). There were two cases of women which constitute true 'mysteries' (one found dead at the spot on the beach where she routinely sunbathed in the nude, another found dead as a result of a stab wound in her bed – in neither of the cases was the victim sexually assaulted), but even these did not conform to the pattern of most serial killings. There may be, of course, cases of missing persons whose bodies may be found later, which conform to the pattern. As matters stand, however, it would appear in Victoria at least that among known homicides serial killing is exceptionally rare.

By 1993, however, it had begun to appear that a pattern of serial killing of women may be developing in the Seaford-Frankston area of Victoria (these homicides not falling within the present study). A suspect has been charged with these killings, but only time will determine if the arrest has brought this series of deaths to an end.

Multiple homicide: observations

There is one sense in which multiple homicides reported here and elsewhere conform to a major focal point of this research: this involves males as perpetrators. It has not been included as a major scenario form for two reasons. First, these killings are infrequent, so much so that it is difficult on the basis of present data to describe any meaningful pattern. Secondly, where the motivations for such killings have been described, they have tended to focus on psychopathological interpretations (Lunde, 1975; Holmes and De Burger, 1988: Vetter, 1990), rather than on the systematic features of masculinity which are part of the present analysis. The horror and public outrage provoked by these dramatic forms of homicide assure that these will be on the agenda of criminological analysis (for an illustration, see Kapardis, 1989). In all likelihood, however, research on multiple killings will require data which spans across time and jurisdictions in order to generate enough cases for systematic analysis as accomplished in the United States by Hickey (1990). For present purposes, however, the data are too scanty to provide a base on which to construct a meaningful analysis of the interplay between masculinity and violence in multiple homicides.

Family killings

There is a second general area where killings are similarly infrequent and yet masculine, these consist of killings that occur in family relationships other than spouses or children. Despite the claim made by some that violence is endemic in family relationships, in fact, outside the immediate relationships of sexual partners and children (as victims), homicide is exceptionally rare. Among the 1373 victims found in Wallace's (1986) study of homicide in New South Wales between 1968 and 1981, only 96 (or 0.7 per cent) were the mother, father, brother or sister, in-law, grandparent or other family relation (other than spouse or child) of the offender. Similarly, in the present more limited time period, there were but nine such homicides within the family network, these making up 2 per cent of all homicides.

As is true of many other forms of homicide, these are again distinctively male homicides. In New South Wales, among offenders who were some form of 'other family' relation to their victim, 90 of the 96 were male, and in the present study, all 9 of the offenders were male. Little is known about these homicides involving other family relations. Regarding one form, Wallace (1986: 135) observed that 'there seems to be very little written on parent killings', and she adds a few pages later that 'Very little is known about violence between siblings in Australia, or elsewhere for that matter' (Wallace, 1986: 139).

The few cases available in the present analysis means that there is little that the present research can add. Among the nine victims, five were parents killed by their son (two fathers, one step-father, and one case where both parents were killed), there were two sisters killed by their brothers, there was one case of a victim who was the mother-in-law of the offender, and a final single case where the victim was the grandfather of the offender. While distinctively masculine, these homicides provide too small a base to begin to build any form of systematic analysis. It can be noted that a common element running through many of these, as observed by Wallace, is a theme of exceptional mental illness, with many of these verging on being classified within the 'special' grouping (Chapter 8).

What can be said, of course, is that these forms of homicide are distinctive in terms of their scarcity. This allows some speculation about the view that the family has become a setting where high levels of violence are common. In contrast to the image of the family as a source of comfort, warmth and harmony, there is a growing perception that the family instead can be a major source of pain. The National Academy of Sciences report commented that: 'Recently we have come to realize that our homes may be as dangerous as our streets' (Reiss and Roth, 1993: 221). Another observer has commented:

> The veneer of the family as a harmonious, gentle, and supportive institution is cracking from increasing evidence ... that the family is also the scene of varying degrees of violent acts, ranging from the punishment of children to slapping, hitting, throwing objects, and sometimes a homicidal assault by one member of the family on another.   *(Gelles, 1987: 20)*

What the present data suggest is that while it may be true that there is an unacceptably high level of violence within the circle of the family, lethal violence tends to be restricted to particular bonds, namely those involving marital partners, or perhaps to children who become victims of parental violence. Outside these two specific dyads, homicide is, in fact, so rare within the family circle that this fact itself is worth mention.

The killing of children by their parents

When the focus is shifted within the boundaries of family relationships to children who are victims of their parents, two differences emerge. First, these killings are more frequent. In Wallace's study in New South Wales, child victims of parental violence accounted for 8 per cent of all homicide victims, a figure identical to the present Victorian study where there was a total of thirty-two such victims (if we include for purposes of this analysis one 'special' case involving a woman offender, thus making up 8 per cent of all homicides).

Second, this is one form of homicide which is not distinctively masculine. In New South Wales, 59 per cent of the parental killers were, in fact, women. Overall, among the child victims in Victoria, fourteen were killed by their fathers (or step-fathers), fourteen by their mothers, there were two where the parents were deemed jointly responsible for the death, and there was one case where it could not be determined who had caused the death. From these figures, then, the offending parents were evenly divided between males and females, a striking distribution when compared with other forms of homicide.

It is also important to note that child victims are most often killed by their parents. There were no examples in the five-year period in Victoria where a child was killed by a stranger, although such killings have occurred since 1989. In Wallace's (1986) larger body of New South Wales data, in only 5 per cent of the cases was the child a victim of a stranger, and, in fact, in 85 per cent of the cases the child had been killed by either natural parents (68 per cent of victims) or step/foster parents (17 per cent). Children, in short, when they are killed are likely to be the victims of those with whom they have the closest social bonds.

There are four important sub-themes within the group of child killings. The most frequent grouping involved deaths by some form of traumatic injury, where there were thirteen cases in all. Of these, seven involved the classic pattern of battering (four where the father/step-father was deemed responsible, one where the mother was the offender, one case where the injuries were seen as joint responsibility, and one case where it could not be determined), while six involved other forms of killing (all with male offenders, these frequently involving somewhat older children).

The next largest group of child victims, nine, are found in the situation where the child's death is part of the parent's suicide. In some of these cases, especially where the perpetrator is a woman, the killing is seen as an attempt to protect the child from the harm they might suffer without their mother. Often in these murder/suicides, the offender has a history of deep depression.

Connie H. (age 24) had been married to George. H. for six years. It was a marriage marred by tragedy. When their eldest child was only 4 months old, he suffered severe head injuries in a traffic accident, resulting in extensive brain damage. The child was quite disabled, and did not respond to treatment in Australia. The couple travelled to the United States on three occasions to seek further treatment.

The two in fact did not have the finances to cover the costs of the medical treatments, although they did receive help from volunteers and public appeals. The financial pressures mounted, and this was compounded by the fact that the exceptional disability was not showing significant improvement, and required a high level of care. The birth of the second child created further demands on their time and resources. Both parents began to feel immense stress. Both underwent courses of psychiatric treatment, with George being admitted to mental hospital once, and Connie three times. Connie had attempted to commit suicide twice, and had herself admitted to hospital on the third occasion because she began to hit the children and feared she might injure them.

After two brief attempts at separation, George decided that it would be best for all if he left the household. Connie felt an exceptional sense of isolation. She refused to discuss her problems with a psychiatrist, because she feared being committed again to psychiatric hospital. She felt that George's parents were constantly interfering in family matters, and that her own parents (from Europe and firmly opposed to divorce or separation) did not care.

One night George came over to see the children. Connie asked him to spend the night, but he refused. A day or two later, he informed her that he intended to move into a flat with a fellow worker who was female. This was enough to tip Connie over the edge. She confided to the baby-sitter that she intended to commit suicide, and that she 'loved the children too much to leave them behind.' The baby-sitter spent hours with her attempting to calm her down, and even offered to spend the night with her if that would help. Connie appeared calm and reassured, however, and said that wouldn't be necessary.

After the baby-sitter left, Connie wrote out several long suicide notes. She left extensive instructions regarding their funerals, stating she wanted her son buried to her left, the daughter to her right. She had purchased new clothes for the children's funerals, and laid them neatly on the couch. Connie carefully labelled all the drawers in the house, so that George would be able to find things.

In the note to her parents, Connie wrote: 'I don't feel I am murdering my children, but saving them from sorrow and pain without their father ... it's the only way out ... all I ever wanted in life was a happy marriage and happy, healthy children ... I have tried very hard ... I cannot leave my children behind ... At least with God there will be peace and happiness and no pain, so I will take them where they will be happy, and I will be there to care for them.'   *(Case No. 2886–85)*

These three deaths represent a profound tragedy, one which has sources and elements far removed from the overt external aggression found in much of masculine homicide. Wallace has commented how these have an appearance close to mercy killings:

Altruistic intentions appeared to motivate the offenders to take the lives of the children when they suicided – altruistic in the sense that regard for the well-being of the child was a primary concern ... The primary feature was overwhelming depression and mental anguish in the offender rather than any hostility toward the victim. For various reasons, largely unrelated to the children ... the parents contemplated suicide. But they could not face leaving their dependants behind, defenceless and unprotected (in their view) to face the world alone.   *(Wallace, 1986: 132)*

While there are too few cases for much in the way of conclusive observations, the present data are consistent with other research (Wallace, 1986) which suggests that homicides/suicides involving a parent and children are different for women and men. The following is consistent with accounts of the masculine variant:

In an instance of homicide of a woman caught up in a sexual relationship with an exceptionally jealous and violent male, the evidence pointed to the conclusion that the de facto husband, Bill S., had started off on a purported 'holiday' after he had decided to end their marital relationship by killing his wife, Val, and taking his own life. After travelling from Adelaide to a point where he was just inside the Victorian border, he shot his wife with a gun, set their camper alight, and finally shot himself. The two had a long and stormy relationship, with Val attempting to leave several times, only to return to face Bill's escalating violence.

In a further twist of this story, Bill faced a decision regarding what to do with his stepdaughter (age 11) and his own son (age 15). Despite the fact that there had been frequent arguments with the son, Bill elected to leave the boy behind as they set off on the 'holiday'. He insisted that the stepdaughter join them, however. The consequences were that the son survived, while Bill in his moody, possessive rage killed the stepdaughter as well as his wife.   *(Case No. 8612–86)*

The homicide in this account involving the wife shows many of the common features of homicides resulting from masculine jealousy and control, and has been classified as one of the killings considered within that scenario (Chapter 3). For present purposes, it demonstrates how children can become unfortunate pawns in the violent games played by their parents. A feature demonstrated here is that when husbands kill children, they may also include the spouse, whereas with women this pattern is rare. In the present case studies where the death of a child was part of the parental suicide, six of the offenders were women, four were men.

Almost as frequent was neonaticide (the killing of an infant within the first 24 hours of birth), where there were eight victims (seven known women offenders, one additional case where the offender was never identified but where it is presumed that the mother was involved

in the death). Most of these involved a pattern of exceptional denial
which seems to be characteristic of this form of homicide:

> Except for a brief period at college, Joan M. (age 29) had lived in one small
> country town all her life. She worked as a clerical assistant at two part-time
> jobs. With the coming of the new year in 1985, several of the townsfolk sus-
> pected that Joan was pregnant, but she denied such allegations (the towns-
> folk had held the same suspicion in 1980).
>
> One day in early February, Joan came home from work, and as usual
> started to watch TV. She had felt 'fine' throughout the day. Feeling
> uncomfortable, she retired to her room, and then went into labour for an
> hour and a half. As soon as she gave birth, she covered the baby with a towel
> and put it in a plastic bag, and hid it in her clothes basket. Joan then changed
> and washed her bedding, had a shower, and then started reading a book.
> Later that night Joan's housemate noticed that Joan had almost completely
> lost her voice.
>
> Five days later, friends found the body in Joan's room. She had unsuccess-
> fully tried to conceal the smell with air-freshener. They notified the police.
> When the police officer carrying out the investigation approached Joan and
> stated: 'I've checked your bedroom and I've seen what's inside the basket',
> Joan's response was: 'Yes, what's wrong?' The police described her as
> 'extremely confused' and she indicated that the incident had occurred 'a
> long time ago'. When asked why she did not tell anyone about the preg-
> nancy, she replied: 'I didn't think it was true', saying at another point that
> she 'just hoped it would go away.'
>
> Joan volunteered that a similar death had taken place some five years
> previously. She stated that she had placed a pillow over the child's face, and
> then buried it in the back yard. As with the first death, Joan had little
> recollection of the event. She did not notice the sex of either baby. When
> asked by police if she wanted the babies to die, she stated: 'I don't know if I
> did nor didn't ... I didn't know what else to do, I suppose. I was worried
> about what the people in town would have said ... '   *(Case No. AG96–85)*

The psychological pressures on the women who are caught up in this
pattern are extreme, and result in psychological confusion and an exceptional capacity to deny to themselves and to others that the pregnancy is
real, even when confronted with the birth itself. Wallace (1986) has
observed the extraordinary levels of denial in this form of homicide:

> Without exception, the neonaticides were accompanied by the concealment
> both of pregnancy and of the birth itself. All of the women had their babies
> alone, most commonly in their own bedroom or bathroom – even, in some
> cases, when others were present in the home at the time. That these women
> could successfully conceal their pregnancy and the ordeals of childbirth
> from others close to them may appear somewhat incredible, but once again
> is a typical feature of neonaticides reported elsewhere.   *(Wallace, 1986: 118)*

In the previous narrative, the young woman was unable to face what
'the people in town would say', and she then followed the path of

denying the pregnancy, these mental processes being strong enough to carry her through the birth itself. The fact that this happened twice to this young woman makes these facts even more striking. As observed by Wallace, in the present narratives the women experience childbirth either in their bathrooms or bedrooms, often with others present in the house at the time. This pattern, clearly, is a distinct form of homicide, being hugely different in content and meaning from the major forms of masculine violence that account for the bulk of homicides.

The final form of child homicide, which involved one case, is a case of neglect where the death occurred when the child was place on a lengthy fast in the belief by the parents that this would result in a cure of the illness suffered by the child. The child was otherwise carefully tended by the parents, but because of the extended starvation, the child succumbed to the effects of malnutrition. Both parents (trained nurses) were deemed to share the responsibility for this death, which was deemed to constitute criminal homicide (the parents were both convicted of manslaughter).

What these data tell us is that the killing of children is very different to other forms of homicide. It tends to be almost exclusively a matter which takes place within close relationships, with the great proportion of offenders being parents. The gender distribution of offenders is distinctive, although it is also clear that the proportion of women offenders varies in terms of the particular form of child killing. Such killings overall, however, are certainly not an exclusive domain of masculine violence.

Women as killers

While the major purpose of this investigation is to examine scenarios of masculine violence, the data on children provide but one indication that women, too, can kill. In general, of course, women are responsible for lethal violence much less often than men. In New South Wales, 15 per cent of all offenders were women (Wallace, 1986), while the figure from Wolfgang's (1958) Philadelphia data was 17 per cent. In the present case study data, in 11 per cent of the cases a woman was involved in the killing as offender or accomplice, while women alone were offenders in 9 per cent of the lethal violence.

More important than these numbers is the issue of why women kill. It was possible in an earlier time to argue for a view that women are 'more perfidious by nature' (Rasko, 1976: 398). This was been expressed in what is perhaps an extreme form in the writings of Sparrow:

Women being different from men in their mentality, thought-processes, intuition, emotional reactions and in their whole approach to life and death, when they murder, do the deed in a way that a man often would not contemplate. Their crime does not bear the mark of Cain, it is stamped with that characteristic subtlety and horror that has distinguished the rare evil women of all times.   *(Sparrow, 1970: 8)*

This view of women's crime as more subtly evil has been called into question by more recent research in Australia and elsewhere (Naylor, 1990). Certainly the homicides of women take a different form to those of men. Empirically it has been found that when women kill, it is more likely to involve a family member than is true for men. Wallace (1981), for one, reported that the victims of women killers were overwhelmingly family members (81 per cent), whereas for men the family victims accounted for roughly only one in three homicides (36 per cent, Wallace, 1986: 74). Equally important is the fact that there are different reasons for the family violence of women (Wilbanks, 1982).

When women kill within the family circle, in roughly half the cases the victim is likely to be the spouse of the offender (Wallace, 1986). In their examination of incarcerated women who had killed their spouses or boyfriends, Bacon and Lansdowne (1982) reported that in fourteen of sixteen cases the woman had been assaulted by the man she was subsequently accused of killing. Thus, the violence of these women can be viewed as both reactive and defensive. In an important way, what it represents is violence mirrored back on to precipitating behaviour which has its origins in the willingness of males to use violence in their attempt to control the actions of women. Consistent with this view is the finding of Wallace that: 'Women killed their husbands against a background of violence; they killed in response to and because of violence perpetrated by their husbands on them and/or other members of their family.' (Wallace, 1986: 108)

Conforming to this finding, in the present case study data just over two-thirds (71 per cent) of women took the lives of a victim that was close to them, the victim being either a male sexual partner (12 cases, these making up 29 per cent of women's homicides) or the child of the woman (16 cases, or 38 per cent of homicides where the killing involved women). When women killed their sexual partner, most often it was in direct response to the violence of the male (8 of the 12 cases). Several of these narratives where women had experienced violence suggest a pattern of consistent violence raised in commentary on what has come to be known as the 'battered women's syndrome' (Browne, 1987; Gillespie, 1989; Easteal, 1993). In only two cases was the killing a response to the threat of the male to leave (one other followed an argument), and there were no recorded examples in this five-year period of a woman killing her male partner because of jealousy. There was one case where a woman and her lover contracted with another male to kill the husband in order for the two to be free to start a new life together. In this limited period, when jealousy was a factor in the killing by a woman, the victim was another female. In two cases, the victim of the woman killer was the sexual rival, while in one other case the victim was a lover who provoked a jealous rage in her lesbian partner. The vast majority of lethal violence around the theme of possession, jealousy and control is emphatically masculine in it makeup, and when women kill within sexual relationships, it is most likely to be a defensive reaction to prior male violence.

From these data it is clear that the pattern observed in Victoria regarding the ratio of female/male to male/female violence is quite different to that observed in the United States. In cities such as Chicago or Detroit, it has been reported that the number of women killing their husbands is roughly equal to the number of men killing their wives (Wilson and Daly, 1992). The present data casts the net a bit wider by including all forms of sexual intimacy, and within that bond men are emphatically much more likely to kill their woman partner (73 such cases) than are women to kill their male partner (12), with the ratio of women killers to men killers being 16. This figure is comparable to the 'sex ratio of killing' (that is, the homicides perpetrated by women per 100 perpetrated by men) observed in cases of spousal killings in England and Wales (23), lower than that found in Canada (31), and significantly lower than that observed in Chicago (102) or Detroit (119).

As such, these data do not support the hypothesis of the sexual symmetry of spousal violence (McNeely and Robinson-Simpson, 1987; Straus and Gelles, 1990) which argues that wives and husbands behave alike in assaults. More importantly, the patterns observed here provide confirmation of the contention made by Wilson and Daly (1992) that it is critical to observe the differential pattern of motives in violence of males as distinct from females (see also Dobash et al., 1992). The violence of women toward men observed in the present case studies arises from fundamentally different sources than does the violence of men toward women.

As indicated above, women may be involved in the killing of their children, although most often it involves either neonaticide (8 of 16 cases where women were involved in the killing of their children), with most of the others being killed as part of the suicide plan of the mother (6 cases), and relatively rarely were women responsible for traumatic deaths of children (there were no cases of shooting, and only one case where the woman alone was responsible for a battered child, while in another case the woman was held jointly responsible).

As seen in previous sections, women are rarely involved in the distinctly masculine scenarios of violence. Women rarely kill in a desire to control their male sexual partners (only two cases, and as observed above, in sharp contrast to male sexual violence, no male lost his life to the jealous rage of his woman partner). There were no cases where a profoundly depressed woman killed her male spouse as part of her suicide plan. In confrontational violence, over 90 per cent of offenders were male (4 of the 84, or 5 per cent, of confrontational homicides being committed by women), with comparable figures being found where the violence occurred in the course of other crime (5 of 61, or 8 per cent, of offenders being women) or in conflict-resolution situations (2 of 38, or 5 per cent, of offenders being women). Further, in these last two situations, most women if they were involved, were accomplices of males who were likely to have played the dominant role in the death. Only one of the homicides in the course of other crime involved women (two co-defendants) acting alone, and in conflict-resolution scenes, both cases involved women as accomplices rather than as sole offenders in the death.

There is a strong stamp of intimacy, in other words, on women's violence. This has been captured in the following observations:

> While murder in general, is a very personalised crime, ... female murder appears to be an especially intimate act. That is, women are more likely than men to murder another family member ... particularly a husband or child; outside of husbands and children, the only significant choice for women appears to be a lover.   *(Blum and Fisher, 1978: 192)*

Masculine aggression is broad ranging, and lethal violence reaches out across a range of social situations as victims. Female lethal violence is much narrower, is focused on a close circle of intimacy, and is often reactive to the breakdown of that intimacy. There is tragedy in these killings, and often a long period of great personal hurt, but there is little here to support the view of women as subtle, vicious and evil killers.

Pulling it together

Homicide can take many forms, and flow out of a multitude of motivations. Not all homicide is a playing out of the themes of masculinity described within the four major scenarios identified in the previous sections of this book. Women, too, can kill, although often when women kill their sexual partners they are responding to prior violence of the male, so at least some of these can be seen as spinning out of masculine violence as well. Men can kill for reasons other than the four major themes that are identified here. For all that, it is also true that over two-thirds of the present homicides result from the playing out of the four masculine scenarios identified here (269 of the 380 homicides, or 71 per cent of the total). Further, while other forms of violence are significant and merit further investigation, within the present body of data there are too few cases upon which to build an analysis. One, serial homicide, in fact, is totally absent from these data, at least as far as can be seen from information based on these known and solved homicides. What is striking in looking at the overall patterns, then, is the degree to which lethal violence in general is masculine, and from a theoretical point of view how much of it can be subsumed within a coherent view of masculine scenarios of violence.

CHAPTER 8

Problems in the study of victim-offender relationships

The task up to this point has been to distil from the various case studies the major themes, or scenarios, which describe the relationships between homicide victims and offenders. It is possible now to shift the analysis to the question of the implication of this thematic method for the more general study of victim-offender relationships in homicide.

There are significant barriers to the development of schemes of classification of such events which need to be acknowledged. Some derive from the initial sources of data. At least three issues are paramount: (1) the problem of unsolved homicides; (2) the issue of homicides where the motivation cannot be assessed from the existing information; and (3) the problem that in any case the voice of the victim is likely to be absent.

Unsolved cases

One of the useful components of the suggested 'syndromes' of homicide of Block and Block (1992) is their use of the term 'mysteries' to cover those circumstances where it is not possible to distinguish the nature of the interaction between homicide victims and offenders. The first of these concerns those cases where the offender cannot be identified, since in such cases it follows that it may not be possible to specify the dynamics which link the unknown assailant with the known victim.

In some instances, despite the fact that the specific offender is unknown, it has actually been possible in the present research to make some presumption about the nature and character of the events which led to the homicide. There were a number of present case histories, for example, where the unsolved homicide could reasonably be presumed to have evolved out of other criminal activity. In one of these, an attendant was found dead from a gunshot wound, late at night at the service station were he worked, and the till had been broken into. In a second, a security guard was found dead, also from a gunshot wound, late at night, with the physical evidence suggesting that he had come across an armed burglar during the course of his nightly rounds. In both of these (and two similar cases) all of the evidence points to the homicide arising out of the course of another criminal act, and these thereby can be classified within these scenarios.

There were additional cases where the death resulted from a masculine confrontation, but where the offenders had not been identified. In one of these, a young Chinese male had wandered down the main street of Melbourne's Chinese quarter shouting insults to Vietnamese in Chinese. Shortly afterwards he was attacked and killed by a group of young Vietnamese who remain unidentified. A similar case involved a fight among a group of Vietnamese men where the lack of language and cultural skills on the part of authorities meant that an offender could not be identified. A third case also concerned a Vietnamese, but in this instance the victim was one of a group of young Vietnamese males who were attacked by a group of whites (who remain unidentified) as they were outside a pub waiting for friends who had gone inside to buy beer. In all three of these accounts, the known facts point to a masculine confrontation between the known victim and the unknown killer which began initially as a fight or disagreement. As such, despite the fact that the homicides remain unsolved, it is possible to place the killing within the scenario of masculine confrontation.

Other cases, however, are more troublesome. These are made up of accounts where the offender was unknown, and where it was not possible on the basis of the scanty facts to determine the nature of the relationship between the victim and offender. Two of these unsolved cases involve women victims:

> At the time of her death, Inga Mayer (age 47, part-time garment worker) was living in a caravan park in Rosebud (a seaside resort in outer Melbourne). She had been through two marriages, and was considered to be a 'free spirited' person who had relationships with a number of males. She was one of those persons who was known to 'love life' and in the phrase of the police, had 'no known enemies'. There was no evidence of any recent antagonism with any specific male friend.
>
> Her daily routine consisted of doing a bit of work in the morning, then (since it was summer) at 11 am she would drive her car to a nearby beach, and then walk to an isolated spot well removed from the more frequented beaches, where she would sunbathe in the nude. The day of 13 February began as had many others. The last time Inga was seen alive was as she drove away from the caravan park at 11 am. She was found by a passer-by at

3.30 pm, who alerted police. Inga, who was nude when she was found, had been beaten about the head with a piece of wood. She was not sexually assaulted. The police were unable to establish either a motive for the crime, or an offender.   *(Case No. 445–85)*

This is clearly a case of homicide, but from the facts available no assessment can be made regarding the nature of the motivations of the offender and the role played by the victim in the homicide. The investigation was unable to reveal known male associates with whom sexual intimacy might be presumed to provide a basis for the homicide. Forensic evidence did not support the hypothesis that the victim had been sexually assaulted. She had not been robbed. In short, no motive could be established which might explain why this homicide occurred, nor was it possible to place the killing within one or another of the homicide scenarios.

Similar circumstances are echoed in the following case:

Inez Watson (age 26, nurse) had just decided to return to her career as a nurse after recovering from a long period of emotional stress connected with the death of her husband from cancer. When her neighbours noticed that they had not seen her for a few days, and that her mail was piling up at her letter box, they entered her house and found her dead, in her bed.

Subsequent investigation revealed that she had been stabbed to death, but very little else. She had last been seen some five days before, when a male friend had dropped her off at her door after they had been out to a pizza. Inez was due to return to work that night, but did not appear. Investigation revealed that a male friend, a physician, had actually been by to see why she had not shown up to work. This friend had entered the apartment, and found her body. In his statement he said that he had 'panicked, and didn't know what to do'. He was unable to provide an explanation of why he didn't report the death to the police, other than to say that he was 'in a state of shock'.

The police were unable to establish any motive or possible offenders of the crime. Inez had not been sexually assaulted. At the time of the inquest, the police noted that the death 'was still being investigated', and the Coroner found that he was 'unable to say whether death resulted from unlawful and malicious conduct or otherwise'.   *(Case No. 879–86)*

The Coroner was being unusually cautious in his conclusions, since a death by stabbing would appear almost certainly to constitute a case of criminal homicide. As in the previous case, factors which are most likely to account for the victimisation of women (sexual intimacy or sexual assault) cannot be established. There was no evidence of either robbery or burglary as possible explanations for the homicide.

Another three cases illustrate killings involving individuals firmly enmeshed in a marginal world of drugs, crime and unemployment:

Paul 'Mouse' Atwater (age 19, unemployed) was described by police as a 'young unemployed person who appears to have led a nomadic lifestyle. Although relatively young, he had appeared before various courts on seventeen separate charges including burglary and assault. He was a member of a city gang known as the 'Westside Sharps', with whom he frequented the Flinders Street Railway Station steps, inner-city hotels, and the nearby banks of the Yarra River. Police allege that this group was 'regularly involved in assaulting and robbing public transport travellers and assaulting and robbing homosexual persons in the city area'.

The last certain sighting of Mouse was by one of his friends, who stated that Mouse had left him at midnight two days before his body was found. Mouse had indicated that he intended to go 'home', although the meaning of that term is not exactly clear since Mouse had no fixed address. His body was found half a kilometre from the highway in a remote country area. He had been shot several times in the head with a .22 rifle (using hollow point bullets). Mouse had consumed considerable alcohol before his death, as his blood alcohol reading was 0.215. Once again, the Coroner concluded that he was 'unable to say whether death was by unlawful and malicious conduct or otherwise'. *(Case No. 1125–85)*

Since the nature of the wounds and the location of the body appear to rule out either suicide or accidental death as explanations, once again for present purposes there is no need to be as cautious as the Coroner since the facts point to the death of Mouse as constituting a homicide. What cannot be established, however, is who was responsible, and what provoked the unknown offender to employ lethal violence.

Similar circumstances are found in the following case:

The movements of Jim Lane (age 24, unemployed) were varied on the weekend of his death. On Saturday night he attended a large party run by the Coffin Cheaters Motor Cycle Club in Bayswater, and he was seen leaving that party with an unidentified girl in the early hours of Sunday morning. On Sunday night, Jim picked up his regular girlfriend at 7.30, and they went to his place where they watched videos and had dinner.

Several telephone calls were received by Jim that night; at just after 11 he told his girlfriend that he had to go out for about an hour, but that she should remain because he would definitely be back. He said that he had to first make a stop, and then go to his friend, Jerry's, place. He never returned. The next morning, Jerry called and asked where Jim was, saying that he had not shown up as they had agreed (it was later established that their meeting involved a drug deal). Jim's body was found on a remote beach near Port Campbell the following day. His death was caused by a gunshot wound to the left chest. The identity of the offender could not be established. *(Case No. 17–85)*

These themes of a marginal existence, involvement in criminal activity, and an unsolved death take a slightly different twist in the final unsolved case:

George Sams (age 22, unemployed) had spent the day with his friends at the local hotel where he hung out much of the time. Earlier in the day, he and his friend 'Mousey' had scored some drugs, and then gone to the home of a friend where they shot up (George had a history of drug use which went back several years, and was suspected to have been an occasional dealer as well). Later that night, George told Mousey that he was going off that night to 'do a job', which involved a task somewhere in the bush where he was to 'burn or blow up something for insurance'. He confided to Mousey that his confederate in the arrangements was the bouncer in their local pub. Before he left, as if he had some misgivings, he gave his bank book to another friend, saying that if anything should happen, he should 'use it for the kids.'

George left at about 8.30 that night, saying that he was late for 'the job'. His body was found next morning, several kilometres away, near Kilmore. He died from multiple wounds which included stab wounds to the body, and fractures to the skull, ribs and fingers. While it was suspected that George's long history as a drug user and dealer was involved, the homicide was unsolved. The Coroner classified this as murder inflicted by a person or persons unknown.   (*Case No. 12–85*)

In all three of these last cases it seems likely that the homicides were related to the other criminal activities of victims. All were participants in a subcultural world well at the boundaries of conventionality. It was not possible to establish definitively, however, who was responsible for the homicides, and the specific bonds that linked these victims with their offenders.

Such unsolved cases constitute one of the major problems of victimology research where the analysis proceeds outward from the relationship between victim and offender. In this investigation 6 per cent of the total cases (22 of 380) must be excluded from the analysis because the basic data are not available from the case studies. This level of residual, unknown cases compares reasonably well with that observed in other investigations. In the work of Maxfield (1989) slightly more than one-quarter (28.6 per cent) of all cases were classified as 'unknown relationship.' In his early research in Philadelphia, Wolfgang (1958: 204) reported a lower rate of unsolved cases, his 6.8 per cent approaching the figure observed here. In the national study in Australia, Strang (1992) found that no suspect had been identified in 45 of 323 homicide incidents in 1991/92, a rate of unsolved homicides of 14 per cent.

From these figures, three points can be made. One, it is likely that data collected by many justice system agencies (such as the Uniform Crime Reports in the United States) will show a very high proportion of missing data because the routine bureaucratic procedures are often not sensitive to the requirements of accurate classification of victim/ offender relationships. Where the researcher is forced to rely on the agency to make the classification, in other words, a high degree of 'unknown' cases is likely to result. Two, with good quality data (such as original case files of homicides), and research procedures which call for the investigator to enter the files to make the classification, it is possible to reduce the number of 'missing data' cases to somewhere in the range of 5 per cent or less. Three, under the best of circumstances it is still inherent that research on homicide which requires information on both victims and offenders will suffer to some degree from missing data, because it is inevitable that some homicides will remain unsolved.

To be sure, in at least some of the unsolved cases a scenario can be drawn from the physical evidence available which allows enough of a classification of the relationship for the analysis to proceed, most commonly when the victim has been part of the scene of another crime such as robbery, burglary or rape. Wolfgang (1958: Chapter 16), for example, did a separate analysis of unsolved homicides and reported that 60 per cent of these cases involved robbery-homicides. Wolfgang went on to establish that there is internal complexity in the unsolved cases. He argued that from a technical point of view there will be four types of unsolved cases, including those where: (1) a suspect is identified, brought to trial, but not convicted; (2) a suspect is identified by the police, but not brought to trial; (3) a suspect is known to police but has escaped arrest; and (4) no suspect has been identified by the police (Wolfgang, 1958: 286).

In the first three of these instances, despite the fact that an offender has not been convicted, his or her identity will be known. Further, the circumstances of the homicide in most can be clearly established. There are numerous instances in the present files where the offender committed suicide, for example, and thus will not be brought to trial. In another case in the present files, a jealous male killed his female partner and then fled the country. For purposes of the present investigation, therefore, such cases need not be treated as 'unsolved'.

Wolfgang similarly concluded that, while technically falling outside the boundaries of solved criminal homicide, these cases can be included in an investigation of homicide. He suggested a more limited definition which provided that an 'unsolved homicide' consists of those killings where the Coroner's inquest determines that the perpetrator or perpetrators are unknown in a case of criminal homicide (thus excluding justifiable or excusable homicides) and where the police are unable to identify a person 'sufficiently suspect' to result in his or her arrest, if they could be located (Wolfgang, 1958: 286).

While Wolfgang's approach provides a starting point, the present study can be even more restrictive. Since in some instances it is possible to make a classification of the social dynamics which link offender and

victim even where the specific offender is not known, the unsolved
cases can be limited to those for which no scenario can be drawn which
links the victim and the unknown offender into a clear pattern of relationship. The group of cases excluded from the analysis can thereby be
reduced to a minimum. As a result, the residual group constitutes only
a small portion of the total cases which are unsolved in a technical sense
of the term. These cases are not so much unsolved as they are unclassifiable within a meaningful scheme of victim/offender relationship.

For all that, it is inherent in the nature of homicide that a pool of
cases will remain for which it will not be possible to describe a relationship between the victim and offender because details remain unavail-
able since the case is unsolved. It is perhaps indicative of the seriousness
with which homicide is treated that, in fact, the ultimate number of
these unsolved and unclassifiable homicide cases is so low, falling in the
range of something under 5 per cent. This is also a reflection of the
nature of the event itself, since in most of the homicides reviewed the
violence was played out in front of a social audience who were able to
provide vivid testimony of the events which led to the death. Even
where the murder has been, in essence, 'behind closed doors', the facts
of the homicide in most cases were clear in terms of what had transpired between an offender and the victim. There were, in reality, few
mysteries in these files.

The problem of 'special' cases

In the grouping of homicides suggested by Block and Block (1992) they
suggest a category of 'mysteries' which, in addition to unsolved cases,
includes those accounts where an offender can be identified but where
there is 'no evidence as to motive'. In any body of homicide data, there
is likely to be a special group of cases that will confound any attempt to
classify the killing on the basis of the social dynamics which link
offender with victim, precisely because these dynamics cannot be determined on the basis of the information available, even when at times
that information is vast indeed.

In the case studies of masculine homicide analysed up to this point, it
has been possible to find a rationale in the critical relationship between
victim and offender which gives meaning to the lethal events that
evolved. The observer can read these accounts and 'understand' how it
was that a jealous husband came to kill his wife, or how a male's
protection of his 'reputation' led to a fatal confrontation with another
male. The various scenarios have a coherence (based on the nature of
the victim-offender relationship) which permits their classification with
other homicides which seem to share central themes and elements.

In the case of those bound by close personal relationships that have been classified here as deriving from sexual intimacy, the male offender and the victim are often attending explicitly to the breakdown of the bond of intimacy as events lead them into lethal violence. In confrontational homicides, victim and offender are likely to have a relatively clear idea of the step-by-step 'transaction' which will lead them to physical conflict (although they clearly do not expect this to be a lethal conflict). In an armed robbery, a scenario can be described in which the victim and the offender each act and react to the other's behaviour during the course of, first, the robbery, and then the fatal violence which results (the 'duet' of crime which Wolfgang, 1958, called attention to in his early work).

There are a handful of cases, however, where this coherence breaks down. It turns out that the assumption that it is useful to classify homicides by virtue of the victim-offender interaction is deceptively complicated. For example, when it is recorded that a homicide involves an offender husband and a victim wife, it is presumed that identifying this relationship tells us something about the homicide in that it provides an initial clue as to such possible underlying issues as possessiveness and jealousy which might be played out in the marital relationship. Establishing the relationship becomes a starting point for the building up of a more elaborate analysis of the specific themes that operate in the given case, and in cases which share with it more general themes and elements.

There are a few cases encountered in these files where what happens between the key actors is so odd, bizarre, or unusual that there is a disruption of the connection between the identification of a particular social relationship (for example, husband as offender, wife as victim) and the building up of an analysis about the homicide. What is common in these cases is that knowledge of the nature of their particular relationship, at least as revealed by the present files, does not lead easily to developing a reasonable account which is able to trace the homicide back to the nature of the bond between victim and offender.

Perhaps the best way to understand this problem is by confronting an example. In the first of these cases, the homicide victim was a wife killed by her husband:

Just before midnight on 2 April 1986, H.S. (age 41, invalid pensioner) came into the South Melbourne Police Station and informed the attending officers that he had killed his wife. In the interview which followed, H.S.'s answers to questions led the investigating police to believe that he 'may have been suffering from some mental disability at the time'. Both H.S. and his wife (W.S., age 31) had long histories of mental illness, including lengthy hospitalisation.

Q: 'What happened between you and W.?'
H.S.: 'I murdered W.'
Q: 'How did you do that?'
H.S.: 'With a knife.'
Q: 'What do you mean by that?'
H.S.: 'I stabbed her.'
Q: 'Why did you do that?'
H.S.: 'To kill her.'
Q: 'Why did you want to kill her?'
H.S.: 'I don't know.'
Q: 'Did you have an argument?'
H.S.: 'I'm not sure.'
Q: 'Where was she when you stabbed her?'
H.S.: 'In bed.'
Q: 'Was she asleep or awake?'
H.S.: 'I'm not sure.'

. . .

Q: 'What were you doing just before you got the knife?'
H.S.: 'I was in bed with W. and then I got up and then got the knife. Then I went back and stabbed her.'
Q: 'Did you decide to kill W. before you got the knife?'
H.S.: 'Yes.'
Q: 'When did you decide to kill her?'
H.S.: 'I don't know, it just sort of happened.'
Q: 'Do you remember why you killed W.?'
H.S.: 'No.'

. . .

Q: 'Did you have an argument during the day at all?'
H.S.: 'No.'
Q: 'Had you planned to kill her before you went to bed?'
H.S.: 'No.'

. . .

Q: 'Did you do anything after you stabbed her?'
H.S.: 'Yes.'
Q: 'What?'
H.S.: 'I kissed her.'
Q: 'Did you do anything else to her?'
H.S.: 'Yeah, I put my arms around her.'

. . .

Q: 'Do you fully understand that you have killed your wife?'
H.S.: 'Yes.'

. . .

Q: 'The only thing you haven't been able to tell me is why you killed her, can you tell me now?'
H.S.: 'I don't know why.'   *(Case No. 965–86)*

What provoked this homicide? When pressed by police in the interview immediately after the event, even the offender professed no
understanding of what he was up to, or what led him to murder his
wife. In all other cases of intimate homicide involving sexual partners

where the victim was female and the offender male, the available information indicated that there was a 'rationale' on the part of the offender whereby the outside observer could see the nature of the mental processes that led the offender to kill his partner. Even where these processes are delusions, as in the case of A.H. who developed the erroneous notion that his wife had arranged for a prostitute to infect him with AIDS (Case No. 231–86), the observer can work through the nature of the dynamics that ultimately led to the killing.

In the case of the invalid pensioner H.S., from these files no such interpretive rationale exists. The wife was not suspected of having affairs with other men, nor had she threatened to leave (the events that provoke the intense possessiveness that leads so many men in intimate sexual relationships to take, ultimately, the steps toward lethal violence). At this point, at least, there was no indication of the deep depression that leads some men to kill their wives as part of their own suicide plans. Even when pressed several times by the police, the offender could advance no reason for him to have killed his wife.

In the mechanical, quantitative data sets on homicides, this killing would pose no problem in terms of how it would be classified. Since by definition the two individuals were man and wife, it would be considered as one of the many which fall within 'spousal' or perhaps 'domestic' homicide. The present research, however, has evolved with the fundamental assumption that classification of a homicide in terms of the relationship between the victim and offender can be justified only if this informs us about the nature of the lethal event. In this 'special' account of homicide among sexual intimates, it was possible to locate the offender and victim in terms of *who* they were within a social relationship (that is, husband and wife), but it was not possible to answer the question of *why* the interaction within that relationship led to homicide.

There is in this account considerable evidence of mental disturbance on the part of both the wife and the husband. Both had experienced long periods of hospitalisation in mental institutions. While this suggests that this might be a case of 'murder through madness', even if it were true that the offender was psychologically disturbed, and thus looked out at the world through a set of lenses which, to our view, were distorted, there still should be some thread of interpretation which leads the individual through the events which provoked his action. What makes this case so special at this point is that the husband repeatedly was asked why he committed the offence, and each time could give no satisfactory answer.

Fortunately, it was possible to round out this account by obtaining supplementary information from another official source. After cases

have moved into and through the trial phase of the criminal justice
system, including the sentencing and appeal stages, a large file has
accumulated and is retained in the office of the Victorian Director of
Public Prosecutions (DPP). These files contain a number of documents
that are potentially useful for gaining further understanding of this and
similar cases. This includes material relating to the trial, as well as psychiatric reports prepared both prior to the trial and prior to sentencing, and the pre-sentence reports prepared by a social worker.

In the case of H.S., it was the psychiatric reports that were particularly
revealing. Consistent with the record of interview prepared by the
police, the psychiatrist who saw the defendant immediately after the
event observed: 'I have no knowledge what the prisoner says regarding
the alleged offence as he says nothing.'

When interviewed many weeks later by another psychiatrist, however,
a tentative picture begins to emerge. This psychiatrist noted that the
defendant said to him that at the time of the offence:

He felt 'racey', ... He said he was not able to think logically, he couldn't
control his thoughts.
    The report went on to note regarding the married couple that:
    They had previously contemplated suicide ... the homicide ... was going to
be a 'suicide/murder combination'. He [the defendant] said he had intended to jump off the balcony.

A third psychiatrist, also examining the defendant much later, supported these observations of the possibility that suicide was contemplated, noting that the husband said that:

He stated that around 10.30 pm he decided to jump off the balcony of their
flat. He removed himself from bed, and started looking down at his wife
feeling very sorry. He related that they had an understanding that his wife
would be unable to live without him. He stated: 'I could not commit suicide
and leave her.'

Both of the last two psychiatrists concluded that the husband was,
in fact, seriously unbalanced mentally. One concluded: 'I have no
doubt that this man was actively psychotic at the time of the commission
of the alleged offence.' Similarly, the other was of the view that 'by
virtue of defect of reason, occasioned by mental illness ... that he
would not have been capable of appreciating the rightness or wrong-
ness of his act'.

This offender was moving through life at the pace of a drummer hidden from our view. He was mentally ill to the point where he qualifies
under the stringent requirements of the M'Naghten Rules of not being

legally culpable for his act in bringing about the death of his wife. That does not mean, however, that the homicide was without motive.

There is here, assuming the psychiatrists are correct in their report of the intended suicide, evidence that this husband was acting in a manner similar to some of the depressed older men observed in the section on intimate homicide (Chapter 3). Such men, suffering from depression and at the same time having a proprietorial view of their wives, decide to take the life of their partner as part of their suicide plan. Mentally ill this offender may be, and perhaps the theme is distorted by that illness, but in the relationship between this male offender and his female victim there may have been a form of the possessiveness that is a dominant feature of homicides committed on women by men.

This can only be advanced as a tentative hypothesis, however. The dimensions of this case remain basically unclear. While a possible interpretation is hinted at from the additional records, it remains the case that a definitive interpretation can not be offered which links the interaction between the offender and his victim. Given that fact, this account should still be kept apart from the main body of case studies as a 'special' case.

Another case, which involves brothers as victim and offender, was similar in that the case study as prepared from the files of the Coroner yielded a homicide with no apparent explanation:

A.G. (age 23, qualified electrician) had been living with his parents and brother, I.G. (age 20) for the three weeks since he had been discharged from the army. Over the past few months, A.G.'s behaviour had become increasingly erratic. He had been in the army from 1983 to 1986, when his odd and disruptive behaviour led him to first be subject to disciplinary action, and eventually to psychiatric and psychological examination and discharge from the army on psychiatric grounds. A.G. returned to the family home, apparently burning with resentment towards the army and the company sergeant-major (whom he had vowed to kill).

One day, some three weeks after his discharge, the two brothers spent a quiet Saturday at home, watching television and videos. They had a few drinks together, and nothing in the accounts available suggests that the day had been anything but pleasant and easy.

In the middle of the evening, I.G. decided to take a shower. A.G. stated later that at this point he began to think upon his resolve to kill his company sergeant-major, and he decided to fetch a bullet from a back shed at the rear of the family home to work on it to make it more 'potent'.

In his testimony to the police, A.G. states that he began to wonder 'what it was like to kill someone.' To find out, he decided to kill his brother. I.G. came back into the bedroom after his shower in order to dress. A.G. placed some earplugs in his ears, raised the gun, sighted on his brother's head, and pulled the trigger. The one shot was instantly fatal. He fled from the house, surrendering to police within a few hours. He could offer no motive for the crime.
(Case No. 4155–86)

As was true in the previous case, here there was no clear motive for the crime. There was no argument between the two brothers as occurred in another case in these files where a brother killed his sister after a series of events and disputes led to an argument between sister and brother, and then the final steps where a gun was fired and the sister killed. That killing can be traced step-by-step from initial disputes to the final violence. In the account of what happened between these two brothers there was nothing in the reported interaction between them that provides any clue as to why the death occurred. The offender himself could offer no motive, other than he wanted to know what it was like 'to kill someone'.

Once again, the files of the Director of Public Prosecutions were consulted to see if a rationale could be found for the homicide. In this case, a number of psychiatrists had seen the offender, and by and large they remained mystified when it came to why the act had occurred. One found that the killer 'specifically denies any resentment towards his brother', another found that 'He is unable to explain why he killed his brother', while another observed that: 'The offence remains apparently motiveless, evidently this man having a good relationship with the victim, his brother.'

No less than four psychiatrists agreed that madness was not apparent in his makeup, and was not a factor in the crime. One commented that there were 'no active psychiatric symptoms present', another that there was 'no evidence of significant psychiatric disturbance at present', while another found that there was 'no formal mental illness'.

The records here cannot provide a definitive reason, then, why this individual, who does not suffer from mental illness, would be moved to kill anyone, let alone his brother. Although not admitted by the offender, one possible reason did emerge in the volume of material available. Some months previously the life of the offender was transformed by a serious motor car accident. He was hospitalised for several months, underwent several operations, and was left with significant facial disfigurement as a result. It was after this accident that his psychological makeup seemed to change, and he began to act in the aggressive manner that ultimately led to his discharge on less than honourable grounds from the army. The driver of the car in that accident was his brother, the victim of the homicide. Was the homicide motivated by a desire to get back at the brother who had caused so much suffering? On the basis of evidence available at this time, we cannot know. At no time did the killer offer this as a motive for the homicide, even when questioned closely by the psychiatrists. In the trial, however, the defence did offer this as a possible explanation for the homicide. It cannot be stated here with any certainty, however, that this was the reason why he was moved to take up his rifle against his brother.

The safest conclusion is that at the moment no clear reasons emerge which account for this killing. What is known is that it was a homicide between brothers. It is not possible at this time to provide a reason why this relationship resulted in the homicide. This case study is placed, therefore, in the category of 'special' homicides because it has not been possible to identify what it was about the relationship itself that contributes to an explanation of the homicide.

Two of the other 'special' cases involve persons who might otherwise be considered as bonded by friendship:

Three days before Christmas, at a few minutes before midnight, S.S. (age 19, invalid pensioner) arrived by taxi at the Russell Street Police Station, where he went up to the desk and announced that he had stabbed someone. Police and ambulances were directed to the address he provided, where they found M.G. (age 75, pensioner) on the floor of his flat, dead as a result of a single stab wound to his abdomen.

Police investigators found that S.S. had been born to parents who had migrated from Yugoslavia when he was 6 years old. After leaving school, S.S. had travelled from State to State working as a labourer. While in Darwin some five years before these events, he had been placed in a mental institution where he was diagnosed as being schizophrenic. He subsequently received psychiatric treatment in Sydney and Melbourne. At the time of this incident, he was being treated for paranoid schizophrenia, including heavy medication.

When asked why he had stabbed the old man, who had befriended S.S. and asked him to his flat several times, S.S. replied that: 'He said I had hands like a female, and said I was a poofter because I wasn't married ... and, he kept talking about Hitler.' S.S. had several times been invited to visit with M.G. and use the TV, as S.S. did not own one. At another point in the interview, when S.S. was asked again if M.G. had called him a poofter, S.S. replied: 'No, he was Austrian and he made me watch German movies all the time. My grandfather had been killed by Germans in the war. I had just had enough.' *(Case No. 3954–85)*

The interaction between the victim and offender as described by the offender were such that the nature of the rationale offered makes little sense. The offender offered a fragment of a motive ('he made me watch German movies all the time'), but this motive, and the others advanced ('he said I had hands like a poofter', or 'he kept talking about Hitler'), were quite unlike the motives of other homicides. Assuming that even the mentally ill have some rationale, however different that might be, for their homicides, it was decided to probe deeper into this case as well. As in other accounts involving offenders where mental illness played a role, before and after the trial the offender was seen by a number of psychiatrists. An important feature of this homicide were the 'voices' heard by the offender. As one psychiatrist observed: 'When asked why he killed the man, he said he heard voices telling him to kill the man. He was deluded that he was the Angel of Death.' A second noted that the offender 'believes that he is the Angel of Death and that God commanded him to kill'. Another put it slightly differently: 'The voices were from the Angel of Death. They said to kill him.'

These psychiatrists all agreed that this was extreme mental disturbance, one finding that at the time of the murder the offender 'was suffering from a psychotic illness and had no real control over his actions'. Responding to the specific legal requirements of the case, a second stated that 'In my view ... he was insane within the M'Naghten Rules at the time of the commission of the alleged offence.' If this case were to be classified within the victim/offender categories employed here, it would be considered as a murder between friends. The actual facts of the homicide, however, require that it receive special treatment. Understanding this homicide dictates that circumstances be considered which go well beyond the nature of the relationship between the disturbed offender and the unfortunate victim who had befriended him. This account has little in common with the other cases where persons tied at one time by the intimate bond of friendship experience the breakdown of that bond to the point where one murders the other in order to resolve their differences.

While there are signs in the brief biographical sketches of some of these special cases that mental illness on the part of the offender plays either a major or minor role in the homicide, this does not always appear to be the case:

Tommy M. (age 19, metal cutter) and Colin E. (age 19, metal cutter) seemed to all outside appearances to be quite friendly. They both worked at the same place, and other workers described them as getting on quite well.

On the Friday before Christmas they both attended work as usual, finishing early, collecting their pay, then attending a company barbecue. The two seemed to be in good spirits, eating and talking together for the three to four hours of the barbecue. Afterwards, they went together to the Excelsior Hotel for a few more Christmas drinks in the public bar.

Before leaving the bar together at about 7 pm, Colin obtained a pocket knife from an acquaintance in the bar, saying: 'I just want to get some money.' His friend gave him the knife, thinking, he said later, that Colin was 'all talk'.

The two left the hotel and headed for home. They proceeded to walk along a nearby creek for a short distance, when Colin suddenly turned on his friend and began to stab him in a frenzy. Tommy sustained over 100 stab wounds, from his eyes to his groin as well as defensive wounds to his hands.

Colin then removed Tommy's pay packet containing some $198 and returned to the pub. He then proceeded to tell the patrons of the bar what he had just done. At first, no one would believe him. In the words of one witness, we thought, 'no, Colin would be bullshitting'. As proof of his claim, Colin then produced Tommy's pay packet. Finally, the patrons believed him.

Their reaction was to assault Colin and drag him out the door of the pub, taking the stolen money from him and giving it to the pub manager. Colin wrenched himself out of the grasp of the group and fled the hotel. He was arrested a few days later and charged with Tommy's murder.

(Case No. 3940–85)

This account is placed among the 'special' homicides because upon reading the case study it is not clear how the killing could be connected to what had previously happened between the offender and his victim. On the basis of information from the files of the Director of Public Prosecutions, it appears that the psychiatrists determined that mental illness did not provide an explanation for the homicide.

The defence, however, advanced the argument that the offender was heavily addicted to stimulating drugs, and at the time of the homicide had been routinely taking very large dosages of 'speed'. There were two effects of this heavy use of the drug, according to this argument. First, it tended to confuse the judgment of the defendant, especially when used in combination with large amounts of alcohol, as was true on the day of the homicide (while it was some time before the offender was apprehended and therefore his blood alcohol level at the time could not be measured, the victim, whom in all accounts had been matching him drink for drink all afternoon, was found to have a blood alcohol reading of 0.229). Second, its costs put the defendant under heavy financial pressure.

The defendant claimed in a pre-sentence statement that 'At the time I was in a bad way with drugs', and referring to the events immediately before the killing stated:

I do remember at the pub worrying about how I was going to cope for money ... I also remember thinking about pinching T.'s money. It's all a bit of a fog, but I remember thinking I needed the knife to scare him.

One of the witnesses testified that the offender was very drunk in the time just before the killing. After stumbling into their table, he apologised and started up a conversation (the witness was a complete stranger to the defendant):

He said that a guy had $1000 holiday pay on him and that he was going to stab him. I then remember saying, 'where's the knife?' and he said 'Here', and tapped his pocket. He kept talking about stabbing this guy for his money, but I heard someone say that they worked together and I thought he was only talking.

This case might be classified under at least three of the categories used in previous sections of this report. First, the two might have engaged in a spontaneous masculine confrontation, but there is no evidence of any argument between them. Second, the murder was apparently motivated by Colin's desire to 'get some money', which resulted in the robbery of his friend, but the facts of the case do not suggest this as anything like a typical armed robbery. Third, since the two had been close mates, it is possible that some rift had developed between them, and that the violence was a method of resolving their dispute. The nature of the homicide indicates, however, that whatever transpired lacked the essential planning and premeditation that is so distinctive among the conflict-resolution killings.

The police investigating the crime asked several questions of people who had observed the two both prior to, and on, the day of the murder, and were unable to establish any indication of conflict between the victim and his attacker. One cannot work one's way from a breakdown of the friendship into the homicide, and more specifically, there is no indication of emergent conflicts within the friendship which impelled the offender to employ violence as a mechanism of conflict resolution. The distinctiveness of this case is preserved, thereby, by placing it among the group of 'special' homicides.

In another case, we find again a combination of a background of psychological disturbance and a set of confusing events which result in homicide:

Kenny D. (age 20) had an extensive history of mental illness. His behaviour attracted psychological attention early in life during his primary school years, where he was diagnosed as 'hyperactive' and placed on medication to slow him down. Kenny was expelled from high school for 'being uncontrollable'. Shortly after that, he was in children's court for charges of sexual assault involving a number of young girls.

After a further offence involving throwing a rock at another boy which caused serious head injuries, Kenny was placed in a mental institution. There followed other offences of violence which led to him being hauled back to court, then back into the mental institution.

Staff involved there in his most recent treatment seemed to feel that progress was being made. Kenny was able to move into a residential program, and he even found and held a job. He was then established in his own flat in Carlton (an inner Melbourne suburb).

Kenny had met Lorrie M. (age 19) while both were patients at the residential facility in Parkville. Lorrie, who was diagnosed as schizophrenic, later became an outpatient, returning to live with her mother in the council housing flats in Carlton.

Kenny had not seen Lorrie for a couple of months, and decided to stop by her flat 'just to see how she was going'. During the visit, Lorrie apparently asked if she could go with him to his place for tea. Lorrie's mother later recalled that Kenny: 'wasn't enthusiastic but he agreed'.

In his later testimony, Kenny's account was that they returned to his place, listened to music and spent some time 'kissing and cuddling on the couch.'

He then fixed tea. After the meal, Lorrie started 'screaming out something, I don't know ...' Kenny asked her to calm down, and he said that he 'even tried to ask her what was wrong, but she started to carry on even worse.' She then went into the bedroom, saying she was going to take a nap.

Somewhat later, Lorrie woke up, and began screaming again. Kenny said that: 'I pleaded with her to be quiet. I then went back into the kitchen and she continued yelling. I went to a drawer in the kitchen, got out my handcuffs and some masking tape, thinking I might be able to shut her up that way.'

Kenny then went into the bedroom, according to his account, first handcuffing her, then winding the 'masking tape around her head and covering her mouth'. Kenny's narrative stated that then: 'She became quiet and I went back to the fridge and had some coke. She must have ripped the tape off, and started yelling again ... I then assembled my crossbow, to try and scare her into being quiet ... I went into the bedroom, and told her to be quiet or leave. I just went off my head. I just couldn't take it any more, and I fired the crossbow ... I had just blown my temper.'

The story doesn't stop there. Kenny went on to relate: 'I put down the crossbow, and realised what I had done. I could see that she was still alive. I took advantage of the situation. I realised what big trouble I was in by shooting her with a crossbow, so I decided to rape her. She tried to fight me off with her arms ... I thought I was in enough trouble as it was, and it couldn't be any worse for me.'

Kenny then gagged her, and left her, still alive, in the flat. He called Lorrie's mother to assure her that Lorrie was all right, then wandered about the city, eventually going to his parents' house to spend the night. Later in the week, he eventually tried to flee, flying to Tasmania under a false name. He was found on the following Sunday in a youth shelter in Launceston, confessed, and was returned to Melbourne to face charges of murder.

(Case No. 3645–85)

As was true with the other special cases, it was difficult to penetrate the rationale offered by this offender. Strapping a person to a chair, and then taping the mouth, are unusual techniques, to say the least, of pacifying a sexual intimate. The rape of the victim, after the fatal wounding, and the rationale offered for the rape, make this case stand apart.

Little additional information was revealed when the files of the Director of Public Prosecutions were reviewed in an attempt to round out this account. These files reinforced data previously obtained which indicated that the offender had a background of behaviour in which violence and mental disturbance were combined. The offender was unable to offer much to attending psychiatrists in the way of an explanation for the homicide, seeing it in his terms as a form of an 'accident'. The psychiatric reports, while commenting on the history of mental illness, did not find that the behaviour of the offender in committing this crime fell within the boundaries of insanity as legally defined.

Because of the extraordinary violence and its rationale, this case does not seem to fit well within the other forms of homicide which have been identified. While the record of the trial indicates that according to the evidence the two had been sexually intimate prior to the homicide, it is not clear what it was about their intimacy that was in any way responsible for the death. In other cases of homicide involving sexual intimacy between the partners, that intimacy (and often its disintegration) can be seen as a central theme which runs through the events which result in the killing of the victim. In this case, while there was intimacy, and certainly exceptional violence, it is not possible to say what it is that connects the two. There is in particular none of the obsessive jealousy or control themes that have featured so prominently in the scenario of masculine violence towards female sexual partners. Accordingly, this case, too, is set aside among the group of 'special' offences.

Some of the same themes of brutality, bizarreness and incomprehensibility are found in the case of Linda G.:

Homicide files will contain many brutal killings, but few found in Victoria were as savage as the homicide of Linda G. (age 21, invalid pensioner). Linda was mildly handicapped intellectually. After spending much of her younger years in an institution for the mentally retarded, she had recently moved in with her mother. Friends and family described her as having a 'lovely and childlike manner'.

A few months before, mutual friends had introduced Linda to Charlie S. (age 29), but they seemed to dislike each other. Charlie often called her a 'dog' and when he saw her would 'bark at her'. Despite this antagonism, Charlie alleges that he had a casual sexual relationship, and would, as he put it, call on her when he 'felt like a root'.

There is some dispute about the set of events that led to the actual murder. There is a suggestion that Linda was angry with Charlie and his brother Arthur, and that she was going to confront them about their harassment of a girlfriend of hers. Charlie's story is that he called her and invited her out.

The story the offenders tell is that they took her to a spot along the Merri Creek, where they all had several drinks (Charlie said that he drank a considerable amount of Southern Comfort during the course of the night). They allege that Linda then stripped, and engaged in various sexual acts with both men simultaneously.

They at first were content with beating her, but at some point, the two decided that 'We'd knock her.' They then moved on and engaged in perhaps the most savage acts that exist in these files. The two engaged in vicious sexual mutilation, gouged out one of her eyes, broke off a piece of wood and forced it up her sexual organs, among other acts.

This case is bizarre also in the way the two responded after the act. Both brothers bragged not only to friends, but even to the investigating police, about what they had done. Arthur said to the police afterwards: 'I'm glad I done it, I don't care what anyone thinks of me. I haven't slept better since I done it. I feel really great. She was a nobody, anyway.' When asked by his sister why he had done it, Arthur replied that it was 'just something to do'. Charlie told the police that: 'We were scared she would call in the coppers ... she was a lowie ...' Both provided graphic details to the police of the numerous sadistic acts they had committed on Linda's body.

(Case No. 1606–85)

As was true with the previous file, this case seems to fall outside the boundaries of other categories of homicide we have reviewed, although in some ways it might initially seem to fit in at least two. There was a prior sexual relationship between one of the offenders and Linda, but the steps leading to the homicide were completely unlike the dynamics of 'intimate sexual' relationships between offenders and female victims of the age of Linda. There was no indication of jealousy or a sense of 'possessiveness' which was threatened by Linda.

A better case might be made that this was an instance of homicide which occurred in the course of another crime, in this case, sexual assault. The initial problem with this interpretation is that the sexual activity engaged in by the woman was apparently voluntary (and this aspect was not questioned by the prosecution during the trial).

Both to see if there was some better explanation for the crime itself, and for the exceptional brutality shown, the files of the Director of Public Prosecutions were obtained for this case as well. Two specific bits of additional information emerged from these records. First, there were some clues regarding the source of the brutality. Further testimony revealed that the brother responsible for initiating and carrying out the greater part of the savage violence had been unable to perform sexually, as found in this exchange from a record of interview:

Q: 'Did you have sex with her at any stage?'
A.S.: 'I tried to ... but it just wouldn't work ... I couldn't get it up.'
Q: 'Did she make any comment about your inability to get an erection?'
A.S.: 'She said, "Have you been giving it to that sheila you're now with?"'
Q: ... 'Was that remark about your inability to get an erection?'
A.S.: 'I can't be exactly sure, but it was to do with that or about the sheila.'

In the accounts of both of the brothers, it was immediately after this that the one brother lost his head, and began to beat her, saying then that they should 'knock her' (that is, kill her). When asked why he had gone to fetch the knife, the same brother replied: 'I was worried that she was going to yell out rape and for the assaults.' [*Q:* 'In order to prevent her from going to the police?'] 'Yes.'

It seems likely that the extraordinary brutality towards the young woman was a response to her challenge of the masculinity of the leading offender. While bizarre, it therefore has elements that perhaps

require it being considered under the issues of gender role that have
emerged so strongly in the section on intimacy. The unique features of
these events, however, suggest that for present purposes its distinctiveness should be preserved by setting it aside in the category of special
cases.

One other of these cases seems to hinge on mental incompetence of
the offender, although at a level not recognised by the courts:

> The life of Georgie Hunter (age 19, unemployed) had not been easy. He was
> retarded both mentally and physically. Throughout his young life, he had
> been exceptionally clumsy, constantly stumbling and falling off bikes. He had
> become such a butt of teasing and jokes that he had reached the point where
> he would do his best to avoid social scenes where he would meet people.
>
> Through a casual contact, he had met Mrs Campbell, a neighbour in the
> suburb, a week before the murder occurred. Mrs Campbell was highly
> regarded by her friends and neighbour, and was known for her friendliness.
> The week after found Georgie in her street again, when upon seeing a group
> of other young people he became fearful. He went up to her door seeking
> the safety of her house.
>
> Mrs Campbell let him in. Through the distorted mirror of Georgie's con-
> fusion, the sequence of events from this point is hard to establish. Apparently
> at one point he asked to go to the bathroom, and while there pulled out his
> knife, which he then used to stab and kill Mrs Campbell. When asked why he
> stabbed her, Georgie said: 'I dunno. I just got frightened. I only wanted to be
> friends.' When asked why he had taken the knife out of his pants pocket, he
> replied: 'I was worried she would see me.' He was then asked: 'Why did this
> worry you?' to which he replied: 'I dunno. I was thinking in the bathroom
> that I should have stayed home.' Later in the same interview, Georgie stated
> that 'I went to the house to make a friend because I was lonely and I haven't
> got many friends.'   *(Case No. AG 870656)*

In this account we have a confused young male, possibly both
mentally retarded and to some degree mentally ill, who first sought the
friendship of his elderly neighbour. He became frightened, and convinced that Mrs Campbell was going to do him harm, he struck out.
Consultation of additional files found that psychological assessment
ruled out insanity as a defence. It was acknowledged that Georgie had a
history of odd behaviour, in which he was easily provoked to bursts of
violence. In this case it is not easy to identify a relevant category of
victim-offender relationship. There has been no need to use the term
'acquaintance' or 'neighbour' for classification in the present study.
Since the offender states that what he was seeking was friendship, then
it might be so classified, if it were necessary to force each homicide into
some such framework. To do so, however, would seem to serve little
analytical purpose.

Homicide and the 'special' cases

This research has proceeded from the assumption that a key to understanding the nature of the events that make up homicides rests in an appropriate classification of the different motivations that link offenders and victims. In most of the cases reviewed in previous sections, the events constitute something like the 'duet' in the metaphor first used by von Hentig (1979). Thus, the major participants, including the offender and victim, move together through a complicated set of moves, each influencing the other, ultimately resulting in lethal violence. Knowing the particular form of victim-offender relationship in most cases will provide a good clue as to the nature of these duetlike moves. Where the victim is the sexual partner of a male offender, at issue is likely to be power, control and masculinity. Similarly, honour or reputation is likely to be central to masculine confrontations which result in homicide, and where the individuals have been bound together in friendship, the dominant pattern that has emerged is one of the readiness of some males to employ violence as a technique of dispute resolution.

The 'special' cases, of which there were 18 in the present investigation (or 5 per cent of all homicides), prove to be a problem for standard forms of analysis of victim and offender relationships in homicide. Each of the special cases on technical grounds would have been classified within forms of victim/offender relationships typically found in studies of homicide. Two involve what might be classified as homicide between friends where the killing is a form of conflict resolution, one is a homicide within the family involving two brothers, while in another three there was some form of sexual bond (however brief) between the male offenders and their female victims, and the final case is a homicide between persons known to each other as acquaintances.

Consider the case where the mentally ill young man was prompted to kill his elderly friend because his 'voices' told him he was the Angel of Death. This event is unlike any of the other homicides involving friendship where the homicide is a form of conflict resolution. While it technically shares with these other killings the fact that the individuals involved were friends, it is radically different in terms of the social dynamics of the relationship between the victim and the offender, especially in terms of the different rationality offered here to account for why the killing took place.

In some of these special accounts, the offender either was clearly mentally ill, or could be considered as functioning in a mentally abnormal way at the time of the homicide. It is not the intent here, however, to shift the analysis away from the interactions between offender and victim onto the mental state of the offender. Instead, in each of these cases the investigators have attempted to isolate as clearly as possible what the circumstances of the relationship were between the two parties. It is this dynamic which has been termed here 'special', rather than the mental state of the offender.

It may be, of course, that the addition of more cases would suggest that a separate category be created for homicides where the violence has its origins in the mental illness of the offender. There is, for example, a persistent theme of offenders motivated by 'voices' which runs through some of these 'special' accounts. Whatever happens, the suggestion for the present analysis is that in these circumstances the ordinary and routine classification of homicide by virtue of the relationship between offender and victim is difficult indeed.

The points to be made from these special cases are twofold. First, it is highly likely that such distinctive events are inevitably part of the events which lead to homicide both here and elsewhere. In investigations of homicide, the materials that provide the base for analysis of the victim/offender relationship ought to be reviewed carefully, in other words, before events are classified simply as, say, an instance of husband/wife, or brother/brother killing. Such a classification may be technically correct in a narrow sense, but as the above accounts suggest, it may not be an accurate reflection of the particular events of special cases.

Second, these cases demonstrate that there are ultimate limits in what can be done in analysing homicide through the victim/offender relationship. In a handful of cases, there may not be enough material available to make clear what it was that was going on between the two parties. Where some interpretation cannot be made regarding the nature of the interaction which has taken place between victim and offender, simply classifying the event along one or another of the standard categories of victim/offender relationship will not prove theoretically or empirically meaningful.

The approach which focuses on this relationship as the major vehicle for the analysis of homicide presumes that it is possible not simply to classify such accounts, but to provide some meaning for what has transpired between the parties. It is suggested here that even where the body of data is reasonably good, as the present set tends to be, in a few cases the nature of the events may be hidden from view by mental confusion on the part of the offender, the absence of accurate accounts of those events, or even the obvious deliberate twisting and misstating of these events on the part of those who survive the homicide.

Put another way, building up an understanding of homicide by focusing on the critical relationship between the victim and the offender inevitably will lead to some classification of such relationships in order to reduce the observations to meaningful conclusions. In the various themes and variations reviewed in previous sections the accounts tended to share common features not simply in the objective relationship observed between offender and victim (for example, women victims of male sexual intimates), but in terms of the factors within these cases which led the events down a path towards homicide (such as sexual proprietoriness and jealousy). A distinctive feature of the special cases is that while they might share with other cases an objective classification of the relationship between victim and offender (wife and husband), the essential facts of these cases are quite unlike the other accounts within the category.

There is, in short, something distinctive about these events which sets them apart. The interactions, motivations and dynamics of other cases simply do not fit for these 'special' events. Accordingly, we are arguing here for a procedure which places these cases in a category of their own, where their distinctive features can be preserved. These are properly considered, in the term suggested by Block and Block (1992), as true homicide mysteries.

The issue of the missing voices

There is as well the problem that the development of any narrative, such as a case study or a police file, on a killing will be a social construction based on available evidence from which some voices will be absent, and others either deliberately or inadvertently less than well-focused. It is an elementary fact of social psychology that the same act viewed by different observers, even under laboratory conditions, may yield substantially different accounts. This will be no less true with the real life circumstance of a killing, especially since the voice of one of the most central parties, the victim, is absent in nearly all cases (there are a few instances where the victim lingers before dying). Further, there are some circumstances where the different observers have oppositional and partisan points of view. If the killing involved a collective argument between two groups of young people, they may give vastly different accounts of who 'started' the violent encounter.

There is no simple way out of this problem. Fortunately, most homicides are definitively social events, where most available accounts agree on the steps which led to the homicide. Often, there will be available either relatives or close friends of the victim who can provide their memory of the actual words of the victim before the homicide (memories which frequently can be cross-checked with other witnesses).

For all that, there are cases which pose significant problems for the
external observer. There are a small number of cases where the actual
killing was not observed, and where the alleged offender denied the
killing. In one case which took place in San Remo (a seaside holiday
resort), a woman was drowned after walking along a dock with her
husband, from whom she had recently separated. The couple had many
violent arguments in the days immediately before the death, the man
expressed to friends his rage that his wife had moved in with another
man, and he had further said that he was going to 'do her in'. When
the wife, who was a good swimmer dies, is it reasonable to presume that
he had pushed her into the water and caused her death?

In a similar case, a woman is found shot dead in the family home, and
her husband is found tied up in the boot of the car outside the house.
It was the man's story that the couple had been set upon by a group
of thieves, who had shot his wife and bound him and placed him
in the car. The couple, it transpired, had experienced great difficulties
in the marriage, including the woman taking a lover. The police were
able to uncover a great number of inconsistencies in the story of the
husband.

Both of these accounts demonstrate the problems that can arise as a
consequence of lack of access to the missing voices which might round
out the story of what 'really' happened. While the police argued that
both of these men were guilty, in fact, while the second husband was
convicted of murder, in the first narrative the husband ultimately was
not brought into court for the death of his wife.

There are other ways that these events can become clouded and
uncertain. In more than a few cases, the available witnesses, and perhaps even the offender, have ingested such exceptional levels of alcohol
that no amount of probing can reveal a very clear account of the death.
In one illustrative case, an infant was found battered to death after it
had been in the care of a rather large family grouping. The accounts
given agree that all of the adults present at the party that night were
exceptionally drunk, and none of the group admitted responsibility for
the beating. No charges were laid in this case.

For all of these reasons, the unknown cases, the special circumstances
where the motivations of the killing are not easy to assess, or because of
the limits imposed when voices are absent or distorted, the investigator
who sets out on the important task of unravelling the interactions
between homicide victims and offenders must recognise the limits of
what that analysis can achieve. Some homicides must remain outside
such an exploration because the available information is not sufficient
for appropriate classification. Others, even where it is known what the
static social relationship between offender and victim is (such as

husband-wife, or brother-brother), should be excluded because in fact the reasons for the killing remain hidden from view.

Despite these limits, with a reasonably rich body of data it is not unreasonable to expect to be able to describe meaningful narratives in close to 90 per cent of cases of homicide. Where cases can be reviewed in detail, and where the inquiry is directed by explicit theoretical interests, it should be possible to describe reasonably coherent scenarios which capture the basic patterns which run through such data.

On the study of homicide

Having now examined the present data on homicide scenarios, what implications do these raise for how studies of homicide are conducted? A review of existing literature will show rather distinct differences between traditional approaches to the investigation of victim-offender relationships, and the present analysis of scenarios of homicide. Typically, previous investigations, drawing upon the pioneering work of Wolfgang (1958), have tended to focus either on relationships defined in terms of the nature of the social bonds between the participants, or on the motives which bring and hold the individuals together.

The first of these deals with a dimension of social relationships which ranges from intimate familial roles at one end of a continuum, to those involving strangers at the other end. These can vary from relatively sparse schemes, which pose an intimate category such as 'family', an intermediate category involving 'friends/acquaintances', and then a more extreme category of 'strangers' (Hewitt, 1988, and Huong and Salmelainen, 1993). Many others attempt to fill out such schemes, posing a number of other categories, most of which will round out the possible forms of known or intimate relationships (spouses, boyfriend-girlfriend, mother-child, etc.). Among these is the eleven-category list proposed by Wolfgang in his original study, and the even more extensive list of the Supplementary Homicide Reports which calls for more than two dozen specific categories (Maxfield, 1989). Silverman and Kennedy (1987) have pointed out that the theoretical content of such schemes is based on notions of 'relational distance', where the social bonds range from those involving close relationships of family intimacy to the extreme of strangers where the link is the most distant.

The category problem: 'stranger homicide' as an illustration

While the approach of Silverman and Kennedy has proven insightful in its treatment of available secondary data on homicide, there are a number of problems with this form of treatment of 'victim-offender relationships' which can be thrown into sharp perspective by a brief examination of the concept of stranger homicide. Though the notion of stranger homicide looms large in media accounts of contemporary crime, and has even been the target of a number of recent accounts of homicide (Kapardis, 1990; Langevin and Handy, 1987; Zahn and Sagi, 1987; Silverman and Kennedy, 1987; and Reidel, 1987), it is significant that at no point in the grouping of the scenarios of homicide from the thematic analysis of the present case studies was it necessary or relevant to make use of the term 'stranger homicide'.

Every single one of the nearly 400 homicides could be grouped into a meaningful scenario or the important residual categories without giving primary emphasis to whether the event involved strangers in contrast to persons known to each other. There were no killings that could be described within a scenario which would be labelled 'stranger homicide'.

The reasons for this finding are straightforward. Put simply, people don't kill each other because they are strangers. Homicide tends to involve exceptional tensions and emotional extremes. With rare exceptions (to be discussed below), these tensions are not found among people who remain totally unknown to each other. There were homicides which involved persons who were not known to each other. The great majority of what are called stranger homicides elsewhere, however, are to be found in two of the present masculine scenarios of homicide. Many will be where the homicide occurs in the course of another crime, for example, during the course of armed robbery. Another large number will occur as a result of a masculine honour confrontation. It is the present conclusion that the thematic material within the scenario provides a better description of the ongoing dynamic between the parties in the homicide than does the designation that the event is a 'stranger homicide'.

In masculine confrontations, for example, it appears to be quite irrelevant whether the persons know each other or not in terms of the basic dynamics of the emerging dispute over honour. It is a social game played out by understood rules, most often by willing participants, which may involve persons known or unknown to each other. Put another way, if they haven't been acquainted before, they come to 'know' each other by virtue of the confrontation itself. If it is necessary to preserve a category of 'stranger homicide', it would follow that there would be two groupings of confrontational homicides, one for those involving persons previously known to each other, and one for those involving strangers. Since there appears to be no difference between the two, the present suggestion is that there is no need whatsoever to retain the term 'stranger homicide' as a major indicator of the social relationship between victim and offender.

Homicides do occur between strangers. Large numbers of confrontational killings, and those which arise in the course of other crime, will involve persons previously unknown to each other. Mass killings, discussed previously, also would fall into this category.

At issue, ultimately, is the theoretical importance of the underlying dimension of relational distance, as expanded by Silverman and Kennedy (1987). While of some use for particular arguments, as in its connection to notions derived from 'routine activities' approaches (see Kapardis, 1990), this conception of 'distance' is exceptionally static. While descriptions of relationships such as those involving persons tied together because they share family bonds, or those linked by friendship, or strangers, define a social status between victim and offender, the content of these relationship categories provides few clues as to why the homicide has occurred. Thus, it is a commonplace observation in criminology to point out that a majority of victims of homicide know the person who took their life. While this is an empirically verifiable observation, it adds little information to our knowledge of why that homicide has taken place.

On the motivations muddle

It is partly to address these kinds of problems that investigations attempting to unravel the dynamics of victim-offender interaction have also probed what are referred to as 'motives' (Wolfgang, 1958) or 'circumstances' (Maxfield, 1989) of homicide. In some respects, such classifications come closer to the present scenario approach, at least in the sense that these give explicit attention to the fact that homicide can result from circumstances concerned with the commission of another crime. Thus, in Wolfgang's (1958) groupings there is recognition that homicide can result from 'robbery', the 'halting of a felon', or as a consequence of an attempt at 'escaping arrest'. The Supplementary Homicide Reports (Maxfield, 1989) provides a much more extensive list and includes specification of homicides as an outcome of the commission of 'instrumental' felonies (for example, rape, robbery), 'property' felonies (burglary, larceny, auto theft), or 'other' felonies (including arson).

Other aspects of such lists have been unsatisfying. It is here that Wolfgang (1958) included his well-known notion of 'trivial altercations' as a motivation for homicide, as well as such categories as 'domestic quarrel', 'jealousy', 'altercation regarding money', or 'revenge', among others. While helpful and an important starting point for research which has followed, obvious problems with such a list emerge from close reading of homicide files, including the fact that an event can involve a significant mix of jealousy and a domestic quarrel, yet at the same time start from an immediate apparently trivial argument (put in other terms, the categories are not mutually exclusive). Further, from present findings it would seem that many male confrontational encounters appear from the outside to be the kinds of events that Wolfgang was aiming at in his use of the term 'trivial altercation', yet in that early research he does not narrow this term to identify fundamentally masculine violence.

While much more recent, even less satisfying is the treatment of a large category of 'conflicts' within the Supplementary Homicide Reports (Maxfield, 1989). While within these 'conflicts' are provided more specific forms which include 'lovers' triangle', 'brawl under alcohol', 'argument over money', and a rather odd inclusion in this context with the label 'killed by baby-sitter', in fact the vast majority of conflict homicides reported within the Supplementary Homicide Reports are found in a residual grouping of 'other arguments' whose content is unspecified and unclear. While many masculine brawls involve alcohol, some which are virtually identical in form do not. Arguments over money may be spontaneous, but many involve definitively premeditated and calculated homicides. In sum, there are many like things that are not placed together in this scheme, there are many unlike things that are grouped together, but most homicides in this scheme fall into the residual categories, either of 'other' (and therefore undefined) arguments, or those where the circumstances are 'unknown'.

Close in many important ways to the present use of scenarios are the various 'syndromes' of homicide suggested by Block and Block (1992). These investigators propose a general grouping of 'instrumental' homicides that encompass most of the specific forms of homicide which have been grouped in the present investigations as homicides consequent to the commission of other crime, these 'instrumental' homicides including killings resulting from robbery, burglary, arson for profit, or contract and gangland deaths (rape is provided for in a separate category). Block and Block provide a distinct grouping for street-gang killings (which would not emerge in Victoria given the absence of formally structured street gangs), and a residual for such 'other' homicide syndromes as murder-suicide pacts and mercy killings.

Particularly problematic for present purposes is a broad band of killings which are grouped as 'expressive' homicides, and include 'neighbour or work-related killings', 'bar-room brawls', 'spouse abuse', 'child abuse', and 'elder abuse', among others. From the present data, despite the utility as a general classification scheme for homicide, there are important theoretical, logical and empirical problems with this form of grouping. Probably most important is that there is no separation of homicides by gender, most critically in the treatment of killings between spouses. Quite different scenarios of violence hold when men kill their sexual partners (at issue most often is some form of masculine control over the life of the woman), than when women kill their sexual partner (where commonly they are responding to the often extreme violence of the male, and very rarely are such killings motivated by jealousy – the common male motive). Further, the deep and long-term planning involved in some of the killings by men of their women partners stretches in uncomfortable ways the implications of the term 'expressive' homicide.

There are, as well, questions regarding the comprehensiveness of the groupings suggested by Block and Block (1992). The present data would suggest that the term 'bar-room brawl' is much too narrow, since the masculine confrontations involved in such killings can occur in streets, in parks, at parties, or in public transport settings. It is, further, not clear where killings which are a form of planned, rational dispute resolution would fit, since these could hardly be considered 'expressive' in the common understanding of that term.

In general, whether the focus is on the static dimension of social relationships, or whether the issue is motivation or circumstance, it would be hard to argue with the assertion of Daly and Wilson (1988: 171–2) that the existing methods of grouping the events which link homicide victims and offenders are a conceptual 'hodgepodge'. One indication of the absence of coherence is that over the many studies it is virtually impossible to find two which have the same list of either relationship forms or motivations.

On the classification of homicide

While the main purpose of the present analysis has been to probe and explore in a highly inductive fashion four particular scenarios of predominantly masculine violence, as a prior step (as indicated in Chapter 2) it was necessary to evolve a way of grouping all homicides (see Table 1, Chapter 2). It must be emphasised that this form of grouping was definitively emergent and it resulted from the attempt to read and identify coherent patterns for clustering each of the 380 case studies. As the study evolved, the following kinds of guidelines were used to establish the groupings.

A starting point was: did the killing develop out of a sexual relationship (marital, de facto, boyfriend-girlfriend) among the participants? If so, what was the gender of the offender? If the offender was male, and the victim female: (a) was the offender using violence as a result of jealousy or in an attempt to control some behaviour of the woman, such as to keep her from separating, to control her sexual behaviour, or perhaps to conclude a fight?; or (b) did the offender exhibit a pattern of profound depression, and was the killing a part of the offender's planned suicide?; or (c) had the offender initiated a new sexual relationship, and was the killing a way of discarding an unwanted partner? If the offender was male and the victim was male, was the victim a sexual rival or was the victim involved in a homosexual relationship with the offender, and did the killing represent an attempt to control the behaviour of the victim?

If the offender was a female, and the victim was male, was the killing in response to prior violence of the male or an attempt to control the behaviour of the male (for example, to prevent his separation), or a way of discarding a no longer wanted sexual partner?

In confrontational killings, the key questions concerned the origins of the conflict. These occurred in male-on-male (or in a handful of cases, female-on-female). The critical question would be whether or not there was any evidence of the violence being precipitated by an insult, jostle, or other form of unplanned exchange. Did the violence proceed spontaneously from an insult to the honour of the participants?

In homicide in the course of other crime, most cases could be classified easily by simply asking the question: did the homicide result as a direct consequence of the commission of a crime? Was the victim the victim of the original crime (a double victim) or did the offender in the original crime become the ultimate victim? If a reverse victim, was the offender either a member of the police force, or a citizen? In some cases (such as killings of police) the cluster is expanded by asking the question: was it some other crime, or another crime pattern, that led to the commission of this homicide?

Conflict-resolution homicides are somewhat troublesome because virtually all homicides can be seen as the last state of some conflict. The scenario here is reserved for those cases which can be reached by the following kinds of questions: was the killing a planned and intentional device for resolving some long-standing personal dispute between the victim and offender? Were there factors present which indicate that it was not possible to resolve the dispute in other ways? Is it clear that the homicide was not spontaneous?

The above guidelines would address the four major scenarios examined in detail here. The other forms can be addressed as follows. Regarding multiple homicides (those involving three or more unrelated individual victims), the guide would ask whether or not the events were part of a 'murder spree' or separated in time and therefore evidence of serial killing (Egger, 1990).

Cases of homicide arising out of family relationships (other than spousal bonds) show considerable internal complexity. If the victim is a child, and the offender involves one or both of the parents, then the questions need to address whether the child was a victim of trauma (what form?), the parent's suicide plan, neonaticide, or neglect. Relatively few homicides involve family dyads other than spouses or children killed by parents, and while not theoretically satisfying, for a complete scheme of classification it will be necessary to answer the simple question regarding the nature of the relationship between victim and offender.

While all of the present homicides, save the one mercy killing, could be classified in the above groupings and questions, there were two kinds of remaining categories. One consisted of the 'special' cases where the relationship information could not produce a meaningful explanation of the homicide (previously discussed). The second consisted of the unsolved homicides where not enough information was present to provide a meaningful classification (also discussed previously).

Since these categories are emergent, and derive from a relatively small number of homicides, it is highly likely that attempts at replication would lead to modifications. Certainly if employed in the United States it might be necessary to add a grouping for gang homicides, and perhaps a category that makes specific reference to conflicts flowing out of drugs.

It needs to be acknowledged that raw homicide data are exceptionally diverse, and developing any systematic form of clustering is difficult. While there are many cases, for example, which come close to the ideal types within the scenarios described above, there are other, more troublesome cases which may either fall somewhere between two groupings, or perhaps in its own unique space.

For an illustration, there was the instance of two young males who had been close friends for years. They had enjoyed the outdoors together, and spent much time camping and hunting. One of the men was involved in a motorcycle accident, and became a quadriplegic. After many months, he became deeply depressed and decided to take his own life. The only method available to him was to refuse sustenance. The young man was returned to hospital, and was kept alive through alternative feeding procedures over which he had no control. His depression continued, and with it his desire to terminate his life. He finally was able to convince his young friend to kill him with a hunting rifle, after which the friend committed suicide.

There is no question of this not constituting, as well as a great personal tragedy, criminal homicide, since the acts involved were fully intentional. But it clearly stands apart from most other forms of homicide observed, making up the one example in this time period of mercy killing.

Most often, however, the problem lies not in the fact that the case stands alone, but that it contains elements of two scenarios. There were two instances where men met in a street after drinking, insults were exchanged, a fight started, a participant was felled, and then afterwards one of the offenders relieved the victim of his money. While the inter-action contained some elements of homicide during the course of another crime, both of these were classified as confrontational homi-cide since the dynamics which produced the killing fitted the elements of that scenario, and the robbery came after the fatal injuries had been inflicted.

There were specific problems noted with the 'conflict-resolution' grouping. There were a few instances where cases could be considered as having elements of both that scenario and homicide arising out of the course of other crime. This is in part because one of the major factors that puts individuals outside the system of conventional arbitra-tion procedures is their participation in a criminal way of life. An argu-ment over a drug debt, for example, is both a conflict which cannot be negotiated by the legitimate legal system, and also arises out of partici-pation in criminal activity.

Similarly, there were some instances where conflict-resolution homi-cides displayed elements of confrontational homicides, especially in the sense that the final episode might contain a fight. There are no easy ways out of these problems. What the classification scheme can do is be clear about what the guidelines are for classification. Where a case has elements of both types of homicides, in the present circumstance it has been classified in the grouping where it shares the most elements. If the procedures are tried in a replicative analysis, especially if there are many more cases, it may be necessary to create sub-categories which recognise the shared features.

Putting this another way, while the use of clear criteria should result in the differentiation of most homicides into the three predominantly male-on-male scenarios, some small amount of overlap is likely to occur, because it is the nature of the phenomena that elements may mix and fuse. Individuals whose lives revolve around drug use and sale, and other criminal activities, may have a long-standing disagreement about a debt that provokes one party to consider the use of violence to settle the matter, but that decision may be acted upon in a leisure setting where the two encounter each other and begin to argue. What is important is that the account be described so as to preserve the critical elements which evolve around the masculine readiness to call upon violence as a way of responding to particular social stimuli.

It also can be noted that occasionally it is necessary to step outside the literal relationship between the specific offender and victim to determine the nature of the scenario. This occurs in such cases as those where the victim by accident intrudes into a scene which has been set in motion by other forces. The man who walked out of a pub and became the victim of another man's violence in the parking lot of a pub was just as much a victim of a confrontation (much of which had taken place earlier in the pub between the offender and the bartenders) as other victims who perhaps participated more directly in confrontational violence. Understanding a scene, in other words, may give a deeper and richer meaning to situations which would not otherwise be revealed by such static terms as 'accidental' victim or 'father-daughter' homicide.

One further factor that became clear as this analysis proceeded was that it was much more complicated in terms of the diversity of elements than was anticipated at the beginning. Originally a plan was established to qualitatively analyse the thematic material in each case study (which was done), and then after writing out the summary, to utilise a set of 'key words' which could apply across the cases.

The problem that emerged very quickly was that the different scenarios each require a distinct set of questions. The essential features of one pattern are quite irrelevant to another. In cases of homicide arising out of sexuality, where the offenders are male, the investigator would be interested in knowing what evidence there was of violence as a control technique, of prior violence on the part of the male, whether or not that violence had been reported, if it was reported, what action was taken, or whether there was evidence of profound depression on the part of the male, and if that led to a plan for suicide.

In cases of confrontational homicide, the specific features which round out the scenario concern the nature of the initial provocation (insult, gesture, jostle, etc.), the location of the events (pub, party, street, park, etc.), the role of peers, the presence of alcohol, and perhaps the role the victim played in precipitating the violence.

In cases of conflict-resolution homicide, the pattern dictates an examination of the nature and length of the bond between offender and victim, the nature of the intended use of violence (for example, was it the victim who first used violence?), the factors that restricted access to other forms of conflict resolution (criminal history of offender, the source of the conflict – such as a drug debt, etc.).

In narratives dealing with homicide in the course of other crime, the primary focus of the narrative would be on explicating the nature of the pattern of criminality that resulted in the homicide (armed robbery, burglary, etc.), how that set up the scene where the homicide occurred, and the particular role of victim and offender (double or reverse victim, for example).

The point is that the enterprise needs to be seen as leading to a complex logical tree that quickly branches out into unique sets of data, each requiring a distinctive set of questions in order to round out the pattern. There is no single protocol, or simple set of questions, which apply across all cases uniformly which can produce much in the way of useful data.

It must be emphasised that the whole inductive and exploratory thrust of the investigation indicates that further and future work may alter to some degree the patterns reported here. This happened, in fact, even as this work progressed. In an original formulation, for example, drawing upon earlier work, there was an attempt to preserve a category of homicide which took place within the intimate bond of friendship. As the work evolved, and especially when 1987–89 data were added to the 1985–86 collected in the preliminary phases, it became clear that this category was not appropriate. Careful reading, and the development of tighter case study guidelines, indicated that this grouping actually contained two different forms of homicide. On the one hand, there were homicides between friends that were identical in content to confrontational homicides, and these should be so classified. On the other, what further analysis demonstrated was that what was at issue between friends who became involved in homicide was some conflict that they were unable to resolve through conventional means.

This illustration of how these conceptual schemes evolve and change provides recognition that it is likely further exploration will dictate further modification of the overall set of groupings. This should not detract from the importance of the present work, and its attempt to differentiate the major scenarios within which masculine violence is carried out. These are compatible with case study narratives in other accounts, and flow along the lines suggested in the theoretical writings of writers such as Daly and Wilson (1988).

Conclusions

The present review of case study data raises serious questions about what can be achieved through secondary analysis of some of the large-scale data sets such as the Supplementary Homicide Reports in the United States. The individual groupings within which such data report information on either relationship or motivation have been revealed to be of limited usefulness in describing the nature of the social dynamics that have transpired between victim and offender. In individual circumstances, homicides may be pressed into categories of relationship even when further analysis would demonstrate that knowing that relationship reveals nothing about why the killing has taken place. Throughout, the exceptionally large residuals, the unknown or unclassifiable cases, raise important questions about the general quality of information available. In the Supplementary Homicide Reports, for example, 28.6 per cent of the relationship data are 'unknown', and in the case of the 'homicide circumstance codes' overall 16.7 per cent are classified as unknown, and within the data recorded as 'conflict' 32.8 per cent (of all homicides) are recorded as 'other argument' (Maxfield, 1989: 675–7).

In general, the weight of the present analysis raises several questions about the common schemes for classification of homicide data. On the one hand, the major underlying dimension of social distance throws up categories ('family', 'friends/acquaintances', 'stranger') that are static and devoid of much in the way of theoretical content. On the other hand, these do not preserve the important dimension of gender which has been found in the present instance to be essential in reviewing homicide data.

In the hands of inventive investigators, secondary analysis of large national data sets may reveal some amount of useful information. From the present data, it can be suggested that such research will be sharpened by clear differentiation by gender in its earliest stages. It would appear much more likely, however, that advances in an understanding of the social dynamics of homicide will be revealed by original data collection from files which are sufficiently detailed in information regarding behaviour of both victim and offender.

The weight of the exploratory analysis of masculine scenarios of homicide which has been undertaken in the present investigation comes down on the side of substantiation of Wolfgang's (1958) claim that an important feature of homicide research should be an untangling of the social dynamics linking victim with offender. What this discussion has raised are the general limits of that analysis, including those imposed by the maintenance of previous categories of analysis which appear of negligible value in guiding present day research. Further advances in understanding homicide are likely to require new categories, sharpened theoretical directions, and original data sufficiently abundant in data regarding the 'duet' of interaction between victims and offenders. Even with that, however, analysts must initiate such work with a clear understanding of the forces operating in the data which will set boundaries on what can be achieved.

One final issue along these lines concerns the overall ability to generalise about the findings observed within these scenarios. Are the conclusions reached here limited to Victoria, or can the patterns be inferred to have wider applicability? Some of the data speak to the caution that must be considered in making any simple inferences to a country like the United States. The overall homicide rate in Australia is much lower (Strang, 1992; Reiss and Roth, 1993), certainly in Australia there is not found the dense Afro-American ghettos that so clearly have impact on the picture of homicide in America (Reiss and Roth, 1993), and there is a much lower level of use of hand guns in homicide than in the United States, firearms contributing to 23 per cent of homicides in Australia in 1990–91 (Strang, 1992: 14), compared with 64 per cent in the United States in 1990 (Bureau of Justice Statistics, 1992).

There are some issues that arise specifically with respect to the playing out of the scenarios as well. For one example, it is clear that the ratio of wives killing husbands to husbands killing wives is much lower in Australia than in the United States (Wilson and Daly, 1992), although the Australian ratio is roughly in the range of countries such as the United Kingdom.

Despite these differences, it can be argued that the general patterns isolated within the scenarios do generalise across national boundaries. The use of violence as a technique of control of women by men has been widely commented on in the research commentary (for an analysis, see Daly and Wilson, 1988), and the phrase uttered in Victoria by a violent male 'If I can't have you no one else will' echoes through literature in the United States and England (see Campbell, 1989; Rasche, 1989, or Mowat, 1966).

The notion of violence as a defence of masculine honour derives from considerable overseas research and thinking as well, in particular the work of Daly and Wilson (1988). The readiness to use violence to defend masculine reputation was commented on specifically by Wolfgang (1958: 188), and features clearly in a number of the case studies observed by Lundsgaarde (1977). This scenario is hardly unique to Victoria.

Most other research provides a specific place for the analysis of homicides which occur in the course of other crime (for example, Wolfgang, 1958: 238–44; Maxfield, 1989; or Block and Block, 1992). In the Philadelphia data, for example, roughly 12 per cent of the homicides took place in the course of other crime (Wolfgang, 1958: 207 and 240), in comparison to the slightly large 16 per cent in the present study. What the present study contributes is a conceptualisation of this particular scenario as deriving from the exceptional *masculine* willingness to take risks which is argued for as a way of looking at this pattern of homicide. This readiness to engage in highly risky criminal behaviour is hardly unique to Victoria, nor is its masculine quality. In fact, all of the 'felony-homicides' (the term employed by the author) in the Philadelphia investigation were male (Wolfgang, 1958: 241).

While the final scenario, involving violence as a form of conflict resolution, has not explicitly been addressed in previous research, it is hardly a new phenomenon. The homicides that occur between various groups within the organised crime networks in the United States would represent this pattern, since these, too, arise often as the final mechanism for resolving competing claims over territory or control of criminal activity. In a way, what the specification of this scenario enables is a sharpening of terms employed in previous research, such as where homicide is viewed as arising out of 'arguments' (Maxfield, 1989) or 'altercations over money' (Wolfgang, 1958: 191). The present usage sets the violence more directly into a theoretically relevant context, and also specifies its masculine content.

Looking at the patterns overall, then, it would seem that the present data are in fact consistent with what has been observed in other settings, although of course there has been a distinctive shaping of the data into the suggested scenarios. There is widespread agreement among the various available studies that homicide is predominantly masculine and lower or under-class in character, and what this book has advanced are particular ways of looking at such violence that appear generally consistent with homicide data across a wide range of previous investigations.

CHAPTER 9

Towards a theoretical analysis of homicide

Roughly 4.5 million people currently live in Victoria. Among these, only a handful, somewhere in the neighbourhood of seventy persons a year, will find themselves in the extraordinary position where they take the life of another person. What is it that pushes individuals to this extremity? Answering this as a theoretical question must be central to any serious discussion of homicide. From the case study material reviewed here, as well as previous research, there appear to be two factors of particular significance in understanding homicide: masculinity, and under or lower-class position.

There is a wealth of literature that establishes the indisputable proposition that homicidal violence is masculine in its makeup (Wolfgang, 1958; Wallace, 1986; Daly and Wilson, 1988). Males overwhelmingly account for most offenders, and to a slightly lesser degree, most victims in homicide. Even where women kill men, it has been demonstrated that the major reason is that the women are defending themselves against prior, and extreme, violence on the part of their male sexual partners (Blum and Fisher, 1978; Gillespie, 1989; Polk and Ranson, 1991b; Easteal, 1993).

The purpose of the present investigation has been to address the particular forms that such masculine violence can take. Throughout, there is strong support for the general proposition that a theme of masculine competitiveness runs through homicide. It is males who feel compelled to compete for resources, for status, for dominance and control of sexual partners, and who are willing to employ violence against other males if called upon in order to assure successful competition. Four specific scenarios of masculine violence have been identified.

The first general scenario consists of the use of lethal violence as a feature of the control over the behaviour of sexual partners. Essential to this scenario is the idea that men view women, to use the apt concept employed by Daly and Wilson (1988), in proprietory terms, where women are seen as possessions over which the male is expected to have exclusive rights. In some situations, the male perceives that the woman is moving out from under his control, as when there is an attempt to break away and form a sexual liaison with a new partner. In such instances the competitive theme is direct and paramount, and the male will feel challenged, as a test of his maleness, to bring the woman 'under control', including, if necessary, the use of violence. In extreme cases, of course, the male announces to the woman and to the world, 'If I can't have you, no one will', in essence destroying the woman to deny the attempts of a competitor to gain authority over the disputed property. Another variant of this theme, where the issue is control of the sexuality of the woman, is where the violence is aimed directly at the sexual rival, with the homicide taking the form of the challenged male taking the life of the male he perceives to be his sexual competition.

Equally proprietory are the cases where depressed males take the lives of their sexual partners as part of their suicide plan. Here again, the woman is viewed as a commodity, over which the male has rights regarding the proper disposal. For such men, it is inconceivable that the woman should be left alone to fend for herself.

What is noteworthy in the present data is the dramatic asymmetry of these major variants on this first scenario. There were no women who killed their sexual partners out of jealousy, and no women killed their husbands prior to their own suicide. This willingness to call upon lethal violence as a feature of sexual control is distinctly and definitively masculine in its makeup. In form and substance, the thematic materials which have emerged from the present case studies are consistent with the ideas of sexual proprietoriness laid out by Daly and Wilson (1988).

The remaining three scenarios all relate to forms of what are mostly male-on-male violence. One such scenario, again drawing closely on the ideas of Daly and Wilson, has been termed 'confrontational' homicide. These are killings which begin in some form of honour contest between males. These tend to start spontaneously from some form of exchange which to an outside observer may appear to be 'trivial' (Wolfgang, 1958), and can be started by an affront to the male, perhaps disrespect to a female companion or a family member, even by simply what is seen as an insulting glance or look ('eyeing off', for an example). A distinctive feature of this scenario, in other words, is that when it begins, what is initially intended is the defence of honour, and the participants may not in any way intend that the violence ultimately take lethal form (evidence for this can be found in the fact that quite commonly it is within this scenario that we report 'victim precipitation', to use the term suggested by Wolfgang, 1958, where the person who becomes the victim is the one who precipitates the actual violence).

A further distinctive feature of this scenario is that, with rare exceptions, the parties are relatively willing participants in the escalation of violence, in that they actively engage in the combat that leads to the death. Accordingly, the terms 'victim' and 'offender' when applied to this form of homicide may not convey the willing involvement of the various parties in the escalating violence. The social audience plays a crucial role in this form of homicide, providing not only social supports for the violence as it emerges, but in many accounts those who are initially part of the audience may become directly involved in the violence itself, ultimately becoming either offender or victim of the homicide.

Another of these masculine scenarios, again most often male-on-male, consists of violence arising out of the course of other crime. Here the essential feature seems to be the exceptional marginality which leads some males to take extraordinary risks with life.

The final scenario is one where violence becomes employed as a device for resolution of conflict. Males caught beyond the boundaries of conventional life find themselves in a bind when it comes to disputes over such issues as unpaid loans, since the ordinary mechanisms of arbitration, including legal remedies, are closed off. Violence, in such circumstances, becomes an ultimate arbiter of the dispute.

These scenarios are all distinctively masculine. Women rarely attempt to control their sexual partners through the use of violence, are unlikely to deal with threats to their honour through violence, nor are they prone to either risk life in the course of other crime, or to feel it necessary to resolve a dispute by killing their opponent in the conflict.

At the same time, especially in terms of the male-on-male scenarios, the use of lethal violence is definitively working- or under-class behaviour as well. Middle- or upper-class males rarely become involved in confrontations which become lethal, nor are they likely to engage in street forms of criminality which result in the loss of life, nor do they commonly employ violence as a form of resolution of conflict.

What might account for the patterns observed in these case studies? There are a number of theoretical traditions that might be drawn upon. Two recent formulations have attempted to delineate general theories of crime, proposing that a common thread of elements runs not only through forms of homicide, but virtually all crime. Other formulations are more specific to homicide, and are focused on such issues as its gender or class makeup.

A general theory: seductions of crime

One view of homicide which has provoked considerable discussion is Katz's *Seductions of Crime* (1988). Katz in an analysis of what was termed 'righteous slaughter' raised the following questions: (1) what is the killer trying to do in a 'typical homicide'? (his phrase); (2) how does he understand himself, his victim, and the scene at the fatal moment?; and (3) with what sense and in what sensuality is he compelled to act? He then develops the notion of 'righteous slaughter', in which he argued that the typical homicide:

> is an impassioned attempt to perform a sacrifice to embody one or another version of the 'Good.' When people kill in a moralistic rage, their perspective often seems foolish or incomprehensible to us, and, indeed it often seems that way to them soon after the killing. But if we stick to the details of the event, we can see offenders defending the Good, even in what initially appears to be crazy circumstances.   *(Katz, 1988: 12)*

Katz then reviewed several case studies of homicide, drawn from writers such as Lundsgaarde (1977), many of which have elements similar to the cases reviewed in the present study. From these, Katz argued that the 'typical homicide' has the following features (Katz, 1988: 18–19). First, such a homicide is a 'self-righteous act undertaken within the form of defending communal values' (Katz, 1988: 18). Second, the 'typical homicide' is characterised by its 'lack of premeditation'. The third characteristic is a bit more cumbersome. What he is concerned with is the fact that the actual killing may not be what is intended in the homicide: it is artificial to take a 'killing' as the act to be explained. What the non-predatory assailant is attempting to do is more accurately captured by the concept of sacrifice: the marking of the victim in ways that will reconsecrate the assailant as Good. The victim's *death* is neither a *necessary* nor a *sufficient* element of the assailant's animating project (Katz, 1988: 18).

With these characteristics assumed as the attributes of typical homicides, Katz then moved on to develop notions about the role of humiliation as it contributes to the rage which leads to homicide, saying in a typical paragraph:

> When the assailant suddenly drops his air of indifference, he embraces and creates his own humiliation. He then makes public his understanding, not only that he was hurt by the victim, but that he was falsely, foolishly, and cowardly *pretending* not to care. In this double respect, the once-cool but now enraged attacker acknowledges that he has already been *morally* dominated just as he moves to seek *physical* domination. He becomes humiliated at the same time and through the same action in which he becomes enraged.
> *(Katz, 1989: 23, emphasis in the original)*

Katz spent several more paragraphs on the question of how humiliation interacts with rage to set the stage for the homicide, as for example:

> when a person becomes enraged, he confirms his humiliation through transcending it. In rage, he acknowledges that his subjectivity has been overcome by implicitly acknowledging that he could not take it any more. But now the acknowledgment is triumphal because it comes just as rage promises to take him to dominance over the situation.   *(Katz, 1989: 26)*

The language is richly textured, the argument complex, but how accurate is Katz's work as an account of homicide? Given that he builds his analysis from the three observations about the 'typical homicide', its value can be partly judged by the degree to which these observations correspond to reality.

Initially it can be pointed out that Katz is in immediate trouble when he employs the phrase 'typical' homicide. He explicitly excludes 'predatory homicides' from consideration, but one must presume that all others are contained within his concept of the 'typical homicide'. Does this mean that the various forms of intimate homicide (sexual or familial), confrontational homicide, conflict-resolution killings, or even negligent work death (all of which legally can be defined as criminal homicides), will fit within the boundaries of his term 'typical homicide?' Since this seems obviously not the case (given the substance of his discussion of humiliation and rage), then Katz might help by providing a little clearer guidance regarding what is, or is not, a typical homicide.

After expending the effort in the preparation and analysis of the present case studies, as well as reading many other accounts of homicide contained in the works of investigators such as Lundsgaarde (1977), the present analysis would not be as bold as Katz and suggest that there is a 'typical' homicide. None of the specific scenarios identified constitute a distinct majority of all homicide cases, and most of the individual forms of homicide themselves have features which are distinctive enough to set them well apart from the others.

Granting Katz for a moment the use of the term 'typical homicide' for purposes of discussion, problems develop quickly when one asks how well his three features of 'typical homicide' bear up when compared across a set of homicides. First, there are many homicides that are not 'self-righteous' acts whose purpose is the upholding of the communal good. Neonaticide is characterised by a form of extreme denial of the pregnancy, the birth, and then the act of homicide, and as such falls far outside the criterion held out by Katz. The depressive, elderly males who kill their wives before they commit suicide would not seem to be likely candidates for consideration as 'righteous' individuals up-holding the common good. The bungling criminals who kill their friends in order to destroy evidence against themselves for other and more minor crimes are clearly acting out of self-interest rather than any interest in the wider 'good'.

Second, there is the question of premeditation. This is an important issue in the argument developed by Katz, since it is the rapid and spontaneous shift from humiliation to rage that provides the core of his conception of the typical homicide. Here, again, the data are not kind. It has been found that a majority of men who kill their wives have given careful thought to the murder they are going to perform (although often the accounts display an exceptional level of rage). Certainly, the criminals who kill to destroy evidence also have given considerable thought to what they plan to do.

In discussing what happens after rage has overcome humiliation, and then resulted in a killing, Katz observes that:

> After their lethal attacks, killers often retrospectively acknowledge a determining sense of compulsion. They frequently say, 'I got carried away'; 'I didn't know what I was doing'; 'I wasn't myself'. These are not only face-saving devices or ploys to reduce punishment, since, as was already mentioned, killers often do not attempt to escape or spontaneously call the police and confess. At times, the urgency with which they bring in the authorities and condemn themselves seems to be an attempt to prove that they have regained control of themselves – that they are typically rational and that the killing was an aberrant moment that disrupted their characteristic state of moral competence. Thus, the killers may be truly disturbed by the question, 'Why did you do that?'   *(Katz, 1988: 25)*

Some killers in the present files utter such phrases, but many do not. Many husbands who kill their wives know exactly what they are doing, and if anything express a sense of relief once the goal, the wife's death, has been attained. In many of the cases of confrontation, the killers left the scene quite unaware of the seriousness of what they had done, but certainly not in a state of mind such that they would say they didn't know 'what they were doing', or that they 'weren't themselves'.

Katz's third characteristic is a bit harder to examine, since his unique use of language makes it difficult to divine precisely what he means. It can be presumed that what is at issue is that the homicide in his view should serve the effect of establishing at its conclusion a situation where the offender is seen as a defender of the 'Good', then again events such as neonaticide (where the homicide is denied in the con-sciousness of the offender) or elderly suicide/murders provoked by extreme depression would not seem to fit. When criminals kill friends to destroy evidence against themselves, it is not likely they would see such acts of self-interest as a defence of the common 'Good'.

Within each of the specific variations of homicide that have emerged from the present data, many killings do not fit the formula which Katz describes as constituting a 'typical homicide.' This creates a peculiar bind in the assessment of Katz's formulation. It seems likely that much of the problem arises out of the method employed by Katz in his analysis. What Katz apparently did was first to theorise about the nature of homicide, then selectively enter the available volumes of case studies (such as can be found in Lundsgaarde, 1977) to isolate those cases which 'verify' his idealised conception of how the act proceeds.

Certainly some homicides can be found, both in other studies and in the present one, that correspond to Katz's notion of a 'typical homicide'. Many confrontational homicides show some correspondence to what Katz seems to have in mind, but there are simply too many examples of homicides which do not fit the patterns described by Katz to conclude that his account is an accurate description of homicide in general.

Also, it must be granted that in some homicides there appears to be a strong interplay between humiliation and rage. When the middle-aged drunk confronts a younger and fitter male over comments made about the older man's de facto wife, the beating the older man received in front of both his wife and the male onlookers was deeply humiliating (Case No. 3778–85). When his wife left him, the 'old-country' husband was humiliated to the point where he said: 'I am no longer a man' (Case No. 231–86).

In these cases, and several like them, the humiliation boiled over into a lethal rage. What is important, however, is that the subsequent violence was most often far from the spontaneous variety described by Katz. There was a clearly premeditated, intentional quality in these homicides which at a minimum meant that the person left the immediate scene to fetch a weapon, and in many of the other cases (especially involving sexual intimacy) this was accompanied by a rather complex plan for the actual killing.

In fact, if one examines closely the dynamics of the homicides most closely corresponding to Katz's notion of 'spontaneous' homicide, which would appear to be confrontational homicides, it is not clear whether there is a good fit of the humiliation-rage model. One male challenges the honour of another as a start to the sequence of lethal violence, that much is clear. But in an exact sense, is it true that one has 'humiliated' the other? Is it not the case in many of these situations that what the fight is about, and the masculine rage, is the *attempt* of the initiator to humiliate? Often it would seem that it is the fight, that is the violence itself, which will determine who is to be 'humiliated.'

There are some confrontations where the initial steps of the confrontation have, as a matter of fact, resulted in one of the parties being publicly humiliated in front of peers. It is specifically these events which are followed by the humiliated party leaving the immediate scene to return at some later time with a weapon. Thus, Katz seems to be wrong on two counts. First, in those homicides which are most 'spontaneous', while it is clear that there is a threat of humiliation present, it cannot be said that experienced humiliation is what provokes, through some 'spontaneous' transcending experience, a rage which results in the killing. Second, when one of the parties has experienced successful humiliation (that is, he is beaten in a non-lethal fight), this may be followed by a build-up of rage which results in a complex set of events whereby a weapon is brought back into the scene, but the time interval is great enough so that Katz's notion of 'spontaneity' does not apply.

Even in those cases where his analysis might fit, his conception of humiliation, rage, sacrifice and marking is curiously empty of its critical gender content. Despite the fact that Katz concludes his discussion of righteous slaughter with a section which comments on the significance of gender in homicide, his discussion of the basis of humiliation and rage does not treat the concept of masculinity. Instead of commenting on why homicide is so distinctively a male phenomenon, Katz (1988: 48–9) makes a few comments on the scarcity of homicide by women, and makes a few conjectures on why this might be so. He does not reflect, however, on what it is about masculinity that provokes 'righteous slaughter'.

What is at issue are the grounds for the humiliation and rage that are so central to Katz's analysis. The view that has been advanced here is that in scenes of sexual intimacy, males may feel rage when their woman partners begin to move out from under their control, especially if this involves sexual activity with another male. When the conflict is with another male, however, the provocation to rage may rest with an insult to masculine face, status or pride. From a theoretical point of view, Katz's elaborate logical construction is found to be unsatisfying because it is empty of any substantive reference to masculinity as providing the fundamental basis for that humiliation and rage.

There is much innovative and provocative thought presented in the description given by Katz of what he terms righteous slaughter. The present work, certainly, would support an argument for examining the 'foreground' of crime, and, in fact, that is why the analysis has engaged in a close reading of actual narratives of homicide. Perhaps if it were possible to know more precisely what he meant by a 'typical homicide', and it could be assured that such homicides behaved by the rules he described, and perhaps if his conception of humiliation and rage treated the masculine basis for that rage, then the account might be more compelling. The task of accounting for the wide range of homicides found in this present study, has led to the conclusion that the homicides show greater diversity than can be encompassed in Katz's idealised conception of the typical homicide. Further, it is difficult to be satisfied with a set of notions that purport to provide a theoretical framework to understand homicide that does not in its basic structure treat the dominant theme of masculinity which runs through account after account of homicide in Victoria.

Those familiar with Katz's work will realise that he included as well comments on what he termed 'cold-blooded, "senseless" murder' (Katz, 1988: Chapter 8, 274–309). The present work can throw little light on that analysis. What he does is select from major non-fictional accounts three dramatic case histories of 'senseless' killing, and then subjects these to his own unique exploration. Unfortunately, while he makes clear which homicides are not 'senseless' (those which result from 'situationally emergent rage', serial killings, killings where the killer 'goes berserk', that is, mass killings, and killings in the course of robbery because of the resistance of the victim) he is less than clear which homicides meet the criterion of being senseless. As a result, it is not easy to determine which narratives among the cases in this study might fit within his category.

In examining the text of his argument, it would seem that few, if any, cases would meet his criteria. Consider, if you will, his concern for 'cosmological control' where he argues that:

> First, there is a cosmological contingency. The primitive god reigns as master of the universe, throwing thunderbolts from on high or speaking through the silence of the prophet's thoughts. When he sends a message, it will boom forth like thunder or stun a man's awareness, as might the sudden burning of a bush. Thus, if one is effectively to mobilize the form of primordial evil, he needs a situation structured for cosmological transcendence.
>
> *(Katz, 1988: 304)*

Katz, in his search for conditions which 'endow the situation with privileged meaning' (Katz, 1988: 305) is reading a level of higher order mental functioning than seems to be available in the present 380 homicides in Victoria. Some of these involve acts of gruesome horror, but where there is evil one is struck by how mundane it is. There may be in Katz's search for cosmological significance a transformation of acts which viewed through other's eyes demonstrate, quite to the contrary of the visions of Katz, the banality of much of the evil found in homicide.

Homicide viewed within a general theory of crime

A quite different view of homicide is advanced in the recent theoretical writing of Gottfredson and Hirschi (1990). What these writers propose is a general theory of crime, one which they argue can embrace such diverse acts as auto theft, burglary, robbery, rape, embezzlement, drug offences, and among these, homicide. Crime, in their view, in its various forms requires little in the way of planning or effort, it offers few long-term benefits, it provides excitement and thrills, and it causes pain and discomfort for the victim.

In making their case, Gottfredson and Hirschi (1990) review various forms of crime, describing for each a 'typical' or 'standard' form. As might be expected, these descriptions tally with their conception of the existence of a general category of 'crime'. When it comes to homicide, they begin with an assertion which may come as a surprise to readers of these pages, since they argue that contrary to popular and scholarly opinion: 'homicide is perhaps the most mundane and, in our view, most easily explainable crime' (Gottfredson and Hirschi, 1990: 31).

After providing a couple of pages of 'facts' about homicide, Gottfredson and Hirschi then assert that homicide comes in 'two basic varieties':

> people who are known to one another argue over some trivial matter, as they have argued frequently in the past. In fact, in the past their argument had on occasion led to physical violence, sometimes on the part of the offender, sometimes on the part of the victim.   *(Gottfredson and Hirschi, 1990: 33)*

The individuals then find themselves in the present situation, in which: 'one of them decides that he has had enough, and he hits a little harder or with what turns out to be a lethal instrument. Often, of course, the offender simply ends the dispute with a gun.' (Gottfredson and Hirschi, 1990: 33)

The second of their varieties consists of a crime such as robbery which can alter and change when for some reason:

> (sometimes because the victim resists, sometimes for no apparent reason at all) the offender fixes his gun at the clerk or store owner. Or, occasionally, there is a miscalculation during a burglary and the house turns out to be occupied. Again sometimes because the victim resists and sometimes for no apparent reason the offender clubs, or shoots the resident.
>
> *(Gottfredson and Hirschi, 1990: 33)*

It would seem here that Gottfredson and Hirschi have fallen into the same trap as Katz of starting with preconception of typical crime, and from that evolved a view of a 'typical homicide' which is rather removed from reality. To be fair, some homicide fits the pattern they describe.

Regarding the first of their types, however, a relatively small proportion of homicides fits a pattern of people who know each other well, who have argued in the past, and then on this occasion the argument goes out of control. This happens in a few cases of domestic homicide, perhaps most noticeably in the one or two cases where a woman offender is defending herself against the violence of her male partner. A very large percentage of homicides involving sexual intimacy where males kill females are clearly planned in advance (including cases where elderly males commit suicide afterwards), and thus do not correspond to this portrait of a 'typical' homicide. The great bulk of confrontation homicides are not situations where people know each other and have argued previously (although this is true of a handful of such killings).

From the characteristics of typical homicide given by Gottfredson and Hirschi, it can be estimated that, at most, about one-third of all Victorian homicides (and this is an outside limit) come close to fitting within the boundaries of the term they propose. What seems to have happened is that Gottfredson and Hirschi, like Katz, have begun their analysis by first developing a highly crystallised notion of typical crime. From that derived notion, and a selective reading of the literature on homicide, they deduce a view of what constitutes 'typical' homicide. They have then committed the fundamental error of entering the data on homicide, and selecting from the accounts of homicide a portrait of homicide consistent with their preconception (and thus with their general theory of crime).

Unfortunately for their theory, in reality most homicide becomes, thereby, not 'typical'. By itself, this is not sufficient to shake the logical foundations they have established for a general theory of crime. This problem, however, appears to apply equally to other forms of criminality they embrace within the general theory. For example, their claim that white-collar crime fits the general pattern seems even more flawed (Gottfredson and Hirschi, 1990: 180–201). Such crime as insider trading is hardly spontaneous, can hardly be said to involve meagre long-term benefits (when major offenders are able to pay civil penalties which run literally not just into millions, but hundreds of millions of dollars), and clearly requires extensive skill and planning (for example, arranging for off-shore trading through foreign merchant banks in order to protect the participant's identity, see Stewart, 1991).

These are not trivial points for the complicated structure created by Gottfredson and Hirschi. They posit as a focal notion the idea of 'crime in general'. Central to their theory is a particular description of 'typical crime', of which 'typical homicide' or 'typical white-collar crime' are merely sub-types. If such forms of crime empirically do not correspond to crime as they define it, the implications for the theory are serious indeed. The logical structure of their formulation proposes that there are certain conditions (the explanatory variables) which are tied in a particular way to general crime (the dependent variable). If the empirical data suggest that their account of the dependent variable is flawed, then the theory itself becomes untenable.

To be fair, some homicide (like some white-collar crime, or some robbery) fits neatly into the general theory of crime espoused by Gottfredson and Hirschi. These writers, however, have not titled their book 'A General Theory of Some Crime'. They argue that it is a theory of 'typical' or 'standard' crime (the terms are exactly theirs), across a range of specific offences, including homicide. If most homicide (white-collar crime, rape, robbery, etc.) falls outside the boundaries of what these writers see as 'typical', then questions must be raised regarding whether the empirical reality of crime bears a close enough correspondence to their conception of general crime for the theory to merit serious consideration. One is left wondering how it can be that homicide is, as they assert, so 'mundane' and 'easy to explain' when their conception of homicide fits so little of real-world homicide.

Accounting for the masculinity of homicide

Daly and Wilson (1988) have developed a comprehensive framework which is explicitly concerned with accounting for the masculine character of homicide. Men's killing of wives, in their view, is a reflection of the mechanisms which have evolved whereby men strive 'to control women and to traffic in their reproductive capacities' (Daly and Wilson, 1988: 189).

These writers recognise that homicide is diverse in its forms. Observing that males more often kill males than females, they then offer a view that such male-on-male homicides also evolve out of mechanisms which can be interpreted as a process where males are 'killing the competition', arguing that these can be interpreted as:

> an assay of competitive conflict. In every human society for which relevant information exists, men kill one another vastly more often than do women. Lethal interpersonal competition is especially prevalent among young men, which accords with many other aspects of life-span development in suggesting that sexual selection has maximized male competitive prowess and inclination in young adulthood.   *(Daly and Wilson, 1990: 83)*

It is their argument that an evolutionary view can also account for the masculinity of robbery homicides:

Men's minimum needs for survival and sustenance are hardly greater than those of women, and the men of Detroit are certainly no more likely to be desperately poor than their female counterparts. But in a paternally investing species such as our own, males gain reproductive success by commanding and displaying resources that exceed their own subsistence needs. We suggest that the chronic competitive situation among males is ultimately responsible for that sex's greater felt need for surplus resources with which to quell rivals and attract mates.   *(Daly and Wilson, 1988: 179)*

Up to this point, the Victorian data have been consistent with the hypotheses advanced by Daly and Wilson in the large body of their works. Males predominated as offenders in homicides where the social bond was based on sexual intimacy, and the social mechanisms that emerged from case history after case history is that of masculine sexual proprietoriness.

Certainly, the masculinity that virtually defined confrontational homicides and homicides in the course of another crime conforms to the ideas advanced by Daly and Wilson. They have explicitly treated both of these forms of lethal violence in their discussion of homicide, and the present case studies are entirely consistent with the portraits of these which they provide (Daly and Wilson, 1988: 123–36, and 178–9). Without some elaboration and expansion, however, the formulations of these writers seem less well-adapted to accounting for the class characteristics which in the present data rival the gender characteristics of homicide, and for some help in this domain it is necessary to turn to another form of thinking about violence.

Homicide and the subculture of violence

One well-established theoretical position is that homicide can be explained by the existence of a 'subculture of violence'. This thesis claims that the life circumstances of particular social groups generate violence as a common outcome of routine social interaction. One of the first statements of this view is contained in the early work of Wolfgang (1958)):

A male is usually expected to defend the name and honor of his mother, the virtue of womanhood ... and to accept no derogation about his race ... his age, or his masculinity. Quick resort to physical combat as a measure of daring, courage, or defense of status appears to be a cultural expectation, especially for lower-class males of both races. When such a culture norm response is elicited from an individual engaged in social interplay with others who harbor the same response mechanisms, physical assaults, altercations, and violent domestic quarrels that result in homicide are likely to be relatively common.   *(Wolfgang, 1958: 188–9)*

This argument was expanded in the later work of Wolfgang and Ferracuti (1967), where they argued that a subculture of violence does not completely oppose the dominant culture, nor does it require that violence be a response in every situation. What the subculture does is to promote a number of social conditions under which violence is likely to be either expected or required. The carrying of weapons, for example, is viewed as a willingness to either expect or participate in violence, and to be ready for quick retaliation should a threat of violence emerge. In some situations, non-violence may not be a choice, as occurs when a male is expected to defend his masculine identity or lose the respect and friendship of his male peers. Thus, as Wolfgang and Ferracuti (1967: 161) state: 'Violence can become a part of the life style, the theme of solving difficult problems or problem situations.'

The subculture of violence thesis has faced wide-ranging criticism (for reviews, see Gibbons, 1992; or McCaghy and Cernkovich, 1987). Some have argued that poverty is a better predictor of homicide than a subculture of violence, while others have contended that within the types of lower-class communities which are supposed to support such a subculture, research has not been able to establish a higher level of support for violence than is found in middle or upper-class communities.

At the same time, the description of actual homicide posed by Wolfgang (1958) or by Wolfgang and Ferracuti (1967), in fact, has stood the test of time. As the present data on confrontational homicide demonstrate, there are those situations where males stand ready to use lethal violence in defence of their honour, and these situations involve distinctively males in working- or under-class contexts. As Wolfgang noted in Philadelphia in the quotation immediately above, so too in Victoria, Australia, there are situations where violence is a 'cultural expectation'.

McCaghy and Cernkovich (1987: 137–8) argue that rather than simply reject the notion of a subculture of violence, it might be better to examine closely the specific conditions which contribute to homicide. In their thesis of a 'subculture of lethal violence' McCaghy and Cernkovich suggest that some conditions which encourage violent behaviour include placing an emphasis on masculine honour and physical prowess, victim precipitation, alcohol use and weapon availability.

Thoughts on masculinity, vulnerability and violence

A starting point in a theoretical attempt to link up these complex phenomena is to emphasise the fundamental masculinity of lethal violence. Gender stands out as a persistent feature of homicide. Most offenders are male, in the present and in other research (for example, Wolfgang, 1958; Wallace, 1986; Falk, 1990). Males accounted for all but 5 per cent of the cases of confrontational homicide. Males made up virtually all of the original offenders in homicides in the course of another crime (five cases involved women, in four of these the women were accomplices of men who were the principal offenders). Males were the killers in scenes of conflict resolution (two such cases involved females as accomplices, however).

The source of this masculinity can be seen as resulting from inherent competition between males, and in the willingness of males to employ violence as a feature of that competitiveness. Daly and Wilson argue that violence evolves as a device of effective, if high risk, competition among males:

> Competition among males is more intense than that among females in a simple objective sense: the variance in male fitness is greater than the variance in female fitness. Among men as compared to women, the big winners win bigger ...   *(Daly and Wilson, 1988: 140)*

Quoting another writer, they then go on to conclude: 'as a general consequence, the entire life history strategy of males is a higher-risk, higher-stakes adventure than that of females' (Daly and Wilson, 1988: 140).

At this point a conundrum is posed by the finding that violence, especially confrontational and risk-taking violence, is exceptionally rare among economically well-off males. If violence among males can be seen as a feature of successful competition, there would seem initially to be a puzzle posed by the empirical finding that the most successful in the competition for desirable mates are, in fact, the least likely to feel called upon to employ violence. Why are privileged males so unlikely to 'kill the competition', since as the greatest winners, according to this formulation, they would have the most to lose?

One possible line of argument is that while males are competitive with other males, both for attainment of the limited economic resources and for controlling the reproductive capacity of desirable females, in contemporary society that competition has been expanded to widen the devices available to achieve success to include such dimensions as class, wealth, status and power. At the same time, physical prowess has waned in importance. The mature male of established class position, with wealth, recognised status in the community, and power to influence the political mechanisms of community governance, has less need to resort to physical prowess either to subdue his competition or to control his female partner.

Both economic and sexual competition may be problematic. Material insecurity, and jealousy, may be as much a part of privileged life as anywhere else. Thus, the male may feel he has to fight off challenges to his economic position, as well as to insulate his female partner from male competitors. How that insecurity is dealt with, however, may differ according to the resources available.

A possible helpful line of argumentation has been advanced recently by the anthropologist Gilmore (1990). In reviewing data on masculinity across a number of cultures, Gilmore concluded that there were three essential features to masculinity: 'To be man in most of the societies we have looked at, one must impregnate women, protect dependents from danger, and provision kith and kin' (Gilmore, 1990: 223).

In many societies, these 'male imperatives' involve risks, and masculinity can be both dangerous and competitive:

> In fulfilling their obligations, men stand to lose – a hovering threat that separates them from women and boys. They stand to lose their reputations or their lives; yet their prescribed tasks must be done if the group is to survive and prosper.
> *(Gilmore, 1990: 223)*

At this level, the argument is consistent with that of Daly and Wilson. Can these ideas be expanded to include the under-class character of this violence as well? A possible line of reasoning is established in Gilmore's argument about the impact of differential social organisation on masculinity:

> The data show a strong connection between the social organization of production and the intensity of the male image. That is, manhood ideologies are adaptations to social environments, not simply autonomous mental projections or psychic fantasies writ large. The harsher the environment and the scarcer the resources, the more manhood is stressed as inspiration and goal.
> *(Gilmore, 1990: 224)*

If Gilmore is correct, it would seem reasonable to argue by extension that the contemporary male who possesses economic advantages is able to provide the base for the procreative, provisioning and protective functions through his economic resources, and these same resources provide the underpinnings for his competition with other males for a mate. In other words, physical prowess and aggression no longer become necessary for the economically advantaged male to assure his competence in reproduction, provision or protection.

For males at the bottom of the economic heap, however, the lack of access to economic resources has the consequence of rendering these issues, and therefore their sense of masculinity, as problematic. For such males, the expression and defence of their masculinity may come through violence. Messerschmidt, for one, has argued along these lines:

> Some marginalized males adapt to their economic and racial powerlessness by engaging in, and hoping to succeed at, competition for personal power with rivals of their own class, race and gender. For these marginalized males, the personal power struggle with other marginalized males becomes a mechanism for exhibiting and confirming masculinity.   *(Messerschmidt, 1986: 70)*

There are deeply rooted aspects of culture which place men in competition with other men in terms of their reputation or honour. Assuming that Gilmore (1990) is correct in his assertion that the bases of masculine rivalry derive from competition regarding mating, provisioning and protecting, males who are well integrated into roles of economic success are able to ground their masculinity through methods other than physical confrontation and violence. For economically marginal males, however, physical toughness and violence become a major avenue by which they can assert their masculinity and defend themselves against what they see as challenges from other males.

It can be argued that part of the adjustment to contemporary life has been the translation of the general problem of maintenance of masculine control into its economic and political forms, relegating physical violence to a background role in the maintenance of social control for those who can make some claim to economic and political resources. For some, of course, physical violence remains as a potential weapon to be employed when other devices appear to fail. Looking at the control of women, this view is derived in part from feminist observations of the nature of male dominance and power. As Stanko has argued:

> Power, prestige, and credibility ... are awarded on a gender basis: men, as men, have greater access to the benefits of power, prestige and credibility. It is likely that female children, as part of growing up in an unequal, thus-gendered position, learn that they are less valued and have less prestige than their male counterparts.   *(Stanko, 1985: 72)*

Thus, part of the control of men over women is derived from their power. While this extends across the broad range of social relationships (including the world of work), it intrudes specifically into the domain of sexuality. As Stanko puts it: 'Women learn, often at a very early age, that their sexuality is not their own and that maleness can at any time intrude into it ... male sexual and physical prowess takes precedence over female sexual and physical autonomy' (Stanko, 1985: 73).

This dominance, Stanko (1985: 70) argues, is such that as part of 'typical' male behaviour women come to expect, as routine, sexual intimidation and violence. In this view, as expressed by Alder (1991): 'male violence against women in male dominated societies is an expression of male power which is used by men to reproduce and maintain their status and authority over women' (Alder, 1991: 168).

Power, however, derives from a number of sources, and it is argued here that some males are able to maintain their status and authority by means of their economic and social status and the mechanisms which these provide. Males who have an array of resources may be able to maintain their position with respect to their women and other men without recourse to violence. In the first instance, women as wives, secretaries, clients, patients, students, party workers and similar roles, are 'kept in their place' by laws, regulations, ethics, economic sub-ordination, and social expectations. Married women, in particular, are particularly constrained by law and custom, as Scutt has argued:

> Within *his* own four walls any man can do as he chooses – and any women must submit ... Protestations that marriage is a partnership and women and men have equal rights within it are empty in the face of a primitive allegiance to a belief ... that a man is head of *his* household.
>
> *(Scutt, 1983: 279, emphasis in original)*

For persons of established privilege, available resources are powerful enough so when men feel that intimidation of women, or other men, is necessary, steps short of lethal violence are likely to be available. It may be, however, that when those males who possess fewer of these resources are placed in a position where in order to maintain their 'masculinity' in the face of challenges to their status from their female partner, or other males, violence, including ultimately lethal violence, may be called into play.

Occasionally even among those of privilege, the female partner's behaviour may not be brought under control by other techniques, and violence may follow, including ultimately homicide. As we have seen from the present data, relationships involving sexual intimacy is one social context where in the present Victorian case studies instances were found of homicide involving some men of established social position (for example, a bank manager, a primary school principal, and the owner of a car dealership).

In male-to-male lethal violence, including confrontational homicides, the absence of males of privilege either as offenders or victims suggests that the most successful competition among males is waged on economic and social fronts, rather than relying on direct physical assaults and violence. The real winners in the male world of class, wealth, status and power are able to establish their dominance by virtue of their economic and social position in the market place, in the world of work, on bureaucratic ladders, in corridors of power, or perhaps in extreme forms of rational conflict, in the courts.

Those at the bottom of the economic heap, however, will have fewer such resources available. For them, a major vector along which masculinity can be defined and, and the issues identified by Gilmore (1990) negotiated, is that of physical prowess and violence. They may not have much in the way of money, their voices may count for little in City Hall, but they are ready to beat the stuffing out of anyone in the public bar at the Victoria Hotel that 'gives them lip' or 'mouths off.'

Similarly, males who experience extreme economic marginality, with their ties to conventional society grossly attenuated, are more open to taking exceptional physical risks. Such males are willing to expose others, and themselves, to the danger of lethal violence in order to wrest away some of the economic resources of the more privileged. Armed robbery, in other words, can be viewed as a form of competition where males with scarce resources are willing to take enormous risks to seize the riches accumulated by others. In the form of homicide termed here 'conflict resolution on the margins', males who are at the far boundaries of the society, when they become embroiled in heated conflict with a friend (also a member of the under class), may feel that they have little recourse but to engage in physical violence as a way of settling the competitive battle.

The description of the present themes as scenarios of violence folds well into conceptions of subcultures of violence (Wolfgang and Ferracuti, 1968). The scenarios can be viewed as established scripts which are available to guide masculine action. As scripts, these are, in fact, widely known. For one example, middle-class as well as under-class males will know a variety of scenarios that might be acted out when confronted with an insult from another male in a public or leisure scene, including the ones that can lead to an honour contest, confrontation and violence.

What is important at that point is which scenario is drawn upon to determine the action to be followed. What a subculture of violence does is to set the stage for violence, to create the conditions under which males feel impelled toward direct confrontation or physical aggression. Scenes of potential violence are highly conditional, in other words. There are many features which may be operating to create restraining judgments (to use the term suggested by Athens, 1980) to deflect behaviour in the direction of non-violence. Some settings, however, are socially constructed in such ways that violence is likely to be a central feature of the script that is to be played out, and it is here that a subculture of violence is central in providing the essential supports for directing action down a path toward violence. Caught in a situation where the script calls for violence, surrounded by a social audience pushing the action in that direction, the males involved may see little choice but to play out the violence dictated by the scenario.

Segal has argued along similar lines, pointing out that there are widely shared images, or fantasies about violence and masculinity:

> The aggressive masculine style which lower working-class men are more likely to value and adopt is not exclusive to them, of course. It is part of the fantasy life, if not the lived reality, of the majority of men enthralled by images of masculinity which equate it with power and violence (where would Clint Eastwood be without his gun?).
> *(Segal, 1990: 265)*

In a way similar to the present discussion, Segal then goes on to puzzle out why it is lower-class males are more likely to act upon these definitions of masculinity:

> Many social mediators – from school, jobs, friends, family, religion and politics – effect the way fantasies may, or may not, be channelled into any active expression ... It is the sharp and frustrating conflict between the lives of lower working-class men and the image of masculinity as power, which informs the adoption and, for some, the enactment, of a more aggressive masculinity.
> *(Segal, 1990: 265)*

The images of aggressive masculinity are widely spread through male fantasy life. In the mind, across social classes men know the content of the scripts which guide Dirty Harry or James Bond through their violent encounters. Some men, however, are restrained from acting within these scripts, those males being those who have other alternatives for establishing themselves along the needs of protecting, provisioning and providing, especially men who have resources of money, status and power. Lower- and under-class males, however, may find themselves in a position where violence provides a major vector along which they can anchor their masculinity.

The present findings suggest diversity in the patterns of both the masculinity and the class character of the violence observed. The violence associated with masculinity assumes different forms in the sense of resulting in violence to control women, the defence of honour, the willingness to take risks, or the readiness to call upon violence to resolve personal disputes. Similarly, a tentative hypothesis can be advanced that the scenarios may tap into somewhat different points in the class structure. While more data are needed to substantiate the observation, it would appear that the exceptional risk-taking where violence occurs in the course of other crime, and at least some of the conflict-resolution violence, is found among those males farthest from the boundaries of conventional community life. In these forms the sheer physical risks are great, and the course appears to be taken up only by those with the least to lose. This does not mean that the more economically advantaged do not take risks. Rather, as James Stewart's (1991) account of the insider trading and other financial manipulations of the likes of Dennis Levine, Ivan Boesky and Michael Milken in the United States in the 1980s suggests, when the well-positioned take risks: (1) they are able to confine those risks to activities with a low potential for violence (although there is the interesting tale of how one of the circle of traders implicated by Boesky armed himself with an array of weapons only to be arrested as he set off to kill Boesky, described by Stewart, 1991: 366); and equally important, (2) they make a lot more money when they do take risks.

Confrontational violence, while fundamentally lower and under-class in its makeup, would seem to tap into a slightly less extreme part of the class structure. While those involved may draw upon scripts of violence when the subcultural cues indicate that defence of honour is called for, some of those involved would not seem to be positioned as far from the boundaries of conventional lower-class life as those willing to become involved in the risk-taking of engaging in violent crime. If anything, the subcultural supports for violence as a device of males in the control of women would seem to be spread even wider into conventional culture. The present case studies can only hint at this possibility that these scenarios connect up in somewhat different ways to the class structure, however, and further work would be needed to both clarify and substantiate these links between masculinity, class and violence.

Some thoughts on policy

Despite its public prominence, its very rarity makes it difficult to provide easy solutions when it comes to homicide. Still, from the information obtained here, some initial pathways can be established. A first level of concern might be directed at the complicated issue of gun control (Strang and Gerull, 1993: 197–228). While the limits of such a policy need to be recognised, an argument can be made for the continuation and even extension of Australia's existing controls on firearm ownership. Such policies, in all probability, would have their greatest impact in limiting the harm in those situations where the violence escalates rapidly, as in many of the confrontational encounters. There is a form of a subculture of violence in Australia, as found in the description here of the playing out of confrontation violence found in locations such as pubs (Tomsen, Homel and Thommeny, 1989). In the American scene, as found in the accounts provided by Lundsgaarde (1977), where males have ready access to hand guns, these disputes can easily become lethal. The general spontaneity, however, means that any barrier placed between the combatants and deadly weapons, such as laws placing guns out of easy reach, will translate into the saving of many lives.

Realistically speaking, the effects would probably not be great in situations of some of the conflict resolution killings, or in the carefully premeditated spousal homicides. In such situations the offenders are willing to expend considerable resources to obtain weapons, and at least in the immediate future, it is likely that illegal sources of supply would be available. There are recognised limits, in other words, to what can be achieved by gun control strategy.

A more medium-range strategy is suggested by the very term 'scenario'. Many of the situations which turn lethal are relatively easy to translate into dramatic scripts defining the most obvious steps in the duet of interaction that leads to the killing. For at least the jealousy-control and confrontational scenarios, these might be transformed into scenes which could be presented to adolescents as they move into their late adolescent years. In particular, it might be possible to create a variety of 'role playing' situations, in which adolescents take turns in playing both the central actors and members of the social audience. These scripts could be written so that young people learn to play out, both as central actors and members of the social audience, non-violent endings to potentially violent encounters. The intent of these would be to involve in a direct and active way males (in both secondary and primary school) in role-playing experiences which convey that violent and controlling masculine behaviour is unacceptable. In a similar manner, Toch (1969: 232) has suggested the use of such techniques as psychodrama and 'test situations' which allow participants to explore alternative courses of action and their consequences.

While one should not overstate what might result from such an educational process, it is clear that many actors caught up in potentially violent situations are inexperienced with violence. They thereby lack a repertory of established technique for deflecting the interaction down a non-violent path. Educational efforts which role play such techniques need to emphasise both the roles of the central protagonists and members of the social audience, since the audience can exert considerable influence on the immediate interaction, and also because often as the violence escalates it is one of the members of the initial audience who gets swept in to the point where he becomes the ultimate victim of the lethal violence.

Most importantly, of course, there is the persistent issue of economic marginality that must sooner or later be addressed in societies with a minimal commitment to social justice. It is inconceivable, at least writing in the 1990s, that it would be possible to eliminate the economic and social stresses that push some persons to the point where they are willing to risk, or even plan, lethal violence. At the same time, most developed economies have allowed economic conditions to evolve which assure a large, and relatively permanent, under-class population. Unfortunately, solutions to this problem are difficult to come by. Much of this under-class problem is a direct result of structural economic changes which have rapidly closed off entry positions to viable careers in the lower occupational levels. This has been most obvious in the rapid closing down of manufacturing activity in developed nations, but it also includes the disappearance of lower positions which in the past were the entry points to positions of relatively high status, such as clerks in banks, file clerks in offices, or stock boys/girls in retail firms. Economists, especially those close to governmental policy makers, tend to argue for solutions to cyclical downturns in the economy, partly because these would show quick returns for any effort expended (often because they have been slow to recognise, or acknowledge, the structural changes which are taking place).

The result is that governments, whether dominated by left or right economic policies, tend to generate solutions which, if they have any effect at all, have an impact on the most advantaged of the unemployed, leaving virtually untouched the least advantaged among us. Few government pronouncements today speak directly to the issue of the large under-class populations that are bubbling under the surface of the domestic peace of developed economies. The result is a very large population of highly marginalised males, drifting the city streets of Australia, Canada, the United States, the United Kingdom, and the other countries of the western world. In this drifting process, the conditions are ripe for countless scenes in which both confrontation and conflict-resolution scenarios are played out.

Providing the economic alternatives directly aimed at reducing these large under-class populations certainly should serve to reduce the essential conditions for these forms of violence. Jobs, wages, family roles, political roles, and other social involvements would serve to pull many who are currently floating along in disconnected, under-class ways of life into what should prove to be more conventional and acceptable ways of behaviour, including a reduction in the willingness to use, and the need for, masculine violence. Accordingly, it is argued here that a society which is serious about the reduction of violence should look above all else to its economy, and to ways of providing for the deflection of individuals from the economic traps involved in under-class life.

Conclusions

There will be no single theory which accounts for the exceptional diversity of homicides. A conclusion based on the homicide data derived from the present case studies, however, is that some theories seem less adequate than others in explaining the nature of lethal violence. Both Katz (1988) and Gottfredson and Hirschi (1990) have developed a theoretical account which presumes a form of 'typical' homicide which does not appear to correspond to anything close to a majority of homicides. Since most homicides are well outside their description of the 'typical', the resultant theories at best will have limited utility.

In contrast, the virtue of the idea of a 'subculture of violence' (Wolfgang and Ferracuti, 1967) rests first and foremost in its enduring accuracy in capturing empirically a portion of homicide. The notion that there are social contexts in which violence, including at times lethal violence, becomes virtually a required response in the legitimate defence of masculine honour, holds in the present data which are far removed in geographic space and in time from the original observations of Wolfgang (1958) or Wolfgang and Ferracuti (1967).

At the same time, that description applies only to a specific group of homicides. The value of the thesis advanced by Daly and Wilson (1988) is that it reaches across the major forms of homicide. By entering the argument first with the proposition that much of homicide is dominated by gender, and then branching outward from that to discuss situations of masculine control over the sexuality of women, masculine competition for status among themselves, and masculine competition for scarce resources, a conceptual framework follows which embraces the scenarios of homicide which have emerged from these case studies.

Homicides of males where their female sexual partners are their victims appear to be motivated fundamentally out of the view of women as masculine possessions. As such, the violence can be seen as an extreme of the more general pattern of male dominance, including physical intimidation, which feminists argue is a feature of men's control of women. As has been seen, much of homicide where men are the victims of women results from masculine attempts at physical intimidation, since these women in most instances take up violence as a method of coping with the assaultive behaviour of their partners.

Homicides of males where their victims are other males are likely to derive from male competitiveness. Lacking the access to power in economic and social arenas that might allow the competition to take other forms, confrontational violence in lower- or under-class social positions thus becomes their way of maintaining honour or reputation in the face of a challenge from another male, with the resultant violence, according to Daly and Wilson (1988), serving as a device whereby the males are able to destroy their competitors.

The predatory violence which occurs in the course of another crime similarly derives from competitiveness, in this case when economically marginal males pursue crime as their method of gaining access to economic resources. Persons with more resources may be pressured out of masculine competitiveness to take some of the risks involved in engaging in criminal behaviour, but are likely to channel these into various forms of elite crime. It can be argued that white-collar crime has the dual advantages of offering to those whose status is high enough to engage in this form of criminality the opportunity for much higher gains, and at certainly much lower risk in terms of the potential that their own lives might be taken in the course of the criminal behaviour.

The present investigation, thereby, provides a tentative empirical base for theories of homicide which focus on questions of the ways by which masculinity in general is an over-arching feature of homicide, and where masculinity combines with working- or under-class position for some of the specific forms of lethal violence. While the data are limited to a small group of homicides over a five-year period in one state in Australia, this book has attempted to raise theoretical issues which have a broad potential sweep in terms of their implications for further qualitative and quantitative research. Hopefully, the present findings will help serve as a guide to that research.

References

Alder, C. (1991) 'Socioeconomic determinants and masculinity', pp. 161–76 in
D. Chappell, P. Grabosky and H. Strang (eds) *Australian Violence:
Contemporary Perspectives*. Canberra: Australian Institute of Criminology.

Ashworth, A. (1991) *Principles of Criminal Law*. Oxford: Clarendon Law Series.

Athens, L.H. (1980) *Violent Criminal Acts and Actors*. London: Routledge &
Kegan Paul.

Bacon, W. and Lansdowne, R. (1982) 'Women who kill husbands: The battered
wife on trial', pp. 67–93 in C. O'Donnell and J. Craney (eds), *Family
Violence in Australia*. Sydney: Longman Cheshire.

Bean, C. (1992) *Women Murdered by the Men They Loved*. Binghampton,
New York: Haworth Press.

Black, D. (1984) *Toward a General Theory of Social Control—Selected Problems*,
(Vol. II). Orlando: Academic Press.

Block, C.R. (1993) 'Lethal violence in the Chicago Latino community',
pp. 267–342 in A.V. Wilson (ed.) *Homicide: the Victim/Offender Connection*.
Cincinnati, Ohio: Anderson Publishing.

Block, R. and Block, C.R. (1992) 'Homicide syndromes and vulnerability:
Violence in Chicago community areas over 25 years', pp. 61–87 in *Studies
on Crime and Crime Prevention*. Vol. 1, No. 1. Stockholm: Scandinavian
University Press.

Blum, A. and Fisher, G. (1978) 'Women who kill', pp. 187–97 in I. Kutash *et al.*
(eds) *Violence: Perspectives on Murder and Aggression*. San Francisco:
Jossey-Bass.

Boyatzis, R.E. (1974) 'The effect of alcohol consumption on the aggressive
behavior of men', *Quarterly Journal of Studies on Alcohol*
35: 959–72.

Browne, A. (1987) *When Battered Women Kill*. New York: The Free Press.

Bureau of Justice Statistics (1992) *Sourcebook of Criminal Justice Statistics – 1991*.
Washington, D.C.: United States Government Printing Office.

Campbell, J.C. (1989) 'If I can't have you, no one can: Power and control in
homicide of female partners', paper delivered at the annual meeting of
the American Society of Criminology, Reno.

Daly, M. and Wilson M.(1988) *Homicide*. New York: Aldine de Gruyter.

Daly, M. and Wilson, M. (1990) 'Killing the competition', *Human Nature* 1: 83–109.

Daly, M., Wilson, M. and Weghorst, S.J. (1982) 'Male sexual jealousy', *Ethology and Sociobiology* 3: 11–27.

Dobash, R.P., Dobash, R.E., Wilson, M. and Daly, M. (1992) 'The myth of sexual symmetry in marital violence', *Social Problems* 39: 71–91.

Easteal, P.W. (1993) *Killing the Beloved: Homicide Between Adult Sexual Intimates.* Canberra: Australian Institute of Criminology.

Egger, S.A. (1990) *Serial Murder: An Elusive Phenomenon.* New York: Praeger.

Egger, S.A. (1984) 'A working definition of serial murder and the reduction of linkage blindness', *Journal of Police Science and Administration* 12: 348–57.

Falk, G. (1990) *Murder: An Analysis of Its Forms, Conditions, and Causes.* London: McFarland & Company.

Field, S. and Jorg, N. (1988) 'Corporate liability and manslaughter: should we be going Dutch?' *Criminal Law Review* 791: 156–69.

Fisse, B. (1990) *Howard's Criminal Law.* Sydney: Law Book Company.

Gelles, R.J. (1987) *The Violent Home.* Beverly Hills, California: Sage.

Gerson, L.W. (1978) 'Alcohol related acts of violence: Who was drinking and where the acts occurred', *Journal of Studies on Alcohol* 39: 1294–6.

Gibbons, D.C. (1992) *Society, Crime and Criminal Behaviour,* 6th edn. Englewood Cliffs, NJ: Prentice-Hall.

Gibbs, J.J. (1986) 'Alcohol consumption, cognition and context: Examining tavern violence', pp. 133–51 in A. Campbell and J.J. Gibbs (eds) *Violent Transactions: The Limits of Personality.* New York: Basil Blackwell.

Gillespie, C.K. (1989) *Justifiable Homicide: Battered Women, Self-Defense, and the Law.* Columbus, Ohio: Ohio State University Press.

Gilmore, D.D. (1990) *Manhood in the Making: Cultural Concepts of Masculinity.* New Haven: Yale University Press.

Gottfredson, M.R. and Hirschi, T. (1990) *A General Theory of Crime.* Stanford, California: Stanford University Press.

Grabosky, P.N., Koshnitsky, N.S., Bajcarz, H.D., and Joyce, B.W. (1981) *Homicide and Serious Assault in South Australia.* Adelaide: Attorney-General's Department.

Hewitt, J.D. (1988) 'The victim-offender relationship in convicted homicide cases: 1960–1984', *Journal of Criminal Justice* 16: 25–33.

Hickey, E. (1990) 'The etiology of victimization in serial murder: An historical and demographic analysis', pp. 53–71 in S.A. Egger (ed.) *Serial Murder: An Elusive Phenomenon.* New York: Praeger.

Holmes, R.M. and De Burger, J. (1988) *Serial Murder.* Newbury Park, California: Sage.

Homel, R. and Tomsen, S. (1993) 'Hot spots for violence: the environment of pubs and clubs', pp. 53–66 in H. Strang and S. Gerull (eds) *Homicide: Patterns, Prevention and Control.* Canberra: Australian Institute of Criminology.

Huong, M.T.N.D., and Salmelainen, P. (1993) *Family, Acquaintance and Stranger Homicide in New South Wales.* Sydney: New South Wales Bureau of Crime Statistics and Research.

Johnson, C.M. and Robinson, M.T. (1992) *Homicide Report.* Washington, D.C.: Government of the District of Columbia, Office of Criminal Justice Plans and Analysis.

Kapardis, A. (1990) 'Stranger homicide in Victoria, January 1984–December 1989', *Australian and New Zealand Journal of Criminology* 23: 241–58.

Kapardis, A. (1989) *They Wrought Mayhem: An Insight into Mass Murder.* Melbourne: River Seine Press.

Kapardis, A. and Cole, B. (1988) 'Characteristics of homicides in Victoria, January 1984–June 1988', *Australian Police Journal* 42: 130–2.

Katz, J. (1988) *The Seductions of Crime: Moral and Sensual Attractions of Doing Evil.* New York: Basic Books.

Kiger, K, (1990), 'The darker figure of crime: The serial murder enigma', pp. 35–52 in S.A. Egger (ed.) *Serial Murder: An Elusive Phenomenon.* New York: Praeger.

Langevin, R. and Handy, L. (1987) 'Stranger homicide in Canada: A national sample and a psychiatric sample', *Journal of Criminal Law and Criminology* 78: 398–429.

Law Reform Commission of Victoria (1988) *Homicide* (Discussion Paper No. 13). Melbourne: Law Reform Commission of Victoria.

Law Reform Commission of Victoria (1991) *Homicide Prosecutions Study.* Melbourne: Law Reform Commission of Victoria.

Levinson, D. (1989) *Family Violence in Cross-Cultural Perspective.* Beverly Hills, California: Sage.

Luckenbill, D.F. (1977) 'Criminal homicide as a situated transaction', *Social Problems* 26: 176–86.

Lunde, D.T. (1975) *Murder and Madness.* Stanford, California: Stanford Alumni Association.

Lundsgaarde, H.P. (1977) *Murder in Space City.* New York: Oxford University Press.

McCaghy, C.H. and Cernkovich, S.A. (1987) *Crime in American Society*, 2nd edn. New York: Macmillan.

McNeely, R.L. and Robinson-Simpson, G. (1987) 'The truth about domestic violence: a falsely framed issue', *Social Work* 32: 485–90.

Maxfield, M.G. (1989) 'Circumstances in Supplementary Homicide Reports: Variety and validity', *Criminology* 27: 671–96.

Messerschmidt, J. (1986) *Capitalism, Patriarchy and Crime: Towards a Socialist Feminist Criminology.* Totowa, N.J.: Rowan & Littlefield.

Messerschmidt, J. (1993) *Masculinities and Crime: Critique and Reconceptualisation of Theory.* Lanham, Maryland: Rowman & Littlefield.

Miller, W.B. (1980) 'Gangs, groups and serious youth crime', in D. Sichor and D. Kelly (eds) *Critical Issues in Juvenile Delinquency.* Lexington, Mass.: Lexington.

Mowat, R. (1966) *Morbid Jealousy and Murder.* London: Tavistock Publications.

Naylor, B. (1990) 'Media images of women who kill', *Legal Services Bulletin* 15 (February): 4–8.

Naylor, B. (1993) 'The Law Reform Commission of Victoria homicide prosecutions study: the importance of context', pp. 93–120 in H. Strang and S. Gerull (eds) *Homicide: Patterns, Prevention and Control.* Canberra: Australian Institute of Criminology.

National Committee on Violence (1990) *Violence: Directions for Australia.* Canberra: Australian Institute of Criminology.

Polk, K. (1993) 'A scenario of masculine violence: confrontational homicide', pp. 35–53 in H. Strang and S. Gerull (eds) *Homicide: Patterns, Prevention and Control.* Canberra: Australian Institute of Criminology.

Polk, K. and Ranson, D. (1991a) 'Patterns of homicide in Victoria', pp. 53–118 in D. Chappell, P. Grabosky and H. Strang (eds) *Australian Violence: Contemporary Perspectives*. Canberra: Australian Institute of Criminology.

Polk, K. and Ranson, D. (1991b) 'The role of gender in intimate homicide', *Australian and New Zealand Journal of Criminology* 24: 15–24.

Polk, K., Haines, F. and Perrone, S. (1993) 'Homicide, negligence and work death: the need for legal change', pp. 239–62 in M. Quinlan (ed.) *Work and Health: The Origins, Management and Regulation of Occupational Illness*. Melbourne: Macmillan.

Ranson, D. (1992) 'The role of the pathologist', pp. 80–126 in H. Selby (ed.) *The Aftermath of Death*. Annandale, NSW: Federation Press.

Rasche, C.E. (1989) 'Stated and attributed motives for lethal violence in intimate relationships', paper delivered at the American Society of Criminology, Reno.

Rasko, G. (1976) 'The victim of the female killer', *Victimology* 1: 396–402.

Reidel, M. (1987) 'Stranger violence: Perspectives, issues and problems', *Journal of Criminal Law and Criminology* 78: 223–58.

Reidel, M. and Zahn, M.A. (1985) *The Nature and Pattern of American Homicide*. Washington, D.C.: United States Government Printing Office.

Reiner, I. and Chatten-Brown, J. 'Deterring death in the workplace: the prosecutor's perspective', *Law, Medicine and Health Care* 17: 23–31.

Reiss, A.J. Jr. and Roth, J.A. (eds) (1993) *Understanding and Preventing Violence*. Washington, D.C.: National Academy Press.

Sanchez-Jankowski, M. (1991) *Islands in the Street: Gangs and American Society*. Berkeley, California: University of California Press.

Scutt, J. (1983) *Even in the Best of Homes: Violence in the Family*. Ringwood, Victoria: Penguin.

Segal, L. (1990) Slow Motion: Changing Masculinities, Changing Men. London: Virago.

Selby, H. (ed.) *The Aftermath of Death*. Annandale, NSW: Federation Press.

Silverman, R.A. and Kennedy, L.W. (1987) 'Relational distance and homicide: the role of the stranger', *Journal of Criminal Law and Criminology* 78: 272–308.

Silverman, R.A. and Mukherjee, S.K. (1987) 'Intimate homicide: An analysis of violent social relationships', *Behavioral Sciences & the Law* 5: 37–47.

Sparrow. G. (1970) *Women Who Murder*. New York: Tower Publications.

Spergel, I.A. (1984) 'Violent gangs in Chicago: In search of social policy', *Social Service Review* 58: 199–226.

Stanko, E.A. (1985) *Intimate Intrusion: Women's Experience of Male Violence*. London: Routledge & Kegan Paul.

Stewart, J.B. (1991) *Den of Thieves*. New York: Simon & Schuster.

Strang, H. (1992) *Homicides in Australia 1990–91*. Canberra: Australian Institute of Criminology.

Strang, H. and Gerull, S. (eds) (1993) *Homicide: Patterns, Prevention and Control*. Canberra: Australian Institute of Criminology.

Straus, M.A. and Gelles, R.J. (1990) *Physical Violence in American Families*. New Brunswick, N.J.: Transaction Publishers.

Toch, H. (1969) *Violent Men: An Inquiry into the Psychology of Violence*. Chicago: Aldine.

Tomsen, S., Homel, R. and Thommeny, J. (1991) 'The causes of public violence: Situational vs. other factors', pp. 177–94 in D. Chappell, P. Grabosky and H. Strang (eds) *Australian Violence: Contemporary*

Perspectives. Canberra: Australian Institute of Criminology.

Vetter, H. (1990) 'Dissociation, psychopathy and the serial murderer', pp. 73–92 in S.A. Egger (ed.) *Serial Murder: An Elusive Phenomenon.* New York, Praeger.

Victorian Community Council Against Violence (1990) *Violence in and Around Licensed Premises.* Melbourne: Victorian Community Council Against Violence.

von Hentig, H. (1948) *The Criminal and His Victim: Studies in the Sociobiology of Crime.* New Haven: Yale University Press.

Voss, H.L. and Hepburn, J.R. (1968) 'Patterns of criminal homicide in Chicago', *Journal of Criminal Law, Criminology and Police Science* 59: 499–508.

Wallace, A. (1986) *Homicide: The Social Reality.* Sydney: New South Wales Bureau of Crime Statistics and Research.

Walmsley, R. (1986) *Personal Violence.* (A Home Office Research and Planning Unit Report). London: Her Majesty's Stationery Office.

Wilbanks, W. (1982) 'Murdered women and women who murder: A critique of the literature', pp. 151–80 in N.H. Rafter and E.A. Stanko (eds) *Judge, Lawyer, Victim, Thief: Women, Gender Roles, and Criminal Justice.* Boston: Northeastern University Press.

Wilson, M. and Daly, M. (1985) 'Competitiveness, risk taking and violence: The young male syndrome', *Ethology and Sociobiology* 6: 59–73.

Wilson, M. and Daly, M. (1992) 'Who kills whom in spouse killings? On the exceptional sex ratio of spousal homicide in the United States', *Criminology* 30: 189–215.

Wolfgang, M. (1958) *Patterns of Criminal Homicide.* Philadelphia: University of Pennsylvania Press.

Wolfgang, M. and Ferracuti, F. (1967) *The Subculture of Violence: Towards an Integrated Theory in Criminology.* London: Tavistock Publications.

Zahn, M.A. and Sagi, P.C. (1987) 'Stranger homicides in nine American cities', *Journal of Criminal Law and Criminology* 78: 377–97.

Zimring, F.E., Mukherjee, S.K. and Van Winkle, B. (1983) 'Intimate homicide: A study of intersexual homicide in Chicago', *The University of Chicago Law Review* 50: 910–30.

Index